LAND OF THE DEAD

HOW THE WEST CHANGED DEATH IN AMERICA

T0300746

TERRY HAMBURG

Prometheus Books

Essex, Connecticut

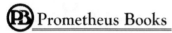
Prometheus Books

An imprint of The Globe Pequot Publishing Group, Inc.
64 South Main Street
Essex, CT 06426
www.globepequot.com

Distributed by NATIONAL BOOK NETWORK

British Library Cataloguing in Publication Information available

Library of Congress Cataloging-in-Publication Data

Names: Hamburg, Terry, author.
Title: Land of the dead : how the West changed death in America / Terry Hamburg.
Description: Lanham, MD: Prometheus, [2024] | Includes bibliographical references. | Summary: "At the turn of the twentieth century, a 1901 decree ordered the exhumation and relocation of more than 150,000 graves in San Francisco—the only major metropolitan city in the United States to order a complete eviction of its dead. Land of the Dead uncovers this fascinating and forgotten part of American history"—Provided by publisher.
Identifiers: LCCN 2024004340 (print) | LCCN 2024004341 (ebook) | ISBN 9781633889866 (paperback) | ISBN 9781633889873 (epub)
Subjects: LCSH: Cemeteries—California—San Francisco—History. | Odd Fellows Cemetery (San Francisco, Calif.) | Masonic Cemetery (San Francisco, Calif.) | Laurel Hill Cemetery (San Francisco, Calif.) | Calvary Cemetery (San Francisco, Calif.) | Cook, Edith Howard, 1873–1876 | Burial laws—California—San Francisco—History—20th century. | San Francisco Bay Area (Calif.)—History.
Classification: LCC F869.S362 A253 2024 (print) | LCC F869.S362 (ebook) | DDC 979.4/6—dc23/eng/20240226
LC record available at https://lccn.loc.gov/2024004340
LC ebook record available at https://lccn.loc.gov/2024004341

To Beverly

CONTENTS

CHAPTER 1

MIRANDAMANIA

MAY 2016. HOME RENOVATION CREWS IN A "POSH" SAN FRANCISCO neighborhood strike something unexpectedly hard in the ground— a diminutive lead and bronze coffin, tightly sealed. Brushing away debris, workers peer through glass portals to behold a "remarkably well-preserved" child in a handmade white christening dress and ankle high shoes. News accounts spare no details: "Her curly blonde locks were laced with sprigs of lavender. A rosary and eucalyptus seeds were placed on her chest. She was grasping a rose in her right hand." But there is nothing to indicate who she is or when she died. The house sits in the middle of what used to be the Odd Fellows' Cemetery removed almost a century earlier. Local television stations run with the story, and "Mirandamania" is born—a meme that will generate headlines well beyond San Francisco and well beyond that day.

Close ancestor encounters of the third kind are familiar in American cities, typically during construction over long-forgotten burial grounds. Fast-growing urban areas at the turn of the twentieth century face à labyrinth of old cemeteries—early civic renditions, church graveyards, and sprawling "pauper" grounds as well as African American and Native American spaces. Sooner or later, this land is coveted by the living. It is common but seldom contemplated knowledge that layer upon layer of ancestors lay beneath the urban landscape today. Most large American cities relocated some of their dead over the past two centuries. Subsequent finds reveal such efforts as careless and incomplete. William Gladstone famously said, "Show me the manner in which a nation or a community care for its dead and I will measure with mathematical exactness the tender sympathies of its people, their respect for the laws of the land and their loyalty to high ideals." By this standard, we all fail. In San Francisco, a convenience turns into a campaign. During long and unrelenting anti-cemetery agitation, the city bans burials in 1901. Then in a sweeping set of government mandates, it takes the extraordinary step to evict all its ancestors, some 150,000. No other modern metropolis has gone to such vast and deliberate means to establish a civic dead-free zone.

Ancestor pop-ups always come as a surprise to the living. The dead should not be there. Consternation and explanation follow. Miranda is just the latest in a long line of deceased who periodically emerge in San Francisco but arguably the most dramatic individual discovery. Older San Francisco residents are shocked and inured. Recent and younger residents are shocked and indifferent. As a Miranda reporter blithely explains, removal of cemeteries from one spot to another occurs almost everywhere in America. Ancestors can be accidently left behind and "every now and then turn up in residential construction."

What makes this incident a national story is the spectacle itself: a child lovingly arranged in an elaborate Victorian setting secured by an "airtight" premium coffin replete with viewing windows—all in exceptional condition. Withered remains in a moldy coffin will make newsprint, but the story has no legs. Even a well-preserved forty-niner might garner only passing attention unless he had been rushed to rest in a pair of old Levi's that can fetch five figures at auction. Miranda is gold. There had not been a significant underworld discovery in San Francisco for some years, and the media abhor a vacuum.

The homeowners where the Victorian child is rescued are staying with relatives in Idaho during renovations. They feel an immediate connection to the lost-and-found child. "That could have been my little girl," John Karner says. Erika Karner confesses to "a lot of emotion as a mom." She contacts the San Francisco coroner. A medical examiner cracks open the coffin for inspection. He declares that the body is the responsibility of the homeowner, not the city, which had overseen a legal burial at the time and is therefore not liable because the corpse currently rests on private property.

Now what? A city official has broken the original seal that inhibited decomposition. Real, if not eternal, time is ticking.

The Karners immediately inquire about a reburial on proper cemetery grounds. The cost is formidable, quotes ranging from $7,000 to $22,000. Erika complains, "I understand if a tree is on your property, that's your responsibility. But this is different. The city decided to move all these bodies 100 years ago, and they should stand behind their decision."

Enter the Garden of Innocence, which provides burials for abandoned and unidentified children. Its founder, Elissa Davey, offers to take custody of the child: "I said yes, not realizing what a mess I got into . . . the homeowner was stuck with a child in a yard that she didn't know what to do with. She was told she had to keep the child under the house or bury her." Paving over the abandoned soul is not an option for the family. But here's the rub. By local law, you can't bury a person without a permit. The only way to get a permit is to produce a death certificate—and no one can produce even an identification. However, there is now a moniker: The "housemate" is christened "Miranda" by the Kanter girls, ages four and six.

The Garden of Innocence arranges transportation and mortuary refrigeration as a new, larger cherrywood-paneled casket is constructed that will serve as a liner into which the vintage coffin can be placed. Davey scours public library archives for a solution to the burial catch-22 and discovers an obscure city ordinance: If a person died more than twenty-five years earlier, a special death certificate could be issued. A proper reinterment can now take place.

Enter Jelmer Eerkens, an anthropology professor at the University of California, Davis, with expertise in drawing DNA from ancient peoples and even woolly mammoths. He is upset to learn that Miranda will be sent back to the soil without any analysis. "As an archaeologist, I thought, that's not right. That is our collective heritage, and we can't just rebury things. All human societies recognize the importance of ancestry and history. But rather than a general story of war and history, this is a story about an individual person. People can understand and connect with how sad it must have been to lose a young daughter."

The Garden of Innocence agrees. Strands of Miranda's blond hair are cut for laboratory analysis before carefully resealing the coffin. That delicate operation is headline news. There is now hope that the child might someday be identified, but such a finding will take time and is far from certain. In fact, it is a long shot. Investigators publicly play down expectations. Eerkens admits he is doubtful that the necessary DNA survived; Davey describes the chances of a specific identity "as slim to none."

On June 6, 2016, a formal "Miranda Eve" funeral is held at Greenlawn Cemetery in Colma. For the Garden of Innocence, it is critical that a nom de guerre be given before burial: "A name is a dignity every human being deserves, to be called something." The additional moniker is inspired by the public administrator; now that the city is embracing the child, it apparently wants to share naming rights. A dozen members of the Knights of Columbus in full regalia hold swords in the air as the body is lifted from the hearse. Another twenty men and women of the Independent Order of Odd Fellows from across Northern California are dressed in black with fraternal insignia draped across their chests. The child is laid to "final" eternal rest. There are poems, prayers, and invocations. "A line formed and one by one, people who never knew Miranda Eve dropped rose petals over her coffin and wished her goodbye," one account notes. Some 140 people are at the service. Millions more attend virtually. The memorial backside is left blank, the *Los Angeles Times* reports, "just in case the true identity was ever discovered."

The burial is not the end for Miranda Eve. It is the beginning. She has become immortal. There are so many questions. First and foremost, who is this captivating child placed with such tender care? Judging from the state-of-the-art coffin, the family has money. Are they also prominent? Is her unexpected death a story back then? Why does she die so young? Could there have been foul play? Do doctors administer medicine in a futile attempt at a cure? And a mourner asks at the funeral, "How could they forget her?"

Psychics and cold-case detectives offer hunches and leads. Davey relies on her personal team of investigators. It takes a few months, but clues begin trickling in from some thirty specialists and volunteers in the lab and field.

Initial hair analysis reveals that "Miranda" is a girl—a foregone conclusion but important to clarify. The Garden of Innocence explains, "Those who know late 1800s society know that sex wasn't demarcated among young children, and both boys and girls typically wore dresses (and had long curly hair, etc.) As I understood, nobody checked the sex of Miranda, so we assumed she was a girl. In any case, it is useful to know her sex for certain."

The child appears to have been weaned from breast milk a year before death, placing her age at two to three and a half years.

Preliminary DNA confirms Miranda to be of European ancestry. Soon after, her mitochondrial DNA is found to be a type most common on the British Isles.

Hair nitrogen isotopes suggest that Miranda literally "wasted" away—a clinical diagnosis of the era called "marasmus." She suffers from malnourishment for approximately three months before death. "We suspect an illness caused her to eat less and less until she was unable to eat at all," the forensic report concludes. That illness could be bacterial, viral, or parasitic but is curable today. Hair is also analyzed for traces of drugs, such as morphine and cocaine—common components of medicines in the late 1800s. None are found.

The story would be amiss without a headline-grabbing brush with the supernatural: *Couple says they heard footsteps before coffin was found in back yard.* At various times, Erika Karner reveals, she and her husband heard the inexplicable sound of children's footsteps on the top floor of their home; her young daughters are asleep or playing in sight at those times. And they were not the only ones to hear strange sounds. "We had a couple of contractors, on separate occasions, who thought they heard footsteps," Karner recalls. "Each time, the contractors walked through the house looking for a child—possibly a wayward kid who had run into the house from a park across the street—and both times, the contractors found nothing."

When Miranda is removed from the property, the footsteps stop. "I'm not sure where I stand on where the soul goes, but my hope is . . . if she was still hanging around here figuring out where she needs to be, that her being identified will give her a little peace and she'll potentially go off and be with her family, where she needs to be. We felt that if anything, she was a friendly spirit. If she wants to stay and play, we're totally okay with that!"

———

Meanwhile, back at the university lab, Eerkens and colleague Ed Green announce that a mere 10 percent of hair DNA belongs to the subject—the rest is fungus and organisms. For Team Miranda, the critical step in the scientific probe is to sequence her DNA to a level where it can be utilized to match a living relative should one ever be located. That process is slow, painstaking, and unsure. So would be the genealogical paper chase—a forensic detective story for the ages.

To determine on which part of the old grounds the Karner residence had been built in 1936, investigators need a detailed "plotted map" delineating the Odd Fellows Cemetery at its most developed, ideally as it stood at the last in-ground interments in 1901. No usable document can be found, hardly surprising considering the sketchy history of San Francisco cemeteries, especially the Odd Fellows. However, an original 1865 plan for the cemetery is discovered at the University of California, Berkeley.

What is not known is how much of that plan is followed as designed. Researchers sift through the thousands of cemetery records. Sections missing from the original plan had been created as the cemetery grew, and a few that were planned never came to be. The Garden of Innocence can soon announce that the general "Miranda" section was executed according to the map.

As investigators using old street overlays and historical records focus on areas intersecting with the Karner home, genealogists are narrowing the search, which includes a review of 30,000 burial records. This research effort will eventually tally some 3,000 hours.

There is plenty of frustration along the way. In the summer of 2016, Elissa reports, "We have exhausted every effort to try to find her name and we have not given up. We get a little closer every day. . . . We have argued about areas, plots, tiers, streets, maps, records, wanted to give up, got mad, got confused, felt injustice, felt sad, felt heartbroken, gotten hungry, blew off steam but in the long run, we have not given up. We will keep trying to find her even if we have to one by one recreate the entire Odd Fellows cemetery. . . . We will not give up until we have exhausted all of our efforts in trying to give Miranda her name."

Finally, it is reported that the grand genealogical search has come down to two "prime family candidates." When an exact location is eventually pinpointed, it leads to the "H. H. Cook" family. The team tracks down a living relative in nearby San Rafael. In the fall of 2016, a DNA sample is obtained from eighty-two-year-old Peter Cook, who is publicly acknowledged but not identified. It will take another six agonizing months to further sequence and compare Miranda's data by examining rates of rare matching DNA variants at specific points across the genome. Ed Green reports that the search is "tantalizingly close."

On May 10, 2017, almost a year to the day of the resurrection, the confirmation arrives: "WE FOUND MIRANDA!!! Miranda Eve is Edith Howard Cook. Born November 28, 1873 and died October

13, 1876." In life, death, and for eternity, Edith Howard Cook will always be two years, ten months, and fifteen days old.

With the mystery solved, 100 devotees trek to Colma for one last ceremony. The previous funeral a year earlier had been shrouded in coastal fog, but the sun shines brightly this June day. A new headstone declares a real name, birth dates and death dates, an image of the child, and a message to mourners and random passersby to "Google Her" for more information. The memorial commences as before, with the Knights of Columbus 4th Degree Color Guard marching, swords at their side. The *San Francisco Chronicle* describes the scene: "The wind whipped their colorful capes and the matching plumage on their hats as they took their places behind Cook's new gravestone, which was still covered up by a dark blue piece of cloth."

The event morphs into an awards show. One speaker calls out a colleague for congratulations, who in turn tosses kudos to another. Geneticists are applauded alongside tombstone artisans. Anthropologists and funeral home directors receive recognition. Genealogists get special praise. The *Chronicle* continues, "After final prayers were said, the Karners stepped forward with their two little girls—both looking adorable in their summer dresses—to pull back the cloth and reveal the new gravestone. After the unveiling, the Karners' eldest daughter left a note written on pink paper with a heart drawn on it at Cook's new headstone. . . . Other mourners and celebrants followed by leaving so many flowers and Beanie Babies on the grave that you could no longer see the new stone."

At the 2016 funeral for "Miranda Eve," the *Los Angeles Times* and the *New York Times* refer to a "perfectly preserved" body. The *San Francisco Chronicle* notes that "its airtight seal preserved everything inside, from the girl's golden locks of hair down to the rose she held in her hand."

But very few have laid eyes on Miranda. At the 2016 funeral, her original glass-window coffin had already been secured inside a new casket. A candid photograph of Miranda taken before resealing is not concealed from the public or press, but one must navigate an internet search to find it. That picture is different than the image from the Garden of Innocence that appears on the Edith Cook memorial and becomes the public face of Miranda.

No less an academic than Eerkens has previously described the child as "mummified," a word picked up by some commentators, including Wikipedia. Miranda was never prepared for traditional "Egyptian-style" mummification. The special coffin acted as a "sort of germicide," he explains, that "preserved soft tissue and clothing." The original photograph does, in fact, roughly resemble the popular view of a "mummy." That image is seldom seen by the public because it seldom appears in news stories.

A few commentators do reference the actual casket photo. One notes, "The original photo was heavily edited by a graphic designer in order to make a decent likeness for Edith's second memorial service." A documentary describes a "rendered photo." The *Atlas Obscura* story of the funeral refers to the picture on the tombstone as a "computer-aided image of what she may have looked like."

The Garden of Innocence clarifies the issue. The public picture is an artist's conception. "We had a photo of the child in her casket the day she was found and she had only slight mold on her jaw and lower lip and a few white spots on her forehead. Elissa asked her cousin, Jennifer Onstrott Warner, who is a graphic artist and owner of Fairy Tale Portraits in Newport Beach, to see if she could remove the mold on Edith's jaw and mouth, close the mouth and make her pretty again . . . and as you can see, she is a beautiful child and so loved by her family and all of us."

There is never an effort to deceive. There *is* an effort to weave a historical story, and the story needs a face. In this sense, that image is just as "real" as the "real" photo taken from the newly discovered coffin. "This is how the last eyes saw her," the Garden of Innocence says, "and this how we should see her."

Edith Cook is a blue blood and a gold blood, eldest daughter of Horatio Nelson and Edith Scoofy Cook, two prominent San Francisco families who merge their fortunes into more fortune and are featured on society news pages. The Scoofy family, on Edith's mother's side, is among the first pioneers in San Francisco at the height of the gold rush. Edith's grandfather marries Martha Bradley, whose family lineage traces back to the earliest Virginia settlers in the 1600s. In proud Victorian manner, they conceive seven children, among them Horatio Nelson Cook and a brother who together establish a family business, M. M. Cook & Son, a leather-belting and hide-tanning company. It remains in operation until the 1980s.

Edith's younger sister grows up to be a notable, even notorious, San Francisco socialite. A newspaper celebrates Ethel Cook as the "reigning bell of San Francisco," who was "made famous by Grand Duke Boris of Russia, who drank a toast with champagne out of one of her slippers at a banquet and declared that she was the most beautiful American woman he had ever seen."

At a more recent stage of lineage, Peter Cook is the great nephew of Edith. Outdoing his Victorian ancestor's fertility, he sires eight children, thirteen grandchildren, and ten great-grandchildren. Already knowledgeable about his wife's and mother's families, he had reached a genealogical dead end with his father, who died when Peter was three. Peter Cook is gifted a first-class genealogy workup.

The choice of location to rebury Miranda is logical and historically correct: Greenlawn Cemetery, nine miles to the south in Colma, which opens as the Odd Fellows Cemetery in 1902, the place for newly deceased fraternal families and, when necessary, the future relocation of those buried in its San Francisco grounds. Miranda's family, unknown at the time of the 2016 reburial, is at rest in Greenlawn. Presumably. No one knows how many remains remain under the bustling San Francisco neighborhood where the child is found.

"Left behind" is often used to describe Miranda's plight. However, commentators hardly discussed what transpired in the old cemetery removal process or the many remains since uncovered, most numerously in the past fifty years. There is passing acknowledgment of the "arduous and ramshackle process of evicting the dead," but most accounts speak of Miranda "interred in a long-forgotten cemetery more than a century ago" without delving into historical details or context.

This journalistic blinder has a long tradition. Why open an old can of worms? Underground discoveries can be indicting as well as engaging. The discovery of Miranda is immediately defined as about the present, not the past. Whatever tragedy trapped this soul in a modern housing purgatory is not the issue. Just as cemeteries are now conceived as havens for the living, the story of Miranda serves as engagement and catharsis for the present. "We came out because she's one of us, it's about something larger and deeper," said one of the mourners. This begs the haunting question: How and why did this happen?

As far as I know, there has never been such a removal of bodies on the magnitude and scale as in San Francisco, and I believe it is the only one that has ever happened like this in the world.
—PAT HATFIELD, FOUNDING PRESIDENT OF THE COLMA HISTORICAL ASSOCIATION

Burials are outlawed in 1901. The final and more drastic step is to reclaim the land. It is universally assumed that the dead will be properly removed before any new developments are started. The public burial ground—"City Cemetery"—comprises some 18,000 remains spread over 200 acres. The region is designated in 1909 for an expansion of Golden Gate Park and a new ocean-view golf course.

Between 1920 and 1940, under intensifying anti-cemetery sentiment, the private cemeteries huddled around Lone Mountain in what is called the "Richmond District" are officially exhumed from San Francisco and relocated to Colma. That removal of 150,000 bodies is fraught with fits and starts, twists and turns, and a political free-for-all punctuated by three contentious elections. The "Big Four"—Calvary (Catholic), Laurel Hill, Masons, and Odd Fellows—are driven out of town at different times and in different scenarios. The Odd Fellows are in the middle of this public ruckus, and its relocation process is arguably the most slipshod and irregular. On its abandoned and repurposed grounds, Miranda is discovered 140 years after her burial.

The past turned up there much earlier. Plumbers laying a sewer line in "big development in the old Odd Fellows Cemetery" in 1941 uncover some caskets. They discuss the situation and decide to open one. A skeleton stares back.

The plumbers remain composed, placing the caskets back from whence they came and dutifully finishing the daily job assignment. The incident is not officially reported—likely regarded as insignificant or, if not, why rock the boat? It takes an "anonymous tip" to alert newspapers. The next day, before official inspection or damage control, the *San Francisco Examiner* blurts out the truth: "From undercover information supplied to the health department, they fear that they will discover that much of the big new development is built over the remains of old San Franciscans, who were once supposedly buried for good and ever in the old Odd Fellow Cemetery. . . . But from yesterday's find, plus the results of other official investigations, it is believed only a percentage of the caskets and bodies were removed from the old burying grounds—and that today, an inestimable number of human remains still lie, under the new houses, streets and gardens being developed there."

Authorities quickly dispatch a special crew "wielding long prodding rods" to conduct a search of the building lots in the area. Only one casket is uncovered—and empty. The Health Department announces, "The result of the operation gives every reason to believe that every vestige of human remains had been cleared out of the old Odd Fellows Cemetery, site of the housing development, when the cemetery was evacuated a decade ago. There is no indication of any bodies—or even any other caskets save the empty one our prober found—remain." Casket closed.

The Masonic Cemetery adjacent to the Odd Fellows is removed at about the same time. The Masons sell most of its historic burial grounds to the University of San Francisco. When the school begins large-scale campus expansion in the late 1950s, troves of caskets and human remains are uncovered. What is found in underground San Francisco depends on the type of new construction. The university is excavating for large buildings. The deeper you dig, the more secrets you uncover. Who knows how many remains are found and never reported, especially in small business projects and private housing?

There is a continuous, if not heralded, stream of discoveries in the "Big Four" cemeteries. Revelations beneath these private grounds will pale in numbers and drama before the headline spectacles of those "left behind" in public burial plots. Perhaps the ultimate irony of "Miranda" is her exceptional burial. Many in early California are not accorded such love and privilege. The gold rush years are characterized by indifference, even disdain, for the dead. This legacy ameliorates but never dissolves, and it will transform traditional cemetery practices in the American West and the nation.

Edith Howard Cook memorial stone at the June 2017 funeral. *Colma Historical Association*

CHAPTER 2

CHARISMA OF THE DEAD

WHY SHOULD WE CARE ABOUT THE DEAD? WHY DOES HUMANKIND go to extraordinary lengths to protect and honor physical bodies after they die? What motivates a nation to retrieve its fallen soldiers years later in far-off lands even when those remains might be mere fragments of bone?

American Revolutionary War leader Joseph Warren is killed at the Battle of Bunker Hill in 1775. A close friend and political ally is determined to retrieve his comrade. Paul Revere arrives at the bloody aftermath to discover that most bodies are indistinguishable from one another. A dentist who has had Joseph Warren as a patient, Revere undertakes steadfast forensic inspections until he finds his man. Why is it so important to recuse those remains?

We may also ask, if a city needs additional commercial or residential space and land is scarce, why should it not remove an inconvenient and dilapidated cemetery to facilitate progress and prosperity? It does. After all, isn't life for the living? Fourth-century BC Greek philosopher-provocateur Diogenes counsels students to take his dead body and fling it unceremoniously over city walls to be devoured by wild carnivores.

In *The Work of the Dead*, Thomas Laqueur considers why Diogenes is "existentially wrong, wrong in that it defies all cultural logic. . . . We endlessly invest the dead body with meaning because, through it, the human past somehow speaks to us." He suggests that this living connection to the deceased depends on the material body itself, not religion per se or belief in an immortal soul. The body of

Karl Marx is the subject of great contention between Great Britain, where he dies, and the Soviet Union, which he inspires. Eventually, the remains are secretly transported to Moscow, where it becomes a pilgrimage shrine that evolves into a burial site for devotees, as if gathered around a saint.

Marx's doctoral dissertation is a reverent study of the third-century BC Greek philosopher Epicurus, who echoes Diogenes, positing that death is the thorough and eternal destruction of the body and that whatever might be defined as a soul never existed or, if it did, perished with the corporeal. No rational argument in the materialist Marxist tradition can justify that the spot where Marx's actual remains sit is special in any way. But could a mere cenotaph—a memorial without remains—have evoked such passion and spawned such controversy? Apparently, remains matter even when it is simple matter, even to those that scorn such reverence. "Marx's actual body," Laqueur contends, "is necessary for this to happen; name bearing stones would not have sufficed for those who choose to surround him."

Napoleon's vision for a grand modern Paris cemetery in 1801 is slow to attract public interest. Administrators devise a marketing strategy to enhance the attractiveness and stature of Père Lachaise. With considerable fanfare, the remains of the great poet Jean de La Fontaine and national icon playwright Molière are transferred to the new resting place. Burials steadily pick up. Another well-publicized relocation occurs in 1817—medieval philosopher Pierre Abélard and amour Heloise d'Argenteuil, whose tragic and sensational affair became the stuff of legends. For centuries, the lovelorn have left letters at their crypt. The transfer precipitates a renewed Père Lachaise rush by nobles and the aspiring to be sequestered among such celebrities. Everybody loves a lover and a poet. Politicians and generals can be another matter. The relocation of those notable remains has often created controversy, underscoring that it is the bones that carry the mystique, not statues or epitaphs.

Grave robbing for ransom makes sense only in this context. The most famous of such ghoulish cabals is the plan to abscond with

Abraham Lincoln. A band of counterfeiters fallen on hard times concoct a daring alcohol-driven conspiracy to kidnap the remains for a king's ransom of $200,000 ($7 million today) plus the release of its imprisoned and apparently indispensable engraver. Getting wind of the conspiracy, the government plants an agent in the gang posing as an experienced grave robber. The scheme is foiled. Plenty of these creepy capers punctuate American history, most notably the remains of Charlie Chaplin and Elvis Presley. Families will pay big money to retrieve small bones.

Laqueur believes that this elevation of the deceased to sacred remains is rooted in the evolutionary human subconscious connected to a higher, metaphysical function—some irresistible power of the imagination propelled not simply by religious belief or a transposition of religion into secular custom. It "blinds' us" to what a corpse really is—inert matter—and represents "a conduct of life that has spiraled out of the order of nature." This belief is primitive in the sense that it is irrational and rests on intuition, but the sentiment may represent a critical cultural demarcation in human history. It occurs as cannibalism recedes in most parts of the world. Laqueur asks, "Did the beginning to care for the dead mark a cognitive border between prehistory and history, between one cognitive status and another higher one?" Over time, treatment of the deceased as carrion or refuge becomes widely regarded as "prehuman" or "uncivilized." Out of these beliefs emerges "the charisma of the dead."

In 1896, the *San Francisco Call* laments the acres of tombstones "standing guard" over the gateway to the "beautiful suburbs of this City," proposing that "mock sentiment alone says it would be destructive of the dead to remove them. Not so; the bodies are but the dust of the earth, to which they have returned. The living souls have fled to another sphere and scorn the mortal clay."

The "charisma of the dead" is beginning to wane across America at this time, most dramatically in California—a distant thirty-first state born in a vacuum, a freak of nature. Its far-western revolution in attitudes and behavior presages the course of social change in the still-adolescent nation. The story of the dead in California begins with the story of the living, and that story begins with the Big Bang of the nineteenth century—the gold rush. In the American West, a new way of death will be born.

The paradox of a great memorial park is the paradox of life and death itself. We establish cemeteries to memorialize the dead, but in so doing, in making the memory of those who have gone before us, we memorialize not death, but life itself. Death has no meaning without the life that went before it.
—LATE CHIEF LIBRARIAN OF CALIFORNIA KEVIN STARR AT THE CENTENNIAL OF CYPRESS LAWN MEMORIAL PARK

CHAPTER 3

GETTING THERE

ON THE ROAD AND ON THE SEA

January 1848. John Marshall is constructing a sawmill in distant "California"—a virtually uninhabited part of the far-flung Mexican empire 2,000 miles from the continental U.S. frontier. He stumbles on shiny yellow flecks in the soil. The discovery will change the world.

At the time, the nation contains less than 10 percent of the present population. The gold rush becomes the largest voluntary mass movement of people in the American story. Oscar Lewis calls it "the most widespread and urgent migration in history." It happens in a historical split second. The young and the restless from around the world abandon families, farms, and foundries in a mad dash for a breathtaking vision of the "American Dream." Almost 100,000 descend on California in 1849, two-thirds of whom are American citizens. With this sudden surge, California becomes an official state the following year, faster than any other new territory in the nation's history.

Some 300,000 will arrive over the next five years. When the gold rush begins, that vast territory is part of a still more vast territory that has just been ceded to the United States after its victory in the Mexican-American War. What is called "California" is a swath of land that goes 400 miles inland from the Pacific Ocean and stretches twice that distance from the Oregon Territory to Mexico along the coast. Residing there are 6,000 of Spanish or Mexican descent known as *Californios*, some 150,000 Native Americans, and a thousand or so "Americanos." The San Francisco port hamlet is one of the most remote places on Earth. By land, you start from the actual U.S. frontier—the Missouri River—and journey by foot for 2,000 miles across terrain brimming with treacherous unknown weather and treacherous unknown Indians or take a grueling six-month sea odyssey around the notorious ship-graveyard southern tip of South America.

Getting there and surviving will test pioneers physically, mentally, and culturally. In the past, a frontier that gradually edges west remains connected physically to the rest of the nation, which is increasingly accessible by a network of railroads and river routes. Suddenly, the new frontier leapfrogs 2,000 miles to the end of the continent. That yawning gap is slow to close. The Transcontinental Railroad will not be operational for another 20 years. Even a transcontinental telegraph system takes until 1861. The difficulty in reaching or communicating with the new land allows California to develop as an outlier, removed from the traditional influences of "the states"—as the rest of the country was now called—especially the blue-blooded Puritan East Coast. California is a virtual colony in the expanding American empire. "Thrown back upon their own resources for two decades," Carey McWilliams observes, "the Californians created, out of the wealth they possessed, a culture of their own."

The speed with which California is admitted to the Union reflects a national apprehension: This vast, rich, and fast-populating land might go its own way politically as well as socially, becoming a separate nation or falling under the sway of foreign or revolutionary parties. The Transcontinental Railroad is a far-fetched dream before the gold rush; suddenly, it is an imperative. The link is psychological as well as physical. California is admitted to the Union two decades ago, notes the *California Alta* on the completion of the grand project in 1869, "but that relation did not a become a real, visible, tangible fact till the last rail was laid, and the last spike driven into the great continental road." Another editorial writer predicts that "California will no longer be divorced from the sympathies and affections of the old states." Assimilation occurs, but could it be that the nation at large is being assimilated by its offspring?

Connection to the exciting new territory is a national obsession. Major East Coast newspapers in circulation wars are quick to report the latest information and misinformation from correspondents dispatched to the cutting edge of manifest destiny. Rumors and speculation abound. California is singular in more than distance. Popular literature reinforces the idea of what some perceive as a budding alternative culture. The American West carves out its own literature. Mark Twain's style of writing—vernacular, satirical, and casual—is characteristic of a national revolution in art and letters that hurls a fresh, frontier perspective into the staid Old World tradition of New Englanders such as Ralph Waldo Emerson, who molded America's first generation of literary greats. California is the national epicenter of the new writing. In general, upstart Western society appears so unorthodox and on such a large scale that it provokes consternation back in the "states." Some pundits compare it culturally to the American colonies and their relationship with Great Britain.

San Francisco is the premier city of the new territory. Its influence is immediate and enormous and lasting. Early settlers forge a temperament, an energy, that spreads across the region and up and down the coast. It becomes the DNA of the new state. Those who shape California are not traditional "elders." The founding generation is dominated by brash young Americans who experience unexpected and unprecedented adventures on the journey there—perhaps the most significant of which is the untimely deaths that will continue unabated well after they arrive. These survivors are still evolving their tabula rasas. Never has so young a generation of leaders built so large a community. They are born and raised with conventional "Victorian" beliefs. The journey to California will challenge that nurture and crack open the door to new perspectives.

The odyssey begins with the state of transportation and communication, both progressing at breakneck speed. The gold rush accelerates the momentum. At the time, however, reliable word of the once-in-a-lifetime opportunity travels only as fast as a human (with the help of a trusty steed). At the American frontier in Missouri, a telegraph can dispatch messages to the East Coast. The gold discovery at Sutter's Mill in January 1848 is a secret bursting at the seams, but it will take until August for the *New York Herald* to report the titillating news. The extent and nature of the find is still unclear, creating more of a restlessness rather than a rush. Soon, it will be "official." A young army officer, William Tecumseh Sherman, who will become a famous and infamous Civil War general, urges his California military commander to visit the goldfields to verify the tall tales. Colonel Richard Barnes Mason treks to Washington, D.C., with an eyewitness account and bearing gifts—chunks of actual California gold. President James Polk is wide-eyed and thrilled. He holds an almost divine belief in the manifest destiny of America to reach the Pacific Ocean and now envisions gold as the key that unlocks the door to that dream. In his annual address to U.S. Congress on December 5, 1848, the president confirms the discovery in California: "The accounts of abundance of gold are of such an extraordinary character as would scarcely command belief were they not corroborated by the authentic reports of officers in the public service." The actual gold, in "lumps and scales," is immediately put on exhibition in the War Office, where hundreds gathered daily to view the dazzling revelation. Rumors are suddenly and dramatically validated. The floodgates burst open. Without that primitive lure of fortune, manifest destiny would have taken a divergent journey, certainly a less direct and impactful one. The ensuing race to riches is a seminal event and so will flourish fabled California and its influence. J. S. Holliday believes that the gold rush "changed the whole West and changed America's sense of itself."

Few of the immigrant "forty-eighters" come from the United States. Without telegraph or railroads, news of the gold strike must travel to the Atlantic coast by the ships sailing south along the Pacific coast, then "around the Horn" of South America to eastern U.S. ports, or an uncertain and dangerous six-month land trek east from those far-away lands to the edge of civilization in Missouri. By contrast, the 7,000-mile journey by sea from China could be done in three months; by 1852, more than 25,000 immigrants from there arrive in California. Tales of gold reach Mexico and South America relatively fast, where a trek to the new "El Dorado" is quicker than to Boston by boat or to Buffalo by land. Not only did news of the gold strike take longer to reach the eastern United States, but in 1848, it came in tentative, unconfirmed stories that tempted few of the comfortable to chance the long, difficult, and uncertain journey to California.

The émigrés from the United States and elsewhere are the most diverse collection of humanity ever to assemble in the United States then or since, certainly more heterogeneous than the English/Irish/Scot/Welsh/German/Scandinavian stock that comprise previous voluntary arrivals. Some foreign émigrés are authentic "refugees," especially among the Chinese and Central/South Americans escaping oppression and poverty. The European and American fortune seekers are generally not the desperate fleeing persecution or economic deprivation but rather the middle class looking for adventure and fortune. "Give me your tired, your poor, your huddled masses yearning to be free, the wretched refuse of your teeming shore" is a generation away.

The decision to embark can be the most consequential moment of your life. Gold seekers are typically young men who have spent childhoods close to their farms and villages. Even as late as World War II, most Americans are born and raised and then die within fifty miles of their birthplace. A typical forty-niner seeks to make a killing and return home; only a few make a killing, but many make a living and choose to settle in California, often without relatives and old friends. The American West is born in social chaos and ethnic diversity.

Gold represents the chance of a lifetime, manna from heaven for those brave enough to claim it—you and yours will be set for life. This is an age of the extended family. Relatives typically live with or near one another. To deliver the dream is chancy and daring—trek thousands of miles over uncharted geography to a remote location to dig alongside fierce competitors for elusive treasure and then make the long journey home laden with riches that will attract cutthroat thieves. The decision can be divisive and heart-wrenching. An eldest son and his young brother are itching to jump in. How many families say, "Don't chase that far off rainbow. It's dangerous, it's foolish, and it's expensive. How are we going to raise the money for you to go traipsing off? We won't hear from you for months, even years, and what if you perish out there? We need you here for the harvest. Your wife is pregnant, you already have a baby son, and grandpa is infirm. How will we get by?" Countless such dramas are reenacted. The plan is to get rich quick and return home quick to share the bounty. It is that promise that grants émigrés the blessing to go.

Most Americans cannot afford to book ship passage or arrange transportation by land to such a far-off place and still have the grubstake to finance a mining adventure where a shovel and pan in the supply-deprived, demand-heavy early goldfields might cost $35 ($1,500 today). By land, travelers confront inflated prices for scarce commodities at trading posts and ferry crossings. Being properly outfitted for both the journey and the arrival runs at least $50,000 in current value. You can raise capital by selling farmland and possessions, borrowing from friends and relatives, contracting partnerships with wealthy stay-at-home sponsors or banks, and, as a last resort, begging for an early inheritance. Life insurance policies are available to ease the potential impact on families. The irony, then as now, is that those who most need this protection can least afford it.

You reside in western New York or Illinois and have spent your life on a farm or in a small village. Why travel for days to the East Coast to join a crowded crew of strangers aboard a ship that will be tossed and turned for some 18,000 miles? Those west of the Allegheny Mountains and inland from the Gulf of Mexico prefer overland routes.

Newspapers across the country in early 1849 report that "tens of thousands" of adventurers are hurriedly preparing to go to the Missouri frontier for the rush that will begin at the first good weather, hopefully in late April. Such a perilous journey begets formal émigré groups, often made up of friends and other locals. There is security and comfort in numbers. Many form joint stock companies, like the Iron City Telegraph Company or the Peoria Pioneers. Each member buys a share in the enterprise, the proceeds used to purchase wagons and provisions. Better organized groups have written constitutions or bylaws to ensure smooth operation over a long and potentially divisive journey. In Ithaca, New York, a company of fifty with a capital of $25,000—plus a $25,000 credit at a local bank ($2 million total today)—establishes a unit that aims to maintain the enterprise in the goldfields. We shall see that most such plans in California do not pan out.

These companies embody the workable contradictions in mid-nineteenth-century American life—a balance of the "independent" New World character with the advantages of voluntary collective action. Eager young men must raise funds and convince families that this wild adventure is wise if not prudent. It is easier to mortgage the farm or coax money from family, friends, and speculators if you are part of a respected organization. And it is easier to convince worried parents and spouses that morale and morals will not be compromised. Company bylaws typically include Sabbath and behavior rules, however unpracticed in fact.

Most fortune seekers travel alone or in small groups with little or no formal organization.

The "official" news—President Polk's presidential declaration of reality in December 1848—sets off "gold fever." The *New York Express* exclaims, "We have seen in our day manias, fevers and excitements of all sort, but it can easily be said never were people so worked, so delirious as they were here and elsewhere yesterday when they read the telegraphic dispatches from Washington chronicling the reception there of intelligence from El Dorado. . . . The fact is, this last gold news has unsettled the mind of even the most cautious and careful among us."

In many places, the reaction is mixed, even anxious. The event could have profound effects on the local economy and culture as communities lose countless young men and resources. Suddenly across America, there are vacuums in families, farms, and factories. Such an exodus is the kind of price that homelands pay for foreign wars.

Under the headline "The Gold Excitement," a candid *Buffalo Morning News* editorial satirizes its own apprehensions: "We are quite sure that it is the duty of newspaper to use all the means in their power to repress rather than stimulate the prevailing excitement on the subject of gold in California. But we must publish all the authentic intelligence from that region and of what avail is sedate or sage of admonitory comment in the face of the glittering, dazzling news?"

The word spreads quickly and everywhere. In normally understated Great Britain, a Liverpool newspaper proclaims, "The gold excitement here and in London exceeds anything ever before known or heard of. Nothing is heard or talked about other than the new El Dorado. Companies are organizing in London in great numbers for the promised land. Fourteen vessels have already been chartered."

Back at Sutter's Fort, there is a hopeless conspiracy by the few who are privy to the find to keep it from locals and especially from 1,000-strong San Francisco, 100 miles away. The news spreads like a virus. Everyone near Sutter's Mill abandons jobs to dig for riches along the American River and its tributaries. A resourceful city resident and Mormon leader, Sam Brannan—regarded as California's first millionaire—seizes the day aboveground. On word of the discovery and before the onslaught of outside adventurers, he accumulates as much mining equipment as can be found and arranges to acquire more, cornering the early market. To promote his wares, Brannan saunters up and down San Francisco's Montgomery Street on May 8, 1848, with a large bottle of gold shavings, announcing,

"Gold from the American River!" The merchandising spectacle is the first concrete proof that residents have of the find. Overnight, the fledgling San Francisco port is reduced to a ghost town as merchants, sailors, soldiers, and laborers rush inland to the goldfields.

The whole country from San Francisco to Los Angeles and from the seashore to the base of the Sierra Nevada resound to the sordid cry of gold! GOLD!! GOLD!! while the field is left half-planted, the house half-built, and everything neglected but the manufacture of shovels and pickaxes.

—*CALIFORNIAN*, MAY 29, 1848,
CEASING PUBLICATION DUE TO A LACK OF
READERS AND JOURNALISTS TO REPORT
LOCAL STORIES THAT ARE NOT HAPPENING

Those who reside in far-off "civilization" are keenly aware that this opportunity is time sensitive, very time sensitive. Who knows

THE WAY THEY GO TO CALIFORNIA.

N. Currier, 1849. *Alamy*

how long or deep the bonanza runs? Go now or forever hold your peace—and regret.

There are two choices in 1849: land or sea. Each promises its own unique hell. By land, you walk. By sea, you lurch. Each take about six months, but the land route in early 1849 poses a major disadvantage: You cannot travel west beyond the Missouri River from November to May. The presidential announcement comes in early December. Until spring melts the vast western tundra, there will be few fish, birds, and animals to hunt and virtually no vegetation for oxen. If that does not kill you, freezing temperatures will. By sea, you could heave-ho immediately and be in the gold diggings months before land trekkers. More émigrés will come by water, but the land route is initially popular for those who live in the "backcountry" and have never beheld the Pacific Ocean. A sea voyage can seem a risky, cramped, and uncertain journey. The blazing of a pioneer route from the Missouri frontier to the Oregon Territory in the 1840s increases the confidence of potential land-goers. Trails from the southern states through Texas and Mexico are passable year-round.

The trail is a great equalizer. On ship, some travel better, much better, than others. The land is egalitarian. Rich or poor, you walk. Rich or poor, you stand the same chance to be dispatched by bears or Indians. On ship, you face the same ocean, but you can buy a "luxury" journey, which did not have its privileged equivalent on land.

Road warriors must get to the "jumping-off" points—the westernmost parts of the United States where one departs "the states" and ventures into what is labeled on maps as "Indian Territory" or the "Great American Desert," "past the bounds of civilization" as one journalist describes the undertaking. At that edge sits the Missouri River and the towns of St. Joseph and Independence, which catapult to prominence as the outfitting stations and launching points for the Oregon/California Trail.

On inland farms and villages, gold hunters pack wagons and head for the roads to the Missouri frontier. Thousands from the East begin on river steamers down the Illinois River or the Ohio River.

The typical cost per person in a stateroom for seven days from Pittsburgh to St. Louis is $9. Some travel west on the Erie Canal across northern New York or through Pennsylvania using the Portage canal system. Others trek north on the Mississippi River.

One of those pioneers is William Swain, a well-educated Youngstown, New York, farmer who keeps a diary of the trip. At age twenty-seven he decides to chase the dream, leaving behind his schoolteacher wife Sabrina, one-year-old daughter Eliza, an elderly mother, and his older brother George. It is a complicated and painful negotiation with loved ones. Sabrina and his mother plead with William to stay home to mind the farm and family. His brother supports the ambitious plan and wants to join, but to suffer both young men away is impossible. George promises to stay home and take responsibility for the family welfare. William contacts friends and neighbors to find traveling companions and picks up three: a thirty-year-old from Youngstown who leaves behind a wife and young son, the still-teenage bachelor son of a local doctor, and a forty-three-year-old widower from Buffalo without children.

In April 1849, William and his companions take passage from Buffalo bound for Detroit on the steamer *Arrow* and then by rail and canal boat to connect with steamers down the Illinois River to St. Louis, where a final transfer to the *Amelia* charges him $6 ($250 today) including baggage for the 387-mile trip west on the Missouri River to Independence. The *Amelia* carries 250 tons of freight and some 100 passengers hankering for a bite at the El Dorado apple. Swain describes a "dense medley of Hoosiers, Wolverines, Buckeyes, Yankees, and Yorkers, including blacklegs [gamblers] and swindlers of every grade. The decks above and below exhibited a stupendous assortment of wagons, horses, mules, tents, bales, boxes, sacks, barrels, and camp kettles; while cabins and staterooms were an arsenal of rifles, bowie knives, hatchets, and powder horns. Every berth was full, and not only every settee and table occupied at night, but the cabin floor was covered by sleeping emigrants." Swain, along with many others, deems it more prudent to stock up on wagons, animals, and supplies at the point of final departure.

He is impressed with St. Louis, which has soared to 65,000 and now absorbs a daily invasion of gold seekers. "Hotels, boarding houses, and steamboats are filled with them. . . . Blacklegs, swindlers and pickpockets are as thick as the locusts of Egypt." He describes some victims losing all their money right there: "They have to forgo the golden dreams and return to the 'old diggings.'"

In the early years of the gold rush, a virulent cholera attacks each spring at the jumping-off towns along the Missouri River. It spreads fast and kills faster, usually within twenty-four hours. The disease claims countless victims before they have a chance to embark across the Kansas prairie.

Cholera is a relentless worldwide killer in the mid-nineteenth century; science has no understanding of its origins, much less a cure. It hitches a ride and wreaks havoc on gold rush wagons and ships. The disease introduces an uninterrupted ordeal of death that will stalk the pioneers into the goldfields and beyond.

The epidemic erupts the first night out on the *Amelia*, spreading quickly among passengers in close quarters, many of whom are immune deficient after weeks of inadequate diet reaching the Missouri frontier. Swain witnesses twenty men laid dead on the deck and then buried, "wrapped only in their blankets, in shallow holes hastily dug by the deck hands on the river islands, the boat barely stopping long enough for the purpose."

He arrives in Independence on May 6 and joins a company from Marshall, Michigan, that dubs itself the "Wolverine Rangers." At least 35,000 gold seekers set out from the western frontier in the spring of 1849 from two concentrated launching points. Swain writes his wife, "Neither the Crusades nor Alexander's expedition to India can equal this emigration to California." His biographer describes the scene at the Missouri border: "Never before had this country, or any other, experienced such an exodus of civilians, all heavily armed or intending to purchase rifles and pistols . . . many organized in formal companies. . . . They were not unlike a great volunteer army traveling from all parts of the nation to mobilize at the frontier."

Waiting for the Missouri weather to clear, fortune seekers settle into sprawling staging camps brimming with wagons and animals. The virus continues to rear its deadly head. As steamboats full of gold seekers arrive in Independence and St. Joseph, the bodies of victims are dragged ashore and pushed into shallow graves. The gruesome, disheartening sight intensifies fear and impatience to start the rush. Rumors swirl. Everyone who keeps a diary during the weeks of preparation and delay at the frontier writes of companions dying, of the paranoia sweeping the camps.

Graves are sometimes dug in advance. Swain reports that in Independence, "cholera is raging to some extent and is very fatal" as he describes the cholera death in camp of Dr. Palmar, one of the Ranger doctors. "Only thirty-six hours ago he was joyful and mirthful with bright hopes, glowing in his prospects." Carrying him up a hill, he records "solemnity, or rather a gloom on all the countenances in the camp. . . . It was a solemn sight to see one of our number carried to his last resting place far from home relations. . . . His relatives little think he is no more. What sad hearts will be at his home when the news reaches them." The next day, he writes that Mr. Nichols contracted cholera last night and is now dead. "So although we have been here but ten days, two of our number are no more, and their remains are deposited beside the Missouri in a lone spot where many exiles from home have been deposited before." The traditions of grief and ceremony these pioneers carry with them are practiced with as much compassion as can be mustered under the circumstances. There is little time for mourning. Swain's next diary words after the subject of Mr. Nichols: "Today our camp is all bustle in preparation for starting."

Those who travel alone or in small, informal groups must rely on the kindness of strangers.

WAGON HO!

To be the leader of an emigrant train through the wilderness is one of the most unenviable distinctions. . . . Some may say the children of Israel in the wilderness were a clamorous set, but they were nothing more than what folks are now.
—CAPTAIN OF AN OVERLAND WAGON CARAVAN

Mrs. Hofstadter, the one thing we don't have to worry about on this trip is witches. Fire, floods, feuds, famine, Indians, disease, stampedes, yes. Witches, no.
—WAGON MASTER IN THE 1950S TELEVISION HIT
WAGON TRAIN, BARKING BACK TO A GROUP
COMPLAINING ABOUT A "WITCH" TRAVELING
WITH THE ENTOURAGE TO CALIFORNIA

Departing Missouri, you are finally off to the final frontier. Expect to average fifteen miles per day over 2,000 miles. That is 133 days mathematically, but figure 180 days in real time if lucky. Pioneers can calculate how many miles traveled in any given time with roadometers or miledrometers—a device attached to wheels of a known circumference. With each turn calibrated on set cogs, the distance can be accurately measured. This is important. Time is money on this trip: There are likely some pangs of anxiety over moments of rest and recreation or even sacred but time-consuming duties like burials and church services.

Welcome to your home for at least six months: the "Independence"-style wagon—about eleven feet long, four feet wide, and two feet deep surrounded with bows of hardwood supporting a cloth bonnet five feet over the wagon bed. With only one set of springs under the driver's seat and none on the axles, folks (including a handful of hearty pregnant women) often chose to walk alongside herds of cattle and sheep. There are few horses, which are expensive to buy and high maintenance, cannot carry heavy supplies, die faster than other animals in hostile weather, and are very coveted (stolen) by Indians and outlaws. Magnificent horses are beasts of war and personal adventure, not burden. Oxen are the wagon workhorses. Donkeys remain untrainable and ornery but will carry anything and go on and on, however reluctantly.

There will be no communication with loved ones. It preys on the mind. "May not the sad intelligence be borne to them that I am left on these plains or rest from the troubles of life in California," pens William Swain. "For how my dear Sabrina would endure the sad news . . . or who would have the care of a father for my dear little Eliza Crandall. May God bless them and George and Mother."

The national mail system is well established but virtually nonexistent west of the Missouri River. Pioneers develop their own information highway called the "Bone Express"—a system of posting messages by writing on cloth, wood, and sun-bleached bones scattered along the way. This communication is not only for those who follow. There are "go-backs" traipsing the same trail who might read a poignant appeal to contact an émigré's relatives at home. Trading posts large and small are plastered with notices for friends expected to arrive later as well as general travel advice. The network continues to California and is especially popular at forks where two or more roads diverge; those become public gathering spots where messages abound. At U.S. forts Kearny and Laramie along the trail, you can drop off a letter that will (eventually) be delivered by the government. In San Francisco itself, the national postal service will serve as a critical lifeline to the home and hearth left behind.

As a gold seeker in 1849, you are not stepping into totally virgin wilderness as you depart Missouri. There was Meriwether Lewis and William Clark, who at the bequest of President Thomas Jefferson in 1803 blazed the original trail. Over the next three decades, trading organizations like the Pacific Fur Company and Hudson Bay Company consolidate the route to expedite trade with the American states as well as British tradesmen in Canada and French merchants in the Louisiana Territory. The trail is becoming part of American folklore. Three years before the gold rush, the Great "Pathfinder" General John C. Fremont, who will run for president in 1856 on the newly formed antislavery Republican Party, publishes his best-seller: *Report of the Exploring Expedition to the Rocky Mountains in the Year 1842, and to Oregon and North California in the Years 1843–44.* Newspapers across the country carry excerpts. It piques interest and yearning, including a small, persecuted western Illinois Christian sect. Inspired by Fremont's account, Mormons set their aspirations on a part of Utah around the Salt Lake Valley that Fremont recommends for settlement.

The Oregon/California Trail is the most prominent route to the West from 1841 until the Civil War twenty years later. Before the gold rush, it runs approximately 2,000 miles from Missouri toward the Rocky Mountains and ends in Oregon's Willamette Valley. That region, replete with fur trading and fertile farmland, is more established than California at the time, capturing the national imagination. Eleven thousand emigrants arrive in Oregon before the gold rush; California attracts only a quarter as many.

It has been called the "longest graveyard in the world." At least one in ten who start on the trail do not finish. An estimated 30,000 crossings in the early gold rush years translates to an average of fifteen graves per mile. Then one in five survivors will die within six months of their arrival in the promised land.

"We are at the mercy of the skies," laments a pioneer. The brave are exposed to extreme heat and freezing temperatures, frightful mountain crossings, rampaging rivers, hailstorms, and lightning strikes. Should you have a (likely undetected) underlying immune-deficiency issue, it can dispatch you at the first available pathogen. A physical injury on the road is different from one at home, where there is better medicine and better care (a licensed physician and mom), including a stable recovery bed, not a makeshift cot on a slapdash wagon bumping over unpaved trails.

Looked starvation in the face.

—Clark Thompson, 1850,
on the way to California

The most popular and gruesome account of land perils to California is the Donner Party saga. In July 1846, a group departs Independence, Missouri, in the general company of other pioneer groups. Approaching California, it decides to take a new route that promises to be faster but proves more daunting than anticipated. The party hunkers down for an usually nasty winter in the Sierra Nevada mountain range. Eventually, some resort to eating dead comrades to survive; there is evidence that two Native American guides are murdered for this purpose. Rescuers cannot arrive until the middle of February 1847, almost four months after the wagon train is trapped. Of the eighty-seven original party members, barely half survive. Accounts of the ordeal that reach New York City in July 1847 become national news as editors provide graphic and often exaggerated detail of the "cannibalism." For many readers, it represents a cautionary tale about such adventures. In 1846, an estimated 1,500 people trek to California. The number declines to just a third of that in the next two years. Donner is sobering, but the drop in emigration is likely caused more by the ongoing Mexican-American War. The 25,000 who rush to California in 1849 deliberately avoid the Donner Party's route.

The prudent pioneer stocks up on flour, dried meat, and other long-lasting, easy-to-transport foods. Supplies of everything, most critically food, is a constant problem as stocks run low or hunting and foraging are difficult. The 2,000 miles from Missouri to Northern California offers few predictable resupply opportunities. There are two dependable stops. Fort Kearny is established in 1848, the first to be built expressly for the aid of travelers along the Oregon/California Trail. Manned by 120 troops, it serves as a general way station and supply depot where travelers can get treated by doctors, visit blacksmiths, repair wagons, and deliver a baby or a letter.

Located 125 miles west of what is now Lincoln, Nebraska, wagon trains reach the spot after only a month into a six-month journey. At the height of the trail's traffic in the early 1850s, as many as 2,000 emigrants and 10,000 oxen might pass through the fort in a single day. Fort Laramie is founded as a private trading post in the 1830s for the overland fur trade. Purchased by the U.S. government in 1849 to protect and supply emigrants, the oasis sits at a point where the westward trail diverges in the direction of either Oregon, Salt Lake City, or California, just east of the long climb leading to the best and lowest crossing point over the Rocky Mountains.

Small, improvised trading posts set up by local Indians or émigrés abound. Caveat emptor reigns. You are stuck in the middle of nowhere. Entrepreneurs fill the supply vacuum, often as movable grocers or blacksmiths. There are stories of travelers who jettison supplies to get up mountains only to buy back the merchandise from resourceful "middlemen" who pick up the discarded goods and dash through secret passes to install pop-up stores on valley floors. Entrepreneurs are everywhere. Enterprising bridge and ferry boat operators typically offer supply depots that take full advantage of the laws of supply.

Émigré wagon trains are reluctant to take on sick and stranded strangers. Every group has limited resources. The military, hearing of the plight of pioneers trying to cross the Nevada and California deserts as well as those who might be trapped in the mountains—with the vision of the Donner disaster still fresh—does what it can to set up relief and rescue efforts in August 1849. The Michigan Wolverines come across two men sick from scurvy and unable to drive their teams. "They wanted us to take them through. But as distressing as is their condition, we declined, the government [wagon] train sent here for the relief of the emigrants will be back in a few days. . . . They have one noble ox, which will enable them to make some deal to get through even before that train arrives." That ox might save your life in a more fundamental way. Some killed their own teams "as a last and only resort to avoid a visit from that lank, lean, old monster, Starvation."

There are many ways to meet your maker on the trail. One of the most recorded and heartbreaking is by wagon. Animal-drawn vehicles are as common as the automobile is today, but a covered wagon over unfamiliar terrain is a novelty. Accidents are most common among women and children.

Mr. Harvey's young little boy Richard 8 years old went to git in the waggon and fel from the tung. The wheals run over him and mashed his head and Kil him Ston dead. He never moved.
—Absolom Harden, 1847

Word was passed that a woman had been accidentally run over and killed instantly. . . . The woman was getting down from the moving vehicle, her clothing caught on the break-rod and she was thrown forward beneath the wheel.
—Ellen James Bailey Lamborn,
September 3, 1854

The beasts of burden are your life and might be your death. In addition to the ox teams pulling the wagon, there are horses, mules, and even cattle herds, all of which can be spooked by a gopher or a gunshot, trampling people and damaging wagons. You might confront wild horse and bison herds overrunning your party. One traveler reports, "We were often compelled to halt our teams and form a circle with our wagons around our stock to keep it being stampeded by the buffalo, which crossed our track at intervals in herds of thousand, sounding like distant thunder as they rushed on with tremendous speed."

The "Great American Desert" inspires the need for weapons—and plenty of them. The perceived Indian danger and the need to shoot for defense and food motivates those who are neither hunters nor soldiers to purchase firearms, many for the first time. Not only are the shooters defective, but so are many of the pre–Civil War guns. There is no learning curve for the jump into the frontier. Gun mishaps are part of the death equation, probably as many by accident as by intention. The guns-to-California demand is unprecedented as manufacturers pour resources into production, leading to shoddy firearms. To make manifest destiny mania even more manifest, the U.S. War Department offers pistols, rifles, and ammunition at cost to California and Oregon emigrants.

Along the 2,000-mile route, you confront countless rivers and creeks that must be crossed or traveled, some for miles. The challenge is met by a new frontier "cottage industry" offering ferry boats and rafts to move wagons, men, and animals. The vehicles are often less than waterworthy. A traveler complains of "makeshift" ferries where "men are daily drowned. If one of those frail boats overset, all on board are lost. Not one in thousand save his life by swimming, no matter how expert at swimming. The water is cold and the current rolls and rushes along with a tremendous velocity." Perhaps as many drown on overland trail routes as on ships traveling the seas for six months. Again, the pioneers are witness to violent, unexpected deaths and ungodly burials. Arriving at a treacherous river crossing moments after a major destruction of equipment and animals as well as émigré losses, William Swain records escaping the "smell of death" as his party navigates the hellish scene.

Most land émigrés have never seen what they fear most. Indians are certainly a menace, and this apprehension accounts in part for the pioneer arsenal. Early gold rush routes traverse vast native lands of little-known tribes, each one distinct. This is an invasion, however inevitable and at times benign. One can expect native peoples to resist. Wagon trains and émigrés are always exchanging the latest news about such dangers, the stories often embellished in the passing. A few highly publicized massacres reinforce the fear. A wagon train attacked by the Shoshones results in nineteen émigré deaths; reports of torture are widely circulated. Soon after leaving Independence, Swain writes about entering Pawnee territory and hearing stories about "emigrants being attacked, plundered and slaughtered by them." Two days earlier, news reaches his company that the tribe has surprised and killed seventy emigrants 100 miles away. Swain remains calm and resolute. "The stories have alarmed some timid men, who retrace their steps. The best intelligence from the plains is that the emigration removes on safely."

His intelligence is correct. The Indians turn out to be more benign than belligerent. Many pioneers would never have arrived in California had it not been for trading and buying with tribes along the trail. Like any profile of humanity, Indians ranged from the dull to the daring to the crazy. Most Native Americans tolerated wagon trains passing through their territories. Many are indifferent or aloof. Some are con artists. Young émigré men are fascinated by young female Indians, a few of whom walk around "*naked!*" as one diarist exclaims. But beware of the bait and run: "I saw more than one man pay a squaw and head for the bushes. She would lead the way for a short distance, then turn and run to a gang of her own people. . . . The squaws would clap their hands and laugh as if they would split their sides."

Throughout history, there have always been those who go for a walk or chase a dog and become the man who never returned. It happens more often on the trail. Or you could get lost straying off main roads and find yourself deep in unexplored country. Should a party lose its way in the arid desert west of the Rocky Mountains, a lack of food or water might mean disaster. Such outcomes are more common for those traveling alone or in small groups. The Donner Party is always lurking in your mind.

The Grim Reaper will usually visit in the form of bacteria. Pioneers carry medicine kits to treat diseases and wounds. The arsenal includes patent medicine "physicking" pills, castor and peppermint oil, quinine for malaria, hartshorn for snakebite, citric acid for scurvy, opium, laudanum, morphine, calomel, tincture of camphor, and, the go-to when in doubt or dying, rum or whiskey. Often the cure is worthless or is worse than the disease.

The most prevalent diseases are typhoid fever, Rocky Mountain spotted fever, measles, mumps, flu, dysentery, smallpox, scurvy, and the king of the road, cholera: fast, rude, and deadly, it causes severe diarrhea and dispatches victims through dehydration. Within hours, your skin is wrinkling and turning blue. "People in good spirits in the morning could be in agony by noon and dead by evening," a pioneer remarks.

The bacteria spreads through water and food contaminated by human waste. The few overused natural water sources are quickly polluted. Abigail Scott laments in an 1852 diary entry, "The great cause of diarrhea, which has proven to be so fatal on the road, has been occasioned in most instances by drinking water from holes dug in the river bank and long marshes. Emigrants should be very careful about this." In time, this knowledge leads to changed behavior, but diligence and judgment are constantly challenged by sheer survival. Once the contagion hits, it can fell a community. An émigré writes, "First of all I would mention the sickness we have had and I am sorry to say the deaths. Francis Freel died June 4, 1852, and Maria Freel followed the 6th, next came Polly Casner who died the 9th and LaFayette Freel soon followed, he died the 10th, Elizabeth Freel, wife of Amos (and Martha's mother) died the 11th, and her baby died the 17th. You see we have lost 7 persons in a few short days, all died of Cholera."

If death does not strike the first day, one usually recovers and acquires immunity. Cholera dispatches more California pioneers than bears and bullets and arrows combined. It also kills untold thousands of native Indians who come in contact with émigrés. The outbreak along the Oregon Trail is an extension of a world-wide pandemic that begins in India. Major U.S. cities are struck, and the disease reaches overland emigrants initially by traveling up the Mississippi River from New Orleans. The epidemic thrives in the notoriously unsanitary conditions along the trail, peaking in 1850. Pioneers originating from Missouri are the most vulnerable. It remains a scourge through the Great Plains, but once past Fort

Laramie in Wyoming, overlanders are usually spared from cholera at the higher elevations.

I look back upon the long, dangerous, and precarious emigrant road with a degree of romance and pleasure; but to others it is the graveyard of their friends.

—OREGON RESIDENT, 1852

Death is a constant companion on the journey west. But everywhere in nineteenth-century America, the loss of loved ones is more direct and dramatic than today. Typically, it occurs at home. The nation is largely rural and Christian, embracing time-honored traditions for the deceased. What erupts on the road will test that tradition. Back at your hearth, there is a pattern and predictability to end of life: You bury old people, not the young and vibrant; the deceased is surrounded by generations who share grief and catharsis at formal ceremonies. A memorial stands as a permanent testament and place of commiseration. After-funeral rituals include bereavement periods communally embraced. It is clearly important to emigrants, especially in the early journey when psychological ties to family are still strong, to mourn and bury the dead with as much ceremony as time and conditions permit. A continuing grim reality will threaten those practices. Wagon trains and ships are mobile communities suffering communal loss, but there is little time for mourning. Travelers experience death in unanticipated, shocking ways and in numbers never imagined. That ordeal will continue in survival-of-the-fittest California. *There but for the grace of God go I. Life is cheap. Death is disposable.* Pioneers are crafting psychological defenses against the demise and sorrow all around them.

I attended the funeral of a child of Mr. Smith's, the man whose wife died two weeks ago where we were haying. The child, one of twin, eighteen months and seven days old, and has died of the same disease which caused its mother's death. Mr. Moore said in a sermon: Suffer the little children to come unto me. He spoke very feelingly upon the death of children, and I thought of my own dear wife and child and Mother and brother, from whom I have not heard these five months. God knows what is their condition. May He protect them from all harm.

—WILLIAM SWAIN, 1849

The service ends, and the wagon train presses on. What is lost is not only the ceremony and context of death but also the grief—a critical part of the loss-of-life experience. The healing process takes time and involves rituals, some formal, some subtle parts of daily experience surrounded by loved ones. When this catharsis is short-circuited, the "survival" mind will form its own closure.

The markers of death are never-ending signposts as common as the trees and the rocks. "For four hundred miles the road was almost a solid graveyard. . . . At one campground I counted seventy-one graves," writes George Tribble on his journey to Oregon in 1852. Of ten Tribble family members who start west, only five reach the destination.

Our knowledge of death on the Oregon/California Trail is drawn largely from diaries of those who walked the walk. Often there is only a simple, stark statement. "August 12. Sabbath. Mr. Seymour is dead. We have buried him beside the road with all the decency that we can here on the wilderness." Disposition of a body is often fast and minimal, often with no memorial. "Buried on the prairie" or "buried on the banks of a little creek in the Hot Spring Valley" are common diary notations.

Passed six fresh graves! . . . Oh, 'tis a hard thing to die far from friends and home—to be buried in a hastily dug grave without shroud or coffin—the clods filled in and then deserted, perhaps to be food for wolves.

—ESTHER MCMILLAN HANNA, 1852

As time passes and conditions worsen, so does compassion, especially for the dead. The collapse of an ox pulling your wagon might cause more dread than a human demise. Fear of disease degrades the care the healthy give the sick: "Many wagons kept moving through heat and dust with dying men suffering inside; and sometimes graves were dug before death brought surcease," records one traveler, a callousness that would have shocked and frightened families back home. "It makes your heart ache to see how some of the companies buried their dead. I have visited graves where the person was not buried more than twenty inches deep and found them dug up by wolves and their flesh eaten off and their bones scattered to bleach upon the plains."

Swain complains that cholera victim Mr. Lyon is the victim of negligence: "His mess and the doctor who attended him seemed to take but little care of him; otherwise he might, in all probability, have been saved." The next day brings a startling scene. The party is at Bull Creek, where the Santa Fe Trail and California Trail separate—a general camping grounds for emigrants. He notes ten newly dug graves. "Poor fellows. They little thought that this would be their fate when urged on by the laudable hope of benefitting themselves and their families. They left their homes and friends to endure hardship and toil, hoping to meet again the loved ones and to make them comfortable through life. Sad is their fate, buried here in this wild of wastelands, where not a mark will their last resting place far from loved ones."

A few are remembered and honored. Twenty-five-year-old George Winslow perishes from cholera on June 8, 1849, soon after his wagon party crosses into Nebraska. A companion, Bracket Lord, writes home: "George is dead—Our company feel deeply this solemn providence. I never attended so solemn funeral—here we were on these plains hundreds of miles from any civilized being—and to leave one of our number was most trying." Friends bury him on a grassy knoll under an inscribed sandstone slab, then send word back to his wife and family in Connecticut. Many years later, Winslow's sons relocate the grave site and erect a monument beside the trail swales. Owners of the family farm where the grave lies protect it to this day.

When Swain lands in California, he writes his brother to stay put and advises others to do the same—too many had died on the tough journey there, he laments, and the gold pickings are getting slim. He decides to return home with his remaining cash, about $15,000 today, arriving in New York City suffering food poisoning and seasickness. His family nurses the adventurer back to health. Swain passes in 1904.

Anchors Aweigh

You decide to chase the rainbow. Pick your poison. Do you want to tempt death by drowning or scalping? On a sea voyage, you will be a chicken in a tiny coop, enduring extremes of temperature as you lurch and pitch for six months over treacherous waters. But it is faster and safer to sail than to walk. Not counting European and Asian émigrés who must travel by sea, more people go this route than by land. In the autumn of 1849, the first 10,000 frenzied adventurers have disembarked in San Francisco Bay. By the end of the year, another 30,000 will rush ashore. Ship adventurers are called "Argonauts." In Greek mythology, Jason led a group of sailors—*nauts* in Greek—aboard a ship named *Argo* in search of the fabled Golden Fleece, thus "Jason and the Argonauts." In the twentieth century, the phrase morphs into sailors star trekking to outer space, as in "astronauts" and "cosmonauts."

You live in or around Boston or New York City. The sea route is calling and compelling as opposed to a frantic, crowded rush by boat and train for hundreds of miles just to plop at a point in frontier Missouri where you hurriedly buy a horde of overpriced supplies and get the opportunity to wait in an endless wagon line to depart by foot for another 2,000 miles across a virtually unmarked terrain with hostile Indians, uncertain supplies, desolate plains, death-defying deserts, freezing mountains, and—let your imagination run wild.

Of the approximately 250 ships setting sail to California from Massachusetts in 1849, more than half will leave from Boston. The demand for transportation is overwhelming. East Coast shipyards operate around the clock. New ships take time, so early enterprises concentrate on repairing and redesigning aging ones. Obsolete vessels get pulled from mothballs, including whaling fleets converted for paying customers by turning cargo bays into temporary—and often dismal—living spaces.

As with land travelers, prospectors form companies for mutual aid and protection; on a ship, it means room, board, and mining tools. Some groups purchase their own vessels and charge others to come on board. In 1849, more than 100 such companies sail from Massachusetts alone. The first embarks Boston scarcely a month after President Polk flags the race—the *Edward Everett* has among its 135 passengers eight sea captains, four doctors, a clergyman, a mineralogist, a geologist, merchants, manufacturers, farmers, artisans, and medical and divinity students.

Nearly half who sail in those first years—the proportion increasing as time passes—are traveling as single passengers.

In December 1848, a group of young New York men hurriedly form the California Mutual Association and solicit by newspaper for individual shares of $100 (cash, about $4,000 today) to buy an old ship, the *Panama*. Money is in hand seventy-two hours later. Each shareholder receives room and board to California, lodging on the ship while it lay in San Francisco harbor, and an equitable share of profits from the eventual sale of the vessel. Transport-only public tickets are offered for $130. Some speculate in public tickets, reselling them for a tidy profit just before sailing. Two hundred and two souls squeeze on board, including four women. The entire space between decks from stem to stern is equipped with bunks on either side, one above the other, each capable (theoretically) of holding two persons. Regular onboard association meetings manage day-to-day affairs and make major decisions, such as where and how often to stop along the route. The *Panama* takes 180 days to get to San

Francisco, typical at the time. Sailing vessels maintain a monopoly on this lucrative trade in the early gold rush.

This is a seller's market subject to wild price fluctuations in fares to California, but a single ticket can be as low as $75 for "steerage" passage, where you are treated as a piece of cargo, up to $400 for a private cabin, where you are treated as the captain's brother-in-law.

Entrepreneurs, most notably Cornelius Vanderbilt, quickly place steamers on both oceans to make the journey in about half the time of sailing ships, which require strong ocean winds far from the faster coastline routes. Sailing also requires stops for water and provisions more often than steamers, adding days to your journey and exposing you to Central American prospectors clamoring on board with who knows what local contagious disease.

The accelerated development of new, sleeker clipper sailing ships is a direct response to the challenges of getting to California as quickly as possible. The *Flying Cloud* makes news in 1851 when it goes from New York to San Francisco in eighty-nine days. That is unusual. The average clipper passage around Cape Horn is 125 days as opposed to 180. The clippers are built for speed. Long and thin and full of sails on three masts, accommodations are tight and narrow with ceilings so low that most passengers must bend over when moving about.

On the company-owned *Duxbury*, Lewis Meyer, a grocer from New York City, spots a "beautiful" clipper bound for California. "She came close along us so as to enable us to have a fair view of her. Her whole company on board consisted of 17 men. Although we were under the disagreeable necessity to see her beat us, still there is nothing discouraging in that for us, because such small vessels have invariably the advantage over larges, where such slight winds prevail as we have."

A ship around Cape Horn is the longest conceivable route from the East Coast, usually taking six months. This involves 18,000 nautical miles—from Northeast ports sailing south past the entire United States, past Central and all of South America, around the treacherous cape, and then all the way back up to about the same latitude as where you left but on the other side of the American continent. It is long and arduous, but what are the alternatives? By land, you must hold your horses until spring to leave from Missouri and then expect at least six months to arrive.

Sailors contemplate a dramatic shortcut, traversing skinny Panama. The grand Panama Canal is a half-century in the future. The Panama alternative, serviced by sailing ships as well as steamers, is theoretically the fastest sea route to get to California ahead of the "around-the-horn" trippers but also the most adventuresome. Disembark on the Caribbean side of Panama and trek overland about sixty miles across the Isthmus of Panama by foot and mule and rafts to reach the Pacific. The shortcut has a steep price. Travelers who carry what goods they can with help of native strangers across treacherous jungles and swamps face malaria, yellow fever, and highway robbers. Then you could get stranded waiting for arriving ships on the Pacific side sailing north from around the Cape. In 1850, *Gregory's Guide for California Travelers via the Isthmus of Panama* becomes a best-seller in East Coast cities. Some 6,500 brave souls had already made that journey the previous year, cutting 8,000 miles and perhaps three months off the Cape Horn route. Steamship companies that open in late 1849 set up scheduled runs in the Pacific to pick up their passengers who have been dropped off on the Atlantic side to traverse the isthmus. It is a complicated and uncertain venture. The Ensign and Thayer travel company issues an advertising broadside:

DIRECTIONS
for emigrating by sail
The Great Sea Adventure to
CALIFORNIA
VIA CAPE HORN
The distance from NY to Sf via Cape is about 18000 miles,
and will occupy nearly five months. Yet it is the surest route.
VIA CHAGRES AND PANAMA
On account of the great savings of time and distance,

the route is chosen by many . . .
The town of Chagres is a village of huts in the midst of a swamp.
The Climate is very unhealthy, producing bilious, remittent, and
congestive fevers. . . . The swamps, stagnant water, reptile etc.
render walking across next to impossible.
The Climate at Panama is more healthy than Chagres, but it is
dangerous to camp out, or live in tents, all it will soon prove fatal.
Avoid the sun, keep within doors during the day, do not
touch oysters . . . and be off at the first opportunity.
VIA MEXICO
Which is said to be "the cheapest, quickest and safest" is
to take passage in a vessel to Vera Cruz; thence overland
to Mazatlán, thence by vessel, mule or horse, up the coast.
To prevent danger of being attacked by robbers throughout Mexico,
persons should go in parties of 50 or more.

Everyone crossing Panama will witness gruesome deaths and rude burials that shock the senses. The nature and number of deceased in it-seemed-like-a-good-idea-at-the-time Panama can be gruesome for tenderfoots.

There are no nonstop ocean voyages. It is necessary to dock at ports along the way for desperately needed provisions and medical care. The *Duxbury*, with its eye on the prize, docks at only two: Rio de Janeiro and the Juan Fernández Islands. Most vessels harbored at more, such as Callao, Peru, or Valparaiso, Chile. When they do, Peruvian and Chilean immigrants buy their way on board, raising alarm among passengers that a tropical disease is hopping on board as well. One diarist notes that nearly all the ships in the crowded anchorage at Valparaiso are American vessels en route to San Francisco for the gold rush.

Welcome aboard! What can you expect? Bad food, bad weather, and stomach-wrenching waves—for six months. The early ships are not designed for long passages through extreme conditions. There is insufferable heat in the topics and freezing cold in other places. Steamers more than sailing ships stuff passengers on board beyond what vessels can accommodate, sometimes twice the number. Eager prospectors dare not complain; most would beg or bribe to board a sardine-packed ship if another sardine-packed ship were not available right away.

Anchors, aweigh! You are surrounded by water as far as the eye can see, bobbing and weaving and exchanging breaths with strangers from all walks of life. The steamer is faster than early sailing ships and soon becomes the most popular transportation "around the horn." The sea, especially the steamer option, perpetuates the inequality of life. Then, as now, first class gets the perks.

"Our vessel carried at least two hundred more passengers than she could comfortably accommodate," observes L. M. Schaeffer on a trip aboard the *Winfield Scott* from San Francisco to Panama in early 1852. "The decks were so crowded that a man really had not a place to spit. . . . The vessel was expressly built for the California trade, and even the smallest space was adapted to some use." An area at the bottom of ship that sat well below the surface—"way down in the hold"—has been quickly redesigned with berths from floor to ceiling. "There was hardly enough room left for a passenger to pass along. The place was dark; daylight rarely penetrated there." Yet fifty eager customers pay $75 ($3,000 today) for this privilege, which in this case is only to Panama, not California. The so-called steerage passengers pay double that to sleep on the second deck—"more comfortable" than the section below and where "they could enjoy a little daylight." Those on the third deck pay still a bit more but get additional "comfort," including bedding. Above them, literally, are those who "concede" another $50 that offers sleeping berths on the quarterdeck just beneath the surface plus early bird access to food (which runs out in quality and quantity as the mass meals continue throughout the day). For another $100, you ascend to first class, which provides "premium" dining and staterooms and "the privilege and hospitality of the whole vessel." Mr. Schaeffer enthusiastically recommends this "cabin ticket" for those who can afford it. James Buckley, on board the *Capitol* in 1849, describes his second deck cabin quarters as "my apartment, a chamber six ft long two ft wide about three ft high." Entire companies often live, eat, and sleep on the main deck; pieces of sail are used as protection from sun and rain.

As for the weather, expect anything—and expect that to change. One sea journalist writes,

February 9: . . . left harbor in buoyant spirits: Amid the adieus of our friends and the cheers of the spectators, we cast off from the wharf and with a flowing sail ran down the harbor.

Saturday 10th . . . it was very rough . . . now upon the top a great foaming sea is dashing across a long dark, blue valley, we again climb to the crest of some rolling mountain, only to again to be hurled from its brink to another mighty frothy valley. The rolling and heavying of the ship already wrought a mighty change in the faces of the passengers, as chests, trunks, boxes, etc. are darting hither and thither in the most wonderful confusion, and as many poor, pale looking devils trying in vain to secure them. . . . The ships sides from morn till night are constantly crowded, and each as he places his head over the rail or inserts it through the rigging, like a prisoner with his face to the grates, seem anxious to vie with his fellow in playing tribute to Jonah!

Sunday 11th—No service today. The minister is too sick to officiate.

Sleep is often whenever and wherever you grab it. "Vainly did the passengers endeavor to obtain rest," laments a traveler, "for how you can expect to sleep, when you are threatened every moment to tumble out of your berth, while the cracking sound of the ship and the noised of sliding and rolling trunks and chests fall constantly on your ear." With temperatures frequently around freezing, clammy dampness permeates clothing and bedding, especially in the lower decks. For days at a time, the hatches are closed as groups huddle in icy quarters, "living like moles in a swamp," seldom venturing onto the deck, which is likely covered with sleet.

There is food, terrible food—and not enough of it. To catch fresh fish on board is the high point of any day, but the effort is never sufficient to feed more than a few, and the precious meat can cause more resentment than pleasure. On ships, you eat in shifts, the order determined by your ticket status. Quality and quantity diminish quickly. Mess halls are small and dingy and typically overrun with mining supplies and general cargo. Mother Nature joins you for every meal, and you can never predict her volatile mood:

The gale became furious last night and seemed increasing in force this morning. We had no little difficulty in eating. . . . We could not sit, and we were in danger every moment of being pitched over the table, and across the cabin. To avoid such a catastrophe, we were obliged to hold by the berths with both hands. We made an effort, however, to eat, but had hardly made a beginning when a violent lurch of the ship sent our pork, bread, coffee, and all, in an instant upon the floor and into a neighboring berth.

Supplies of fresh fruit, meats, and vegetables are used up fast. Until resupply, there is dried or smoked fish, beans, salt meats on the edge of spoiling or well over it, and "navy" bread, that is, bread as hard as a rock. Criticism of meals and kitchen crews abound, as do threats of mutiny and plank walks for the cooks, spewed mainly by upper-middle-class gents who are more bluster than action.

Starvation!!
All those persons on board the Ship Panama famishing for wont of proper food, are requested to meet "en masse" in front of the cabin, at 10½ Oclock in order to ascertain if means cannot be found to obtain such food as will sustain ourselves until we arrive at San Francisco.

Several able speakers have promised to address the Meet & forcible speeches may be expected

The diarist reports the following day, "After waiting very patiently for about eight hours we dined in style, on burnt rice and molasses."

Water everywhere and nothing to drink. Ocean water is not consumable, so the suddenly precious item must be rationed. "We receive half a pint of stinking, rusty, brackish fluid twice a day," complains a passenger. "The fastidious adds to his a dram of brandy . . . the thoughtless gulp it down at once and in a few hours they are to be seen with parched tongues and dry lips cursing the ship, the Capitan, and the day they left their comfortable homes."

Disease can spread on twenty-first-century floating meccas that boast privacy, sanitation, and fresh food unimaginable 150 years ago. The gold rush ships in comparison resemble floating hospitals, if not hospices. The paucity of nutritious food over prolonged periods eviscerates the immune system and invites scurvy. It will continue as a menace in the goldfields. The disease induces mental as well as physical symptoms, including dementia. Beyond common seasickness, weakened and close-quartered passengers are frequently ill on board. In its six-month journey from Boston to San Francisco, the *Duxbury* records thirty cases of mumps and fifteen cases of measles. None are fatal in this case. If you die on board, the sea is your grave, often without ceremony, a tradition that stretches back to ancient times. Assuming that your loved ones back home get notification of the event, it will be many months after the death. There are rare exceptions. A deceased lady on board from Bavaria is transferred to a Dutch vessel bound for Amsterdam—possible because most ships follow familiar sea routes and communicate by signals or occasionally sail into nautical "communities" near port calls. Fifty miles outside Rio, the *Duxbury* had thirty-three vessels in sight.

You are more likely to get sick or die on a steamer than a sailing ship. Although travel is faster, steamers carry more passengers and crowd them closer together. This danger could spike dramatically when ships dock in port. Not only do they take on strangers, but existing passengers spend days in Panama or Chagres and might pick up a slew of festering diseases there, such as malaria, jaundice, dysentery, yellow fever (commonly called Panama fever), and the most feared killer of the era: cholera. Your ship has been cholera free since launch, but a port call can change your world in a second. In October 1850, a San Francisco steamer leaving Panama buries thirty-seven men at sea. None aboard has ever witnessed such a catastrophic and ignominious disposition of the dead. Firsthand accounts record how deeply it affects the survivors. *There but for the grace of God go I.*

Many who perish in Panama and Nicaragua are hastily buried in what becomes known as "American cemeteries." There is little understanding of these deadly diseases and no treatment. On ship, the malady would run its course, infect many, and kill some; hopefully, immunity stops the carnage. In 1852, Frank Marryat is aboard a ship leaving Panama on its way to San Francisco when cholera explodes among passengers "crowed as thick as blacks in a slaver." The two doctors on board are stricken and unavailable. Conditions worsen. "From the scuttle hole of our small we could hear the splash of the bodies as they were tossed overboard with little ceremony."

In 1852, cholera attacks the *Golden Gate* packed with gold seekers and a contingent of soldiers bound for the Presidio military base in San Francisco. Eighty-four military and an unknown number of other passengers perish. The fatalities continue daily until arrival. All are wrapped and tossed overboard. The *Blonde* reaches port soon after with eighteen of 300 passengers gone, which is quickly surpassed by the *Sir Charles Napier*, which records thirty-six cholera burials. We will never know the true number of sea casualties because San Francisco newspapers seldom make mention of the events. Ship company records are lax or lost. But word of mouth spreads the grim ongoing events, and in the absence of reliable information, reports are exaggerated. It is more of the same sad story: Life and death are different out here.

At least there are no hostile Indians or buffalo stampedes on the waves. You are in the middle of a vast ocean. No strangers have boarded for weeks, and few are "under the weather"—a nautical term for when sick passengers are transported to the lower decks. The skies are blue, and the sea is calm. You dare to take a deep breath of relief. What else could happen? One of the deadliest and feared perils is ship fires. Steamers and sailboats are made entirely or mostly of wood.

A galley fire erupts in 1852 on the *Golden Gate*, engulfing the ship in minutes. Of the 300 aboard, two-thirds of the passengers and one-third of the crew is lost. A California mine owner who survives floating and clinging to ship wood for a full day lives with the memory: "I was surrounded by a hundred or more people. To describe that sight, and the death scenes that were being enacted, is impossible. . . . Frantic and crazed men and women, frightful to behold and hear, were struggling in every direction, grappling with one another, drowning one another in ferocious embraces."

Mrs. D. B. Yates and her husband are sailing from Baltimore to San Francisco in the summer of 1850. Down the east coast of South America, the ship catches on fire but remains afloat long enough to reach the Falkland Islands. After being marooned for a month, they finally flag down and hitch a ride on a Scottish vessel. Rounding Cape Horn in a storm, eighty miles from land, that ship suddenly bursts into flames, feeding on cargoes of coal tar and liquors. Clutching her pet goat—"I would not leave her behind"—Mrs. Bates is thrust into a lifeboat as she watches the ship being consumed. But soon "Sail, ho!," and the drifting souls are rescued again, this time by an English ship. Two weeks later, the group is transferred at sea to another vessel that had launched from Baltimore. All is well for a fortnight, then Mrs. Yates reports a persistent foul odor. The captain initially dismisses the concern but soon declares an emergency. Drifting for three weeks in this condition, the *Amelia* finds its way to an uninhabited shore of Peru, where the twenty-six travelers survive as they watch the ship burn in the water. The captain dispatches a rescue boat one week later. Help arrives. Undaunted, the rugged Yates couple continue to San Francisco.

Sailing ships stay far from shore except when entering port; steamers hug the shores, seldom out of sight of land—a strategy to shorten the physical route. But it makes striking something more likely. Nautical charts are notoriously inaccurate. There are no light-houses. The few makeshift markers can be as dead wrong as helpful.

Ships full of passengers are lost at sea. One voyager confesses to his diary, "I go to bed every night with a kind of horror knowing we are so near the Cape." Imagine sailing around the world for six months and surviving what might dispatch a weaker man only to meet your fate moments before you set foot on the promised land. San Francisco harbor is treacherous. A ship must thread the nee-dle of the Golden Gate strait—barely a mile wide and three miles long. Captains call on a lifetime of skills to confront unpredictable weather in crowded, unmarked waters leading to improvised docks without navigation lights. The National Park Service notes, "The waters swallowed up many unlucky ships navigating this inlet just hours before they would have dropped anchor in San Francisco's safe harbor." It estimates that twenty-four shipwrecks occur there from 1849 to 1861. Newspapers ignore or diminish these tragedies, but fortune seekers are well aware of such heinous fates.

By oxen or schooner, the adventure to California captures the popular imagination as no other event of the era. Journalists and chroniclers begin a steady stream of tales from "out West" to an eager and bewitched nation. Millions have a loved one or acquaintance on that odyssey or know someone who does. Letter writing is ubiquitous at the time. Correspondence from lonely pioneers is passed around family and friends back home and featured in local newspapers. The flow of information, often poignant and shocking, allows the nation as a whole to share the frontier drama. Despair is mixed with hope as stories of hardships reach "the states." Pioneers witness death and suffering in unexpected and disturbing ways, in numbers that defy imagination. Kevin Starr characterizes it as a "collective return to primary experience. . . . For a few brief years, in far-off California, the bottom fell out of the nineteenth century. Americans—and not just Americans of the frontier—returned en masse to primitive and brutal conditions, to a Homeric world of journey, shipwreck, labor, treasure, killing, and chieftainship."

That long trek promises redemption. Setting foot in Northern California is momentarily cathartic—a new lease on life. Weary travelers record a strong shot of arrival adrenaline: *The worst is over, I have survived, the great quest can begin.* But that quest, however envisioned, turns out to be as nasty and unanticipated as the journey to get there. The Grim Reaper will continue to stalk the brave.

CHAPTER 4

INSTANT CITY, INSTANT STATE

NEWLY ACQUIRED NINETEENTH-CENTURY LANDS ENDURE PERIODS
as official U.S. "territories" before reaching the 60,000-inhabitant
threshold for statehood. Prior to the gold rush, emigration to California has been sporadic. Statehood seems an impossible dream—
the land belongs to Mexico. Even when the territory is ceded to the
United States in 1848 after the Mexican-American War, joining the
Union lies in the future. Then treasure fever brings 100,000 from
around the globe in a single year. San Francisco dominates the gold
region; by 1850, it becomes four times the size of Chicago and three-
quarters the population of Boston. Faced with such rapid growth
to a vast and valuable land, Congress permits California statehood
without any formal territorial stage.

> San Francisco is a hot-bed that brought humanity to a rapid,
> monstrous maturity.
> —ANNALS OF SAN FRANCISCO, 1855,
> THE FIRST RECOGNIZED HISTORY OF THE CITY

That a hamlet port 2,000 miles from the American frontier, confined by sand dunes as far as the eye could see, would in a mere
generation be called the "Paris of the Pacific" is the most improbable
of fairy tales.

The "City" flexed its metropolitan muscles overnight. Rome
wasn't built in a day. But San Francisco was. In his classic study of
urban development, Gunter Barth calls it a rare "instant city" that

virtually bursts into existence "full blown and self-reliant" in a generation. There is no history, tradition, or roots. A year before gold is discovered, the first census of Yerba Buena, soon to be renamed San Francisco, tallies a hearty 467.

By 1860, the city has more than doubled from the 25,000-strong 1849 invasion force. Throughout these years, there are always another 100,000 frenzied treasure hunters scattered about the goldfields some 100 miles inland. San Francisco is *the* place for recreation and investment.

To appreciate this extraordinary growth spurt, consider that the Bay Area is among the more remote places in the Western Hemisphere at this time—the only way to get there is by horse or ship (until the Transcontinental Railroad in 1869). By that year, it is the tenth-largest city in the United States. At the turn of the century, San Francisco boasts 350,000 residents. It takes Boston more than 200 years to reach that figure.

"Mining towns" spring up across the American West. San Francisco is unique. It is not a mining town per se; nary a nugget of gold is extracted from the ground, but tons of the precious metal are deposited right above, transforming it into the capital of a vast mining empire like no other. How did this happen? San Francisco has a large cove that serves as a harbor for trade. But it lacks the basic resources for a nineteenth-century settlement. Residents must bring water, fuel, and food to the site. A fortune of geography blesses the town. Sacramento and Stockton, located on the Sacramento and San Joaquin rivers, are much closer to the mining action. What gives San Francisco a critical advantage is the faster clipper ships, improving quickly in the 1840s and soon to be the standard for cargo and passengers. In an age before the Panama Canal, it can take 200 stomach-wrenching days in a conventional ship to travel from New York to San Francisco around Cape Horn at the southernmost tip of South America. The sleek clippers will cut the time almost in half. But there is a problem. Due to its unique design, that state-of-the-art vessel cannot navigate the shallow waters of gold country rivers.

San Francisco is able to accommodate any ship and quickly becomes the port of transfer for people and materials to the promised land. It is the end of humble beginnings and the start of great expectations.

The bay anchorage, which typically had a few ships arriving each month prior to the gold rush, quickly becomes home for hundreds of vessels packed with forty-niners and supplies. Crews from merchant vessels are confined to ship, virtual prisoners a tantalizingly short jump to land and maybe fortune. Some risk their lives to get away. Four Malay crewmen on an Australian ship are captured trying to escape in a whaleboat. Undaunted, the gang manages later to float away on a raft fashioned from planks only to die in a flash wave. Even the USS *Ohio* naval ship suffers the desertion of eighteen enlisted sailors. The vessels, most lacking a sufficient crew, often sit in port for weeks or months. The anchored armada becomes a liability. The mayor of the newly incorporated city of San Francisco appoints a "port czar" in 1850 to clean up the mess.

Enterprising developers decide to use landfill to extend the shoreline and build new piers. Part of that landfill comprises rotting carcasses of abandoned ships at anchor. Some are converted to saloons, warehouses, lodgings, churches, and one of the first city jails. The natural shoreline is pushed six blocks into the bay. Excavations for skyscrapers and other development in the late twentieth century uncover many of the once abandoned vessels. The San Francisco port is the largest ship graveyard in the world.

As the harbor is cleared and export trade expands, a sailor labor shortage emerges, especially for vessels traveling west to the Pacific. The crisis introduces "shanghai" to the American lexicon as unscrupulous captains pay "crimpers" to kidnap the able-bodied for involuntary maritime duty: experience preferred but not necessary. Shanghai Kelly's Saloon, still open for business today at the corner of Polk and Broadway streets, is named after a real character who made his living as a "crimp"—filling orders from ship captains who need crews. The most common recruitment method is to drug or ply the victim with liquor in a saloon or brothel. The unfortunate soul wakes up the next morning on board a ship sailing to the Far East, "*shanghaied*," referring to the distant Chinese port of Shanghai. The phrase and deed do not originate in San Francisco, but the city becomes legendary for the practice during the gold rush, when it is nearly impossible to induce men to leave such a potentially lucrative place.

The resourceful Mr. Kelly regularly dispatches "runners" to arriving vessels and offers free liquor to entice the unwitting and exhausted to his cozy establishment. Needing to fill an especially big order, the master crimp concocts a daring plan: charter a paddlewheel steamer and invite anyone to jump aboard and celebrate his birthday with endless free drink and food. Once they are drugged, he delivers ninety men to three awaiting ships. But how to explain returning to shore with an empty boat? Kelly hopes to sneak in "under the fog." As luck would have it, he stumbles on the *Yankee Blade* run aground. He graciously rescues the crew and steams back to the city, no one the wiser. Here is yet another harsh dose of the new reality: Life in the promised land is fickle and dangerous. Back on the farm or foundry, you never contemplated such a horror. You're not in Kansas anymore. You have arrived in that fabled land where the streets are paved with gold—and mud, rats, and even more dangerous predators.

The *Annals* describes an early turbulent atmosphere where there is "no sauntering, no idleness, no dreaming. All was practical and real; all energy, perseverance and success. Their rents, interest on money, doings and profits were all calculated monthly." It will be a scramble for survival more fiercely competitive than these young men have ever experienced.

You land in California, dead tired and weak but bursting with primitive enthusiasm. First, you must navigate the port gauntlet—an array of pickpockets, prostitutes, con men, crazies, beggars, merchants, and employers of all sorts desperate for help of all sorts.

Where to go in this chaos? Pioneers crowd the few hotels, a half dozen or more bodies in a single room, or makeshift lodging halls on rows of cots and hammock bunks hung from the ceiling.

In early 1849, argonauts create an ever-changing ragtag encampment that starts near the water's edge and stretches two blocks, a difficult half-mile trek from the more elegant "downtown" area surrounding Portsmouth Square. You could step off a boat and stumble right into Happy Valley. The name derives from its location in a fortuitous little enclave with patches of greenery and a few springs of water huddled between towering sand dunes that provide a bit of respite from sandstorms. For two years, it is a poignant symbol of what the early gold represents for many folks—both the winners

A Street-scene on a rainy night.

Author's collection

and the losers. Off and on, here and there, it houses at least 1,000 at any given moment.

Lewis Meyer gravitates to Happy Valley when his ship arrives. Amid the bustle, death is always on your doorstep. He writes, "A man died of dysentery (which by the way is very prevailing here) in a tent next to ours; and in the afternoon of the next day, was interred at a gently sandy elevation, here another, was already sleeping the sleep which knows no awaking."

In September 1849, New Englander George Kent estimates that at least 2,000 have pitched tents there. It is a popular spot for new arrivals as well as those who come back empty-handed and empty-hearted from the goldfields. Gary Kamiya describes it as "one of the grimmest neighborhoods in the city's history."

The attraction of Happy Valley is location—and cost, usually free. Newcomers find a temporary squatter home there as new landlords face problems even organizing lots much less collecting rents. Large barrels, dry goods crates, covered wagons, and even beached ships are used as dwellings. Virtually all lots in the vicinity had been granted to investors before the gold rush, but when confronted with serial transiency and a lack of organized perimeters, landlords suffer headaches figuring out which strangers are trespassing and whose property they occupy. Mr. Kent observes, "They locate in Happy Valley wherever they see fit, and any attempt to collect rent of them (there have been several such attempts made) is rejected as absurd."

The prime area around Portsmouth Square is crowded and expensive. It will run you $10 ($400 in current value) a day there, but you can get by on a dollar a day in a nearby tent cooking your own meals. Inhabitants of Happy Valley do what they can to make money. Some use dwellings during the day as restaurants or saloons, fix-it shops, and gambling dens and then as lodging quarters at night. Slapdash enterprises appear and disappear.

In the fall of 1849, Happy Valley becomes the instant city's first instant disease hot spot. Denizens drink water from what a physician there describes as "brackish little seep holes two to three feet deep." Latrines in the sandy campground are primitive at best and quickly become contaminated by human waste. The result is dysentery—a deadly form of gastroenteritis characterized by bloody diarrhea, fever, piercing abdominal pain, and dehydration. Then cholera strikes.

A forty-niner records, "Visited Happy Valley. This name is a great 'misnomer' by the way, for a more squalid unhealthy place I never saw. Hundreds of tents in and about it with vast numbers of sick lying in them on the ground and about them in all directions. Poor fellows, many of them must die from the melancholy fact of having no one to do or take the least interest in them." Making health conditions worse, many of the dead are buried right there. It is not uncommon to walk through the settlement and see deceased men laying unattended near their tents.

In May 1850, John McCrackan spends three hours wandering through Happy Valley in search of a family friend suffering from dysentery. The ailing gentleman is transported to a hospital only to succumb the next day. "It is dreadful to think of him coming out here to suffer so much, and then to die," McCrackan writes to his family.

A young Australian argonaut is the son of a chief justice in Sydney. The demise of Francis Forbes turns Happy Valley into a world story as Australian newspapers urge a pause in the California rush by publishing dark accounts of conditions there. The Sydney *People's Advocate* declares, "The fever and diarrhea and dysentery had made dreadful havoc . . . and the awful pictures of the tent town or encamping ground at Happy Valley are horrifying in the extreme. To multitudes it has proven the valley of the shadow of death." Graves were everywhere, the paper reports, noting the "downcast spirits" of new arrivals as if "they had been thrown by their own voluntary exile into a Golgotha."

But Happy Valley, like every place in San Francisco, changes with stunning speed. A wealthy cabal buys up the distressed lots. With its own funds matched by the town council, the area is transformed. Elegant homes spring up, including a prefabricated Chinese residence inhabited by Colonel John C. Fremont. Industry follows—factories, iron foundries, shipyards, and sawmills. In April 1851, in what may be the first published lament for the city's good old days, a local newspaper comments on Happy Valley's transformation: "One by one the relics of San Francisco's early days are disappearing." By 1852, the tent city has vanished but not the deep-seated memory of the fragility of life and death in the untamed West.

The gold rush is the rush west, then the rush to the goldfields, and then an anticipated rush home. Most pioneers reckon to be in San Francisco for a few frantic years before returning as rich, even celebrated, men. Fewer than one in twenty arrives back home in as sound a financial state as when he left.

Everyone is searching for treasure of one sort or another. Some do strike it gold rich, but the majority survive by other means, and many thrive. Merchants prosper more than prospectors. Enterprising migrants set up businesses to furnish, feed, and entertain the region's growing population. Failed miners became settlers, and the San Francisco Bay Area booms. In the course of 1850, the population of California mushrooms from 18,000 to 92,000.

Northern California at the time is arguably the most vibrant, ambitious, and youthful testosterone-driven spot in the nation. It leads to great building, entrepreneurship, and innovation. The most successful merchants find a product or service, not necessarily the first in the market but the first to think big and establish domination in a unique entrepreneurial vacuum, perhaps the largest such window of opportunity in history. From Levi's to ladies of the night, "mining the miners" is the surest road to success. The cream of that San Francisco crop become enduring national household names:

- Levi Strauss opens a San Francisco branch of the family New York City clothing business in 1853. His customers are miners who complain that their pants fall apart in the rigors of gold digging. Strauss experiments with durable canvases and applies for a patent to fashion riveted trousers. Miners, cowhands, lumberjacks, and railroad workers make the pants legendary. Soon, he uses a durable cotton, known as denim. In 1981, the company moves its corporate headquarters to what is now called Levi Strauss Plaza in the Embarcadero. It pays $46,532 in 2001 for a pair of denim trousers it made in the 1880s—at the time the oldest known. In 2018, a pair of Levi's goes to an anonymous buyer from Asia for almost $100,000; it was originally purchased 125 years earlier by an Arizona Territory storekeeper who stashed them in a trunk after a few wears.

- Henry Wells and William Fargo take the young American Express Company—designed to transport goods and valuables between New York City and Buffalo to various points in the Midwest—and expand its operation in 1852 to banking and express shipping to California. The 1950s television hit *Tales of Wells Fargo* depicts Dale Robertson as the stalwart company agent who rides the West tracking down those who dare to rob Wells Fargo stage and railroad shipments. The Wells Fargo Museum is on the site where the first San Francisco office opened.

- Domingo Ghirardelli has a miner supply store in Stockton and San Francisco. Both burn down in 1851. He embraces chocolate in 1852 and hits the sweet spot. Ghirardelli's Chocolate Factory occupies four different sites before the company takes over the Pioneer Woolen Mills on North Point Street—the present site of Ghirardelli Square.

- James Folger arrives in San Francisco in 1849 as a teenager and purchases a stake in a coffee mill company before leaving to find gold. He carries along samples of coffee and spices, taking orders from grocery stores along the way. On his return to San Francisco in 1865, Folger becomes a full partner of the Pioneer Steam Coffee and Spice Mills. In 1872, he buys out the other partners and renames the business J. A. Folgers & Company.

- Isadore Boudin establishes a commercial bakery in 1853 where he produces the renowned sourdough bread that quickly becomes synonymous with San Francisco itself. Miners acquire a love for the special flavor, taking various sourdough starters on their travels; those who go to Alaska in the 1890s gold rush are called "sourdoughs."

The fabled forty-niners are the most motley crew of strangers in history, thrust together from all corners of the world into a tiny domain. Even a decade later, two-thirds of the city's population is foreign born—either immigrating to the United States before 1849 or arriving from other countries. Most are adventurous young males who, if married, decline to take families on such a perilous journey. The devil's trifecta of drinking, gambling, and prostitution can suck hearty souls into a vortex of treacherous lifestyles. In 1853, a city newspaper counts 537 saloons, forty-eight houses of ill repute, and forty-six gambling dens servicing a population of 35,000, perhaps the highest per capita ratios in history for those "sin" categories. There are two churches.

It is a unique situation in American history. Thousands of eager young men unshackled from family and moral moorings travel to the ends of the earth for a brief adventure where strangers will never see you again and neither care nor remember what you do there. Relatives and friends are literally a continent away. Gold rush California is the original "Las Vegas: what happens here stays here." In this far-off land, traditional social norms dissipate overnight, and reputation seems to have little long-term value—down the hatch and let the devil take tomorrow.

"Gambling," the *Annals* notes, "was a peculiar feature of San Francisco at this time. It was the amusement—the grand occupation of many classes—apparently the life and soul of the place." Gambling is human nature, but the impulse is kept in check by religious and conservative traditions. Remove those and toss in the young, most adventuresome, risk-taking men in the world who have already thrown all caution to the wind, and you will have a gambling problem. And a drinking problem. One forty-niner observes, "Men who in the States never drank are here irreclaimable drunkards." California changes souls.

The thriving gambling dens and saloons encourage a bold *Star Wars* mixing of races and ethnicities in whirls of recreation and recklessness. Whatever cultural prejudice immigrants carry from their homelands can be blown to the San Francisco Bay winds in liquor-fueled soirees. This degree of cross-cultural fraternization is not common at the time anywhere else in America. Practice may not make perfect, but practice makes tradition. It engenders a pragmatic equality in a nation that is already celebrated for egalitarianism.

This unrestrained, live-and-let-live atmosphere offers scant time for compassion or connection or cooperation. It breeds the most tolerant society on Earth as it breeds the most diverse society on Earth—a contradiction that proves to be the answer to itself. Everyone is too focused on personal wealth to pay attention to others except when they get in the way. There are so many different peoples to which to direct hostility that a fortune seeker could get paralyzed in the effort to practice it. Given such a diverse collection of customs and looks, it is either tolerance or civil war. As Carey McWilliams notes, California migration represents "an equality of opportunity almost unmatched in history . . . a poor man's gold rush." Miner claims and

Colored population—Greaser, Chinaman, and Negro.

This illustration appears in the *Annals of San Francisco, 1855*. The authors are Anglo patricians who reflect the common prejudices of the era, especially among elites. They are equal opportunity critics, however, sparing no one, regardless of station or origin, from acid satire. *Virtual Museum of the City of San Francisco*

practices in the early years are largely individual in nature, and no one knows where or how to dig for the treasure. Your family's wealth, your fine education, and your fancy duds mean little on this frontier. It is the egalitarian American Dream writ big and bold. Mark Twain and others who chronicle the early American West celebrate the wild scene as conducive to both democracy and innovation.

Male-to-female ratios are wildly skewed. The *Annals of San Francisco* estimates that a mere 700 women are among the presumed 25,000 who arrive in the city during the first two years of the gold rush. Most calculations for these years hover around fifty to one. Commentators always remark on the paucity of women. Bayard Taylor, sent west by the *New York Herald Tribune* to cover the gold rush, writes that a disparity of this magnitude "has never been seen before."

Some attribute the high suicide rate in early San Francisco—the second-leading cause of death—to the dearth of women. The *Annals* waxes poetic on a male facing his maker in this God-forsaken corner of the world. Unlike the dying man back in his native land "cheered by the sweet, loving attentions of the woman—it may be wife, sister or daughter . . . few of such consolations attend the dying here." This "melancholy" subject is especially poignant in face of "the frequent and unexpected death of young 49ers. . . . At home, the shrinking invalid is cheered by the sweet, loving attentions of a women," but in harsh, isolated San Francisco, "no such consultations attend the dying."

These hardships are enough to drive a soul to madness. It is well reported across the country that there are more suicides in gold rush California in proportion to population than any other state. One pioneer pens home in 1849, "Suicides, caused by depression, are as numerous as the death resulting from natural causes."

"In no part of the world are poverty and affluence so nearly mingled in the same cup," remarks Benjamin E. Lloyd, a well-read commentator at the time. "Nowhere is fortune so fickle, nowhere do so many fall in a day from wealth to wants. Such transition naturally disturb the mental balance. . . . [Some] have not possessed strength of mind to enable them to encounter poverty and disappointment, and who have just enough intelligence to perceive that their lives are worthless to themselves and to society. . . . Perhaps the most potent cause of insanity in California is the excessive indulgence in intoxicating drink."

Bayard Taylor describes a miner returning from the goldfields who has just been set ashore near Happy Valley: "He was sitting alone on a stone beside the water, with his bare feet purple with cold, on the cold wet sand. He was wrapped from head to foot in a coarse blanket, which shook with the violence of his chill, as if his limbs were about in pieces. He seemed unconscious of all that was passing; his long, matted hair hung over his wasted face; his eyes glared steadily forward, with an expression of suffering so utterly hopeless and wild that I shuddered at seeing it."

The best and the brightest settle California, but there are countless souls who fall by the wayside. Some commentators at the time suggest that the very privilege that allows a pioneer to come to California might prove his downfall. Dr. Wake Bryarly is a visiting physician for the Sacramento State Hospital, the first hospital in California established specifically for the mentally ill as well as regular patients. He observes in 1851, "Perhaps two-thirds of the immigrants to the country, since the spring of '49, have been young men of this age—[twenty to twenty-five], have been nurtured in a lap of luxury; surrounded by a host of kind friends and relatives, and where their domestic relations have been most happy and many who were in such circumstances as to ask nothing of dame fortune. . . . They arrive here, one half of them, already worn down and debilitated by sickness; then comes the change of scene; change of living; change of climate; change of country and indeed, everything which tends to about a complete revolution in the whole system and constitution."

Lloyd concurs: "The most excitable and unsettled people have been attracted hither from all parts of the world, bringing with them a temperament favorable to the development of insanity. And the circumstances to which they are exposed are inimical to the exercise of self control."

Sex and the City

There ain't a thing that's wrong
with any man here
That can't be cured by putting him near
A girly, womanly, female, feminine dame . . .
There is nothing that you can name
That is anything like a dame.
—"There Is Nothing Like a Dame," Rodgers and
Hammerstein, *South Pacific* (The musical depicts
young men fighting in World War II sans the
traditional comforts of young females,
a situation akin to the gold rush West.)

A lawyer writes his sister back home, "You have no idea how few women we have here, and if one makes her appearance in the street, all stop, stand, and look. The latest fashion to carry them in their arms (the streets are incredibly muddy). This we see every day."

Miner's Ball by Andre Castaigne. *Alamy*

For a young lady, this could be a boon. "Every man thought every woman in that day a beauty," a Sacramento woman tells her diary. "Even I have had men come forty miles over the mountains, just to look at me, and I was never called a handsome woman, in the best day, even by most ardent admirers."

In 1853, only some 8,000 of San Francisco's 50,000 are women. Well into the 1880s, men make up almost two-thirds of the population. Only in the twentieth century will the sexes be close to numerical parity. No other large American city has such a dramatic gender history. The paucity of family life in those early years will affect how residents perceive and practice death traditions. The attitudes will persist even when domestic relationships begin to stabilize.

The gender imbalance is a subject of marvel to every observer then and since. At the end of 1849, the city population is about 20,000, of which it is estimated that 1,100 are women, and 700 of those are in the sex business. The world's oldest profession thrives in this hormonal tsunami. Most men arriving in San Francisco are in their raging testosterone twenties and deprived of traditional sexual relations for six months or more. The *Annals of San Francisco* calculates that in 1850, some 2,000 women descend, "many of whom were of base character and loose practices." Other writers describe them as "working girls" and "harlots." The earliest pioneer prostitutes, or "señoritas," are mostly indentured Latin Americans imported to entertain men in the mining camps and towns. On the level that most men engage in prostitution in the early years, it is a highly dangerous practice. Venereal disease, often leading to death, is added to the wages of sin and decimates women as much as their clients. There is no germ/bacteria theory of infection and no penicillin.

This trade establishes San Francisco as a world-class carnal attraction, a reputation it still commands and sometimes touts. Most of these female immigrants arrive from Mexico and South America with the same motivation and pluck as the men—to make as much money as possible in the shortest time and depart. But as quickly the sea winds will carry them, more "professional" ladies arrive from the eastern United States and Europe along with savvy madams. Upscale brothels mushroom in the fertile soil. The level of service and cost quickly escalate. Some of the houses are conspicuously opulent, beyond anything young male adventurers—now flush with gold—ever conjured up in their wildest back-home fantasies.

The first celebrated parlor house is that of the "Countess," who arrives from New Orleans in the summer of 1849 with a "stable" of beautiful and cultured young ladies. Obtaining a two-story frame building on Washington Street across from the town center at Portsmouth Plaza, Irene McCrady announces the opening of her establishment with an elegant reception conveyed by engraved invitations to the city's most prominent citizens, including the clergy. The Countess, adorned in stunning evening gown and jewels, escorts guests through a lavishly furnished reception room to a luxurious parlor. Piano music accompanies the fine champagne and light supper. Guests who choose to stay past midnight pay $96 ($3,000 today) to partake of the private entertainment. The Countess becomes the mistress to a successful gambler who runs the famed El Dorado Gambling Hall and Saloon. "The only aristocracy we had here at the time," remarks Caleb T. Fay, a leading politician, "were the gamblers and prostitutes."

These "parlors" are an East Coast adaptation. Since the development of an affluent nouveau riche in New York City a century earlier, such establishments flourish. The transplantation to the western pool of riches is restrained only by the time it takes to get there. A San Francisco customer has an opportunity to indulge in elegant seclusion and luxury available to few in the world. Yes, the ladies are the draw, but the regal furnishings, unrushed companionship, fine liquor and food, attentive service, and live music may be as important as the carnal pleasures, assuming that you could remember those pleasures the next morning. What you do not forget is the nasty climate, rude accommodations, and violent milieu that you may have escaped to enter that fleeting moment of pleasure. French or French-looking women are an immediate hit. They had charm and novelty, French journalist Albert Benard de Russail remarks in 1852. "Americans are irresistibly drawn by their graceful walk, their supple and easy bearing, and charming freedom of manner, qualities, after all, only to be found in France. . . . But if the poor fellows had known what these women had been in Paris, how he could 'pick them up on the boulevards and then for almost nothing, they might not have been so free with their [extravagant] offers."

In the early years, the French presence is "underground" but only formally. Soon *nymphs de pave* stroll the fashionable streets, attend plays, and enter the stores to purchase the best that could be bought or solicited. The *Annals* notes in 1855, "Someone has remarked that in Eastern cities the prostitutes tried to imitate in manner and dress the fashionable respectable ladies, but in San Francisco the rule was reversed—the latter copying after the former."

The most ambitious and sophisticated take quick advantage of the chance for social mobility in the sexually permissive city. Madams move into the upper echelons of San Francisco society. Women at all levels of this industry become part of the wider entrepreneurial culture that "mines the miners." Restaurateurs, bankers, merchants, and purveyors of "sin" garner the most reliable assets. Prominent madams become as powerful as they are legendary—the most successful American businesswomen of the era.

Among the early acts of the new state of California is a radical law in 1851 that allows either a husband or a wife to separate on the grounds of incompatibility and petition for a court-appointed referee in place of a public trial. The district court in San Francisco is known as the most liberal. There are 269 marriages in San Francisco during 1856 and seventy-two applications for divorce—ranking as the number one per capita divorce spot in the country. "Marriage among us," observes the *San Francisco Chronicle* in 1866, "seems to be regarded as a pleasant farce—a sort of 'laughable afterpiece' to courtship. . . . The divorces which are granted here are in a tenfold ratio the number in any other part of the Union of equal population."

In his study of pioneer California culture, Carey McWilliams suggests that "where women are at a premium, women's rights are freely granted.... A remarkable independence was conferred upon women in California." Sparsely populated Wyoming is the first state to confer female suffrage in 1869, a half-century before the practice becomes national law. California never goes that far, but its early liberal divorce laws give females leverage, and they exercise it more often than do husbands. Women get even more unprecedented power when the first state constitution grants them in divorce the ownership of any property, real or personal, possessed before the marriage. The Far West revolution in conjugal relations will infect the nation.

We do not wish to say, or even imply, that San Francisco is the wickedest and most immoral city in the world but it has not yet overcome the immoral habits contracted in the days when the inhabitants were nearly all males, and had nothing to restrain them from engaging in the most vicious practices; when there were no mothers to chide their waywardness and say in winning tones: "My son go not in the way of evil" and fewer virtuous sisters to welcome brothers home, and by their loving kindness and noble lives, to teach them to cease from sinning.
—BENJAMIN E. LLOYD, *LIGHTS AND SHADES*
IN SAN FRANCISCO, 1876

From the earliest days, there are schemes to fill this moral vacuum. The most celebrated is hatched by Eliza Farnham, author and former matron of the female section of Sing Sing Prison. She has skin in the California game. Her adventurous late husband leaves a large tract of land near Santa Cruz that she is keen to develop. But true to her feminist idealism, she concocts an ambitious plan to organize a group of well-recommended marriageable women that would "bring their refinement and kindly cares and powers" to the rough-hewn society of male gold miners. Ideologically, Farnham

LAND OF THE DEAD

goes farther than most feminists of the age, advocating the natural superiority of women. She is prominent, and so are her public supporters, the likes of Horace Greeley and William Cullen Bryant, editors of the *New-York Tribune* and the *New York Evening Post*, respectively, and Henry Ward Beecher, the renowned clergyman and abolitionist.

Farnham shuttles between cities on the Atlantic coast, addressing meetings, examining applicants, and giving press interviews. Soon, she could announce that more than 200 women had "signified" a desire to join up. The *Tribune* praises her and the potential "precious cargo . . . on an errand of mercy to the golden land." Editors on both coasts are captivated by the notion. In California, there is joy. One local mining newspaper reports that "the smiles of anticipation wreathed the countenance of every bachelor in town." However, Farnham is having difficulty finding suitable young ladies and then closing the deal on a wild adventure that would yank a young lady from her family and friends to go halfway around the world on speculation for a small fortune in advance. The ballyhooed April launch is postponed. By June, she is ready to give up the plan and sail anyway with a scant three prospects. Disappointed supporters complain that her personal standards for recruits may be too high and so is the price tag. The *Alta California* accepts the news graciously: "The will is always taken for the deed, and bachelors will unquestionably cherish the liveliest of feelings of regard for the lady who so warmly exerted herself to bring a few spareribs to the market." Farnham expressed no regrets. After experiencing "the moral and social poverty" of California for six years, she is "grateful that my endeavors failed."

There are other grand plans to civilize the Wild West by estrogen. Miss Sarah Pellet pursues a scheme for "amelioration of the condition of Californians." Again, the plan looks solid on paper. Import 5,000 young ladies from New England to be recommended by the Sons of Temperance in New England as "worthy girls." Sons of Temperance in California agree to take care of the ladies on arrival.

INSTANT CITY, INSTANT STATE

If this works, up the contingent to 10,000. Too few worthy girls are willing to be shipped, and the plan is abandoned, again breaking miners' hearts.

One might regard the formative gold rush as a "Lord of the Flies" historical moment analogous to William Golding's tale of proper English schoolboys shipwrecked on an island without women or adult males: It is a gradual descent into hell. Boys will be boys, especially with no females or traditional authority figures to temper behavior. Fewer than one in twenty going west in the early gold rush—even into the 1850s—is female. That male world begins the moment one steps into the journey from anywhere. On the *Duxbury*, a traveler notes that "the entire trip was filled with friction and outright fighting, both among the ship's crew and between passengers."

Kevin Starr describes the "Western era" as "a man's world . . . and yes, it could be wild, free, unconventional. Exuberant." This waxes romantic. There is a darker version: "In the course of a month or a year," remarks Edmond Auger, an early French gold hunter, "there was more money made and lost . . . more sudden changes of fortune, more eating and drinking, more smoking, swearing, gambling, tobacco chewing, and more profligacy . . . than could be shown in any equal space of time by any community of the same size on the face of the earth." California will continue to tilt male demographically and culturally into the twentieth century.

Most readers applaud the sentiment of James Wyld in his 1849 *Guide to the Gold Country of California*: "Society without woman is like an edifice built on sand. Woman, to society, is like the cement to the stone. The society has no such cement; its elements float to and fro on the excited, turbulent, hurried life of California immigrants." This is an urgent subject, widely discussed: Women bring civilization—civil society—which begins and is bred at home. Traditional Victorian family values translate into civic values and rituals, including marriage and funerals.

Commentators at the time recognize the positive female influence on the arts, dress, and public manners. The *Annals*, a harsh critic

The traditional Sabbath turns into the devil's workshop. *Sunday Morning in the Mines* by Charles Nahl. *Alamy*

of French ladies of the night sauntering the city streets, concede that they do improve civic behavior. Men dress and act better to impress them. Refined entertainment venues and restaurants open. Some pundits, then and now, attribute, even corollate, the march of "civilization" *in* California to the march of women *to* California.

Early efforts to export virtue illustrate how keenly and quickly the national obsession with "outlier" California appears. San Francisco earns a reputation as the most wicked and licentious city in the country. The jokes and wry commentary in the 1850s reveal a national anxiety: American values are not being transplanted in the newest state. From civility and the arts to the formation of families and respect for rituals, such as Sabbath and burial ceremonies, this far-off land is going awry. Uncontrolled ethnic and religious diversity is said to exacerbate the crisis. Perception becomes reality: The pace of change, loose morals, crime and corruption, cutthroat competition, willful flaunting of tradition, and tolerance for radical ideas turn California into a symbol of suspicion and awe to the distant thirty states—and the world. Can it be reformed before this shiny new jewel begins to reform the nation? What if young folks all over the country are infatuated and infected with California fever? Even when the great rush wanes, California remains a favored destination, real for some, a dream for many. The sentiment that one pioneer expresses in a letter to his sister back home is widely echoed at the time: "The independence and liberality here and the excitement attending the rapid march of this country make one feel insignificant and sad at the prospect of returning to the old beaten paths back home."

New western perspectives encourage a rethinking of common norms, from sex to death. The San Francisco anti-cemetery movement will feed off this impulse and help to chart a new course on how ancestors are regarded and treated in the rest of America.

However daring and resourceful, young men on the edge of the continent are reluctant to cut the umbilical cord. The rough and ready are lonely and vulnerable—a condition few wish to face. Mail is a lifeline—the one connection pioneers have with the world left behind. J. S. Holliday points out that the exchange of letters "began a dynamic process by which the entire nation was emotionally involved in the rush to California." That correspondence is widely shared and often published in local newspapers. The first letters reach homes in March and April from the Missouri frontier and continue to arrive from drop-offs at Forts Kearny and Laramie and then from California itself. Communication is slow. If you are stuck in the American West and wish to share a thought with your mother back home, it will take at least a month for her to get it and another month to receive a response. At that rate, a serious conversation could take years.

The U.S. government extends postal service to California in early 1849 via ocean steamers. By October of that year, the lone San Francisco post office is buried in 45,000 letters. It will get worse. The following year, more than a million letters pass through San Francisco. Most travelers have had no contact with loved ones at home for at least six months. Lines stretching for blocks form at the Portsmouth Plaza post office whenever a Pacific mail steamer is due, and it is common for busy men to hire surrogates to stand in line. Charles Fracchia observes, "Plaintive, sad letters to family members and sorrowful notes in diaries denote how these men missed family and friends, the familiar comforts of home, and highlights the discomforts of their present situation and loneliness." Local newspapers from anywhere are eagerly snapped up. A prescient gentleman arriving in 1849 brings 500 copies of New York City newspapers and hawks the old print at $1 ($40 today) each in two hours.

SUPPLY AND DEMAND

The population of the city in 1850—in flux and difficult to calculate—quickly bounds to 25,000. The previous year, some 75,000 pass through on the way to the goldfields. They return to San Francisco to cash in, restock, and revitalize, spending money like drunken argonauts. That all the goods, from wheelbarrows to whiskey, must be imported turns early San Francisco into a clinic on supply and demand in an unregulated marketplace.

Prominent resident Sam Brannan knows an opportunity when he sees one. He builds a large general supply store next to Sutter's Fort where John Marshall first discovered gold and another in nearby Sacramento. At the height of the early gold frenzy, the Fort Sutter store is the only major supply depot between goldfield lands and San Francisco. The establishment turns enormous profits, on exceptional days as much as $5,000 ($200,000 today). There is no mention of any security arrangements to protect the gold/cash-only business revenue, but it likely resembles a frontier version of Fort Knox.

The early forty-niners face the rudest sticker shock in history. Here are some examples from the 1849 price list at Sam Brannan's Sacramento store ($1 = $40 today):

Pork: $1 a pound

Chickens: $16 each

The 49er by Ernest Narjot. *Colma Historical Association*

Eggs: $0.85 each

Potatoes: $1 a pound

Tea: $5 a pound

Shovels: $25 each

Socks: $10 a pair

Underwear: $15 a pair

Rifle: $75 each

Bath: $2

Lodging: blanket on the ground ($1 a night, including armed security)

High prices directly impact health. Not only are medical services and supplies dear, but there is less money available for personal attention—you need a pickax more than a dressing for your it-ain't-that-bad bleeding wound.

A cheap place to lay one's head in San Francisco without losing it. *Author's collection*

Walter Colton, a former U.S. chaplain, finds the prices ungodly: "You are hungry—want a breakfast—turn into a restaurant—call for ham and eggs and coffee—then your bill—six dollars! Your high boots have given out; you find a new pair . . . and now what is the price—fifty dollars! Your beard has not felt a razor since you went to the mines and your frizzled hair must be clipped. You find a barber, his dull shears hang in the knots of your hair like a sheep shearer's—his razor he strops on the leg of his boots, and then hauls away—starting at every pull a new fountain of tears . . . and what is the charge for this torture—four dollars!"

The lofty prices prevail during 1849 and 1850, then slowly recede as resourceful suppliers fill the entrepreneurial vacuum. It hardly happens overnight. Supply chains before railroads are cumbersome and unpredictable. There is no Panama Canal. The gold riches unearthed daily buoy up extraordinary prices, creating an atmosphere of reckless abundance—witness the gambling parlors where thousands of dollars are won or lost nightly over the flip of a single card.

It sounds almost incredible now, the many stories that are told of the manner in which persons would waste the gold dust in those early times but it was the truth, nevertheless. In front of Mr. Howard's store, on Montgomery street, from the sweepings of the floor a man got over fifty dollars [$2,000 today] in one day. . . . The man who did the City Hotel sweeping would save the sweepings in a barrel, until full; and on washing it out he obtained over two hundred dollars in gold dust.
—JOHN BROWN, *REMINISCENCES AND INCIDENTS OF THE EARLY DAYS OF SAN FRANCISCO*, 1857

John Brown is an example of the rugged, free-spirited character who makes his way to fledgling San Francisco. "In introducing myself to the Public, I wish to say that I was born in the City of Exeter, Devonshire, England. While still very young, I left home to serve as an apprentice to my Uncle, on the packet ship 'England.' I ran away after the third trip, and shipped for Havana, going thence to Philadelphia, which ended my sea-faring life. From Philadelphia, I went to New York, where I remained a few months, then started for the West, going as far as Cincinnati. Leaving the latter place, to make my home among the Cherokees. . . . I remained with the Cherokees until May 1843, when I started for California, arriving in the winter of the same year." True, exaggerated, apocryphal? These stories are the soul of early San Francisco.

CRIME AND PUNISHMENT

A physician at the time estimates that from 1851 to 1853, one of every five reaching California died within six months of arrival. Alcohol consumption in San Francisco is hard and heavy from the earliest days. The drinks flow nonstop in saloons, brothels, and gambling houses. It is only a slight exaggeration to say that liquor is a contributing factor in every death—the stench permeates crime scenes. Liquor and weapons prove to be a deadly combination.

The pioneers arrive loaded for bear. A passenger ready to disembark after a long sea journey describes the scene: "The deck is looking like a veritable arsenal. Guns, pistols, bowie-knives, power flasks, and other death-dealing apparatus that a man may need in a new, unexplored country can be seen in the process of being cleaned and prepared for action when needed."

Everyone in California is armed to the teeth. Weapons are de rigueur, even haute couture, west of the Mississippi.

Several doorkeepers were in attendance, to whom each man as he entered delivered up his knife or his pistol, receiving a check for it, just as one does for a cane or umbrella at the door of a picture-gallery. Most men drew a pistol from behind their back, and very often a knife along with it; some carried their bowie-knife down the back of their neck, or in their breast; demure, pious looking men, in white neck collars, lifted up the bottom of their waist coat and revealed the butt of a revolver; others, after having already

*disgorged a pistol, pulled up the leg of their trousers, and distracted
a huge bowie-knife from their boot, and there were men, terrible
fellows, no doubt, but who more likely to frighten themselves than
anyone else, who produced a revolver from each trouser pocket,
and a bowie knife from their belt. If any man declared that he
had no weapon, the statement was so incredible that he had to
submit to be searched; an operation which was performed by the
doorkeepers, who, I observed, were occasionally rewarded for their
diligence by the discovery of a pistol secreted in some usual part
of the dress.*

—J. D. Borthwick, journalist, reporting
on his attendance at a "no-weapons"
San Francisco masquerade ball in 1852

Homicide, often fueled by disputes over mining claims or gambling debts, takes as many as 4,000 in the first five years of the gold
rush. Gunfights are common, especially in the camps. The romantic
Old West picture of gunslingers facing a frontier version of the classic European duel over "honor" is largely a myth. More men are shot
in the back than the front. Even if you survive a lead bullet, doctors
lacking the benefit of X-rays typically leave bullets in place, which
can cause fatal infections.

In *Barbary Coast*, Herbert Asbury comments, "San Francisco in
1851 is the nearest approach to criminal anarchy that an American
city has yet experienced." It is a port—and a uniquely grab-it-and-
leave-it port—that attracts a transient population less likely to con-
form to traditional norms. San Francisco's notorious reputation for
street crime draws national attention. The public tends to see much
of the early person-on-person assaults as justified by self-defense
and payback vengeance or as too ambiguous to adjudicate. Informal
vigilance groups often dispense "instant justice" before civil authorities can intervene. Those charged with policing do not exist until
August 1849. It is ragtag enforcement by a ragtag army that is sometimes accused of more crime than it prevents.

Crime can be random, and it can be organized. The most notorious of the notorious are the notorious Sydney Ducks. Of the some 11,000 who emigrate from Australia to San Francisco by mid-1851, as many as 20 percent are ex-convicts originally sent to penal colonies there from Great Britain. Sydney-Town, located on the waterfront at the southern edge of Telegraph Hill, is well known for its dive bars, dangerous gambling dens, and violent robberies. The denizens are suspected of many crimes, the most dastardly of which is arson for the purpose of looting and burglary. In fact, many accuse the Ducks of setting some or all of the deadly fires that sweep through San Francisco in the early 1850s. The First Vigilance Committee lynches three of its members in 1851 and deports twenty-eight more. Gangbangers foolish enough to stay or return are routed for good by the Second Vigilance Committee in 1856. That reiteration, a reaction to the assassination of journalist James King of William, boasts a membership of 6,000, the largest organized vigilante group in American history. It operates parallel to and in defiance of the duly constituted city government, which actively opposes the movement. Members are propertied "rebels" protecting their stake in the new social order while professing to save the city from itself. The interrogation and incarceration of suspects—often denied formal due process—is conducted at vigilante buildings. The group targets what it deems disreputable boardinghouses, suspect ships, and undesirable immigrants. Its militia parades often and with abandon. The 1856 Vigilance Committee hangs four people, including the assassin on the same day as his victim's widely attended funeral.

After the second relinquishment of power in 1857, its tombstone might have read, "Keep the Order or We'll Be Back." And the committee does return in 1878 during a nationwide depression that sparks local labor unrest and virulent anti-Chinese sentiment. The Vigilance Committee is credited with rescuing the San Francisco Chinese community from destruction by angry white mobs.

As late as 1871, San Francisco has only 100 police officers—one for every 1,445 inhabitants. New York City has one for every

464 and London one for every 303. Crime and disorder mushroom. Leading citizens scramble to find additional secure jail space. In October 1849, at a cost of $8,000 ($250,000 today), the city buys the abandoned *Euphemia* and converts the brig into a floating county jail that holds twenty-five, some of whom are booked as "unruly"—a code word for mentally unstable. After the Broadway Jail opens in 1851, the vessel is buried in a landfill as the city expands. It is uncovered during a construction project seventy years later.

Émigrés anticipate a challenging plight in California. What they encounter in San Francisco and the expansive gold country exceeds apprehensions, especially for the young, middle-class lads from farms and small towns. It will be a continuation of the hard odyssey there, hardly a respite. But fresh off the boat or rolling in from the mountains, what better diversion from an arduous journey than to throw yourself into the treasure hunt? The well-documented gung-ho of these weary travelers is in part an impulse to find rejuvenated purpose in the chase—to expunge the dismay of death and personal suffering that you endured getting there.

The goldfields are spread over shifting areas that lay at least 100 miles from San Francisco. There is no time to waste. The hunt requires a boat upriver to Stockton, Sacramento City, or new boomtown Marysville. From these centers, wagon and pack-mule trails lead into the hills and mining camps. For the majority arriving in late 1849, it is a rude awakening. The so-called easy "placer" gold—mined from streambed deposits—is harder to find. And the goldfields are getting more crowded by the minute. At the end of 1848, there are some 6,000 miners. A year later, there are more than 40,000, all digging on the same general terrain.

Those who survive the baptisms develop a psychological as well as a physical immunity. Death becomes casual, a part of everyday life. Strangers, not loved ones, perish. Burials go from sacred and special to incidental and mundane. Rituals that most Americans observe back home are often short shrifted or abandoned. This attitude will ameliorate, even compensate, as California becomes more "civilized." But a cultural foundation is being laid and cannot be reimagined.

Perhaps the most discouraging aspect of early mining is the sheer physicality of the work and over-the-shoulder vigilance demanded by competitive, aggressive, often criminal environments where the only law might be that might makes right. Mining camps are even more violent and disorganized than the city. Habitat can be minimal (canvas tents on dirt floors), turning even more unsanitary when soaked by winter rains. Destitute miners who endure empty pans might escape or drift to the city only to find conditions almost as desperate as in the goldfields. And even those who do strike it rich, the *Annals* comments, could lose it all in San Francisco as they "fell victims to overexcitement and continued debauchery. Gambling and intemperance slew many fine youthful spirits."

Some joint stock companies make formal plans to continue the working enterprise in the goldfields. Such ideas, concocted in theory and leisure, are impractical in the diggings. Small "placer" claims in the early years are not conducive to large groups working as a unit. This helps to explain why the camps' death rate is so high and proper burials so minimal. When these companies break up, the last vestige of the organized, compassionate world that pioneers had always inhabited is severed. The dissolution of the companies is a dissolution of the bonds that have kept young men rooted in their cultural origins and traditional mindset.

IN SICKNESS AND IN DEATH

I do think this is one of the unhelthyist places in the known world but thare is money to be made here in San Francisco.
— A PIONEER IN CORRESPONDENCE
WITH HIS BROTHER, 1849

Early San Francisco is the perfect epidemiological storm. Conditions inspire hyperbole. "Outside of Hell," writes physician Octavius

Howe, "it was the dirtiest, meanest city in the world." Another physician describes it as "one vast garbage heap." Streets of dirt turn to instant mud—or rivers—as torrential, unpredictable rains pummel down. Fleas and rats are a constant scourge. The mushrooming, ramshackle city is a sanitation nightmare.

Into this chaotic petri dish arrive the walking wounded. There is no time for rest. You navigate meagerly and deliberately mismarked trails to a labyrinth of goldfields crawling with tough, young competitors. These two areas—city and camps—are joined at the hip and nurture a deadly symbiosis. A continuous looping caravan to and from San Francisco means that any contagion contracted in one place will quickly spread to the other.

Some on ship believe that the ocean experience makes them more ready and able to dig and survive. They have not worn out their bodies or stressed their minds as have the wandering landlubbers. Regular exercise, sports matches, and group drilling on board made them sharp and toned. Others disagree. On boarding a ship, a pioneer is warned by the captain, "By the time that we arrive, in place of being as a dolphin, as you are now, you'll be as fat as a porpoise." Crowded conditions, poor food, and inclement weather make keeping fit mentally as well as physically a daunting task.

The road journey is the best preparation for a tough mining life, say many a trekker: You have walked 2,000 miles in all types of terrain and weather, adapted, and survived. *That which doesn't kill me makes me stronger.* They endure the sick diet, the stress diet, the high aerobic diet, and intermittent fasting. They are lean, mean gold-digging machines. William Swain writes, "How different the adjustment was for the thousands of men who spent five or more months confined to the narrow decks, stuffy, seasick cabins and steerage of sailing ships and steamers. These men landed at San Francisco as soft, uncalloused and unready for the work of the miners that would prove comparable to the sweaty toil of the Irish laborers who had dug canals across New York, Ohio, and other states."

"Street Conditions in San Francisco during the Gold Rush." *University of California San Francisco*

But overlanders—especially those poorly organized or in small unstable groups, loners, and the unlucky—could face a different fate. A. C. Ferris is working a claim high on the Sierra range in the fall of 1849: "I shall never forget the sight presented by the tired, starved, sick and discouraged travelers. With their bony and foot-sore cattle and teams. Men, women, and children, and animals were in every state of distress and emaciation. Some had left everything along the way, abandoning wagons and worn-out cattle to the wolves—leaving even supplies of clothing, flour and food—and in utter desperation and extremity had packed their backs with flour and bacon . . . and a few of the immigrants had thus made the last 600 miles on foot, exhausted, foot-sore, and starving."

In late 1849, the most feared disease of the era begins its devastation in California. By the autumn of 1850, cholera is a full-fledged epidemic in San Francisco and the gold country, exacerbated by a repeat of the previous year's brutal winter. Five to ten perish every day in the city—some in hospitals but more on streets and tent grounds. Tolls are higher along routes to goldfields and in the camps themselves; the actual number and disposition of the dead "out there" were largely unknown. The disease in San Francisco coincides with a virulent outbreak on the Oregon/California Trail. For another three years at the height of each season's epidemic, the scourge will take at least 100 city residents each week and many more unknown scattered about the gold diggings. Dreaded dysentery is everywhere. "Don't drink the water," one hears, at least without a slug of alcohol—regarded as good advice under any conditions.

Typhus fever competes with scarlet fever and smallpox to be the grimmest reaper. Scurvy abounds in the early gold rush due to the paucity of vitamin C, absent in the typical miner diet of coffee, tea, biscuits, bread, and cheese. Even the most resilient can crumble under a conspiracy of symptoms: fatigue, muscle weakness, joint aches, and nasty leg rashes. It also leads to life-threatening dental problems, rampant among the miners. Some 10,000 will die of scurvy in the first three years. Fruit is as rare as women. The demand for lemons and apples with scurvy-preventing nutrients hits a peak in early 1850 (a single apple might cost $150 in today's value); fruit mongering is a lucrative but dangerous profession.

Should a pioneer arrive with money, it can be spent immediately for outrageously priced mining equipment before any indulgence in personal health—not then or now taken seriously by young males. There are few resources for the ill. Private hospitals emerge, but fees are based on what traffic will bear, and only the affluent can bear them. The number of qualified physicians is drastically inadequate for the public need—and who knows who is qualified? Among the advertised "doctors," how many attended a medical college? Even trained physicians, often fresh from school on an adventure west, lack practical experience. The president of Harvard University remarks in 1869, "The whole system of medical education in this country needs thorough reformation. The ignorance and general incompetence of the average graduate of the American medical schools, at the time when he receives the degree which turns him loose upon the community, is something horrible to contemplate."

Science at that time knows nothing of bacteria, viruses, or sterilization. If you cannot decipher what causes the symptoms, how do you treat the problem? Anesthetics had been discovered only three years earlier and are virtually nonexistent east of the Mississippi River. In general, doctors could provide little more than their medieval predecessors. Bleeding by leeches or purging by laxatives are the tried-and-true go-tos, turning gold rush San Francisco into a clinic on how the cure can be worse than the disease. And you will pay a king's ransom for this privilege. Émigré Henry Meyer remarks, "Physicians here can charge just as much as they please, and I sincerely pity the unfortunate patient who falls into the hands of some heartless member of the medical profession." Some brash physicians are reported to demand an ounce of gold ($2,500 today) for a house call. Prices are unimaginable, but so are the gold finds. Medicine as a body of knowledge and a regulated profession improves significantly after the hard lessons of the Civil War. Eventually, state licensing is established. In the interim, shingles substitute for certificates.

"Some will go into business the moment they put foot on land, in three months will find themselves worth fifty thousand [2 million today], while others will in the same short space of time be breathing their last in some miserable tent without a friend or single dime to pay for their funeral charges," observes Mary Jane Megquier, a successful merchant selling domestic services. Those funeral charges could add up fast. A decent death can be as expensive as a decent life. In a pinch, a coffin cobbled together with available boards might cost as much as $1,000 (in current value); the land itself (assuming it's a protected spot where pigs don't scavenge) plus digger's fees, up to $3,000; and a proper memorial is commonly $1,500, as is a priest, where caveat emptor is tested—clothes can make the man, especially in the Wild West.

Masons and Odd Fellows offer free medical care and burial for indigent brothers and their families. The Hebrew Benevolent Society is founded in December 1849 "to assist poor and needy Hebrews in sickness and want." But the vast majority in those early years do not have such special ties. A decade later, several religious and ethnic benevolent groups are extending aid to their communities.

Responding to the unfolding disaster, the 1849 city council contracts to run a hospital consisting of two hastily constructed buildings on Stockton Street, paying doctors and administrators $5 a day for each patient. The conditions there range from bad for those who can afford to pay to worse for those who cannot. The *Annals* comments, "There was naturally a strong repugnance to enter such a place. By the majority, its door was regarded as the certain gate of death. . . . Nevertheless, the city hospital was filled to overflowing and was the scene of much loathsomeness and misery."

When Reverend William Taylor visits the hospital in the fall of 1849, he is appalled: "I thought the up-stairs rooms were filthy enough to kill any well man . . . but in comparison to others they were entitled to be called *choice* rooms, for the privilege of dying in which a man who had money might well afford to pay high rates. . . . [The] lower wards were so offensive to the eye, and especially to the olfactories, that it was with great difficulty I could remain." The untrained male nurses were "devoid of sympathy, careless, and rude in their care of the sick."

By 1853, improved public assistance is available through the State Marine Hospital of San Francisco, which becomes San Francisco City Hospital. But transportation to the facility is not available. It will take another decade before a small medical school is opened.

CATCH AS CATCH CAN

In pre–gold rush days, the Catholic graveyard at Mission Dolores is the formal burial ground for the unmarked remains of some 5,000 native Ohlone Indians who had perished since the Spanish arrival in 1776 as well as Europeans from Italy, France, Germany, Portugal, and England, some honored with substantial memorials. Natives are commemorated today by a diminutive statue of Kateri Tekawitha,

Our Lady of the Mohawks, dedicated as "In prayerful memory of our faithful Indians." She achieves sainthood in 2012.

The influx of gold rush immigrants prompts expansions of the graveyard intended to serve Catholics well into the next century. As usual in California, the future comes earlier than expected. The cemetery land at Mission Dolores is reduced in stages beginning in 1889, when the city extends 16th Street to accommodate the influx of residents to the area. The rector is reluctant to disturb bodies but succumbs to public pressure and sells a portion of church land for far below what he regards as fair market value. To ensure that final payment is forthcoming, two souls are left in the ground until the full fee is transferred. The remains from this and further reductions are reinterred at Calvary Cemetery in San Francisco and eventually to Holy Cross Cemetery in Colma.

Some 11,000 are interred at Mission Dolores. In addition to Native Americans, there are thousands of non-Indian Catholics whose families cannot afford to move relatives before city construction on the burial grounds paves them over in the 1890s.

In the early city days, a formal funeral cortege there requires a challenging trek through marshes, swamps, and mountainous sand dunes that might take half a day. After rituals and repast, the return home is over the same path by foggy moonlight. Travel improves when a pair of plank roads are constructed from downtown to the mission. It is the road to perdition. A fledgling city begins nibbling at the sacred land itself. The property morphs into a suburban entertainment resort adjacent to and spilling into the graveyards. The church is willingly complicit, jumping on the secular bandwagon by selling or leasing land for saloons and gambling halls. Racetracks, boxing contests, and bull and bear fighting rings follow.

The earliest burial grounds in the city could be improvisational at best. Looking back on those pioneer days a generation later in an article titled "The Rude and Hasty Funeral of the Gold Hunters," the *San Francisco Call* recounts that "the method of burial in consecrated ground was soon unheeded, and in consequence the bodies of the dead were sometimes hastily placed anywhere out of sight."

Since most in San Francisco are on the move and strangers to one another, "there was little incentive to pay more than cursory regard to the dead. . . . Often the corpse of some unknown would be discovered lying in a retired spot, hidden in the bushes or chaparral, or in a secluded tent, and sometimes in the public street. His fellows or nearest neighbors, or those who discovered the corpse, would generally dig a hole in the ground behind or near the deceased's late abode, and there the body would be buried."

Discovering the dead becomes an early fact of city life. The 1855 *Annals* observes, "In grading the streets, sinking wells and digging the foundations of houses in after years, the bones of such as had been buried in this fashion have been repeatedly brought to light." Some spots simply morph into informal burial grounds. One of the earliest sat on top of what is called "Russian Hill," a name that survives to this day. The cemetery is a scrape of land where Russian sailors are buried as early as the 1830s and then unknown dead from the gold rush. Quickly, the one-acre area is beyond full. Scavengers strip the crosses and wooden headboards for firewood. In 1915, the graveyard comes back to grisly life when crews constructing a ramp and staircase on the corner of Jones and Vallejo unearth several old cemetery skeletons. Some estimate that dozens more lay underneath there today. Another nascent burial spot is perched on the top of Telegraph Hill, where sailors are placed from the mid-1820s. Deceased miners will fill the remaining space virtually overnight. The ad hoc burial ground is abandoned and neglected. It is unclear how many (if any) remains are ever removed to other locations, but when skeletons and coffins are discovered in the late 1850s, they are seldom reinterred.

Amid this chaos comes fire and brimstone. Hastily built structures made with wood from abandoned ships, tents fashioned from whatever was available, and drunken outdoor cooking create the conditions for an inferno begging to ignite. From Christmas Eve 1849 to June 1851, six large fires devastate major parts of the city and take countless and mostly unknown lives. The collective events are regarded as the most destructive set of fires for an American city to that point in time. Some blocks are consumed and rebuilt two or three times before the scourge ends. Where the fire dead are buried is unrecorded. An invasion of this magnitude might have discouraged ordinary people. Californians were not ordinary, nor did they see themselves as such. In San Francisco, they construct a new instant city over and over. The calamities do have one beneficial effect: As in most disasters, they inspire improved construction.

Build it, and they will come. A *Californian* proposal that a piece of property in the North Beach area would make a decent burial ground precipitates an informal cemetery rush in 1849. Powell Street between Filbert and Greenwich, just north of what is now Washington Square, quickly becomes the most popular dead venue in the city. The legal landowner initially acquiesces or is apparently ignorant of the unfolding situation. He is never consulted. Neither are city officials, who initially acquiesce or are apparently ignorant of the unfolding situation, which is soon a community fait accompli. Some bodies are buried carelessly and without coffins. The area is not even fenced, and when the property owner, now keenly aware of the trespass, begins cutting streets through the property, remains and skeletons are exposed and discarded. The *Alta California* is chagrined, urging that bodies of "gallant adventurers" who have living friends still in grief be removed at city expense to a protected space. It describes the current situation: "We are digging up coffins with as much unconcern as though there were stumps and let them and their contents lie as carelessly until it suits the convenience of someone or anyone to take them away." Adding insult to injury, another part of the burial land is claimed as a sheep pen.

City officials do act, ordering burials in North Beach to stop immediately. An ordinance in 1851 requires the street commissioner to solicit bids for the removal of bodies there to the new city-sanctioned Yerba Buena Cemetery; as usual, this edict by the Board of Supervisors is seldom read or is simply ignored. Just to approach the spot is jarring; beyond the visual shock, it has an "unmistakable" and "unsettling" odor. Although the North Beach grounds present a slightly more ordered appearance than other dead depositories, in one year, it is filled to the brim with almost 1,000 remains. "Civilization," the *Alta California* proclaims, "may be traced as unerringly by noting the sacredness with which the last dwellings of all are preserved, kept and guarded. What would the philosopher say of us, if his estimate of Californians was based upon what he might observe in and about our cemeteries?"

Those who perish at the official city hospital are loaded in a "dead cart" every morning for a North Beach Cemetery run or dumped on the shore to be carried out with the tides. This cost is assumed by the city, which suddenly finds itself officially in the cemetery business. Corpses can also lay unburied for periods of time just west of Miller's Point, where the first pier in San Francisco will be built, prompting a French government agent to complain of the "pestilent odor" at numerous waterfronts.

DEADLY TRADE

There are reports of body harvesting in the North Beach Cemetery to supply cadavers to the medical profession—to the extent that such a "profession" can be said to exist in San Francisco at the time. In those early days, anyone could call himself a doctor, and anyone did. A city hospital is established in 1849, presumably staffed by trained physicians even if lacking in practical experience; they will get plenty of experience fast. Then there are the "barbers" who nurture a long tradition of treatments from setting fractures to giving enemas to extracting teeth. The signature colored pole outside shops historically symbolized the services: let blood (red), bandage wounds (white), and give a shave (blue). A human specimen to dissect would be nothing less than a treasure to any practitioner of the invasive arts. In the *Devil's Dictionary*, nineteenth-century San Francisco satirist Ambrose Bierce defines a body snatcher "as one who supplies the young physicians with that which the old physicians have supplied the undertaker."

In East Coast cities, grave invasions by so-called resurrection-ists or sack-'em-up men has become a cottage industry that benefits from experienced personnel emigrating from England and Scotland. Body trafficking for profit is largely an Anglo-Saxon phenomenon; European authorities typically distribute unclaimed corpses to medical groups. What has been a haphazard practice in the United States evolves into an established trade when the demand for ana-tomical specimens at newly established medical schools increases. Those in Philadelphia, Baltimore, and New York City are infamous for this criminal activity. In most cases, culprits are either faculty and students or middlemen who have various understandings and contracts with them. Public controversies over this trade periodically erupt, such as the 1788 doctors' riot, where body robbing precipi-tates angry public protests led by poorer New York City residents (the population most likely to be snatched) against physicians and students perceived as entitled elites. Nineteenth-century American urban history is punctuated by these incidents.

This is a ghoulish enterprise no doubt, but in the eyes of many, it is not essentially evil or self-serving, however greedy. It serves a socially beneficial purpose. Comprehension of the human body is woefully incomplete at the time. During the Civil War, doctors learn that rudimentary knowledge can do more harm than good. Ameri-can medicine begins to focus on human anatomy, striving for a more scientific and practical approach. New medical schools are opening in major cities. These future professionals need hands-on experience, and that means more cadavers—many more.

That postwar period is the golden age of body snatching and the golden age of medical and surgical advancements regarded as the dawn of modern medicine. The trade continues into the twentieth century and disappears only when states begin to permit voluntary private body donation and "public" cadavers—expired criminals and the indigent—for professional dissection.

Early San Francisco is an extreme example of the dire "frontier" medical situation that other cities experienced in their early years.

Before medical colleges, amateur suppliers can keep up with demand. It takes until 1864 to establish a fledging medical school in San Francisco, then another decade before it is university affiliated. The founder, Hugh Toland, trains in Paris, where clinical instruction and dissecting are centerpieces of the education. By the time the school opens in San Francisco, the demand for cadavers is met by local government-assisted supply chains. The university medical school employs eight faculty members and offers four-month courses costing $130 ($5,000 today) that awards a doctor of medicine degree. By 1870, it entertains thirty-five students and has graduated forty-five.

In the first decade of the gold rush, folks are dying at an alarming rate; bodies are there for the picking, not digging. With shallow graves and shallow public attention, it is more cadaver culling than harvesting. Go for a working stroll on the Pacific coastline where specimens from the city hospital are deposited to be swept out by the tide—but be careful not to collect any cholera victims. There is never a lack of the willing to learn a new trade, drawn from the constant flow of roughneck, eager-beaver newcomers far from the prying eyes of hometown and family.

Resurrectionists work in the dead of night and in teams— ideally, one lookout, two diggers, and a wagon driver. A mark is made at the head of the grave and excavated one or two feet in diameter straight down. After reaching the casket, ropes are attached to the exposed lid, and using the dirt's weight as leverage, it is yanked hard, cracking the lid. The body is then dragged out by a rope or iron hook placed under the chin. Fill in the hole and tidy up. If no one notices the disturbance, that cemetery will be quickly revisited. It is tradition for the deceased to be decked out in their finest clothing and jewelry, but such is often left behind by robbers. Trying to sell them ran the risk of locals recognizing the goods: Stealing property is considered a felony, but in common law, absconding with a corpse is "mayhem," a misdemeanor. People could not legally donate their body to medicine— common law held that you had no interest in your remains.

Professionals try to steal several bodies in a single swoop, hopefully fresh ones, but will occasionally settle for the lower price procured from skeletal remains. The gang then goes as quickly as possible to the medical school for payment. The fresher the body, the higher the price. A specimen skillfully removed without disease or disfigurement might fetch $25 ($1,000 today) for an hour's labor. Even on a bad hunting night, the desperate might make pocket change with mere "remains." *Chambers's Edinburgh Journal* in 1853 details "a curious and unusual California Industrial practice. . . . Owing to the spongy, springy nature of the soil in the burying-ground of San Francisco, many of the corpses there interred, instead of decaying, have been converted into a substance well known to chemists by the name of adipocerous—a substance analogous to, and intermediate between, stearine and spermaceti. In passing the ground this morning to my place of employment, I saw a person busily engaged in collecting the adipocere from exposed bodies. Struck by the singularity

Colma Historical Association

of his employment, I interrogated him as to its object, when he coolly replied, that he was gathering it to make soap! This practice may account for some of the missing pioneers' dead bodies or remains."

There are tried-and-true ways to thwart cadaver crime, such as guarding the fresh grave (the loot is time sensitive), conducting a stealth or a decoy placement, or securing the burial spot by an iron surround called a "mort-safe." A heavy slab of stone discourages diggers. The Irish wake tradition, where friends and family gather around the body for a community ceremony that might last a few days, is based in part on the fear of body snatching. A variety of ingenious and not-so-ingenious prevention devices are patented. Some are simple booby traps. The "coffin-torpedo" promises to maim or even kill an intruder. One model advertises, "Sleep well sweet angel, let no fears of ghouls disturb thy rest, for above thy shrouded form lies a torpedo, ready to make mincemeat of anyone who attempts to convey you to the pickling vat." The graveyard itself or an individual spot can be outfitted with spring-loaded guns ready to go off on unsuspecting intruders. A coffin collar serves as an inexpensive quick fix: Thieves typically pull corpses from coffins through a hole, so the device secures the body to the coffin itself by an iron collar placed around the neck and bolted to the bottom—for the snatcher, too much work and too much risk of damage. Better to go on to the next-door neighbor.

Fear of grave robbing remains a public concern into the twentieth century. Perhaps most notoriously, Indianapolis maintains a thriving cadaver trade until police stop it by 1910. Cypress Lawn is the first cemetery in the West to have a crematory, which means that fresh bodies are stored for brief periods in vaults prior to cremation. Fear of snatching rises to a new level: aboveground. An 1898 Cypress Lawn promotional piece tries to calm this concern: "The receiving vault is immediately in the rear of the chapel and contains 24 niches, which are supplied with an electric attachment connected with the office by a secret wire, so that those who fear the remains of loved ones being STOLEN can be assured of absolute safety, as the mere touching of the door of the niche will ring a gong in the office."

The newly formed cemetery assuages another angst of the age: "To those having a fear of being buried alive, a ring can be placed on the finger of the deceased, and the slightest movement will ring a bell that notifies the watchman in the office, who is in attendance day and night." At the Sacramento City Cemetery, some graves are equipped with a protruding pipe connected to a "Dread Naught" coffin that, if stirred from the inside, triggers a spring-loaded flair to alert authorities.

By the 1880s, in San Francisco as in urban America, traffic in bodies is co-opted by the government. It is a business too vital and gruesome to be left to the genius of private enterprise. Improved methods of refrigeration preservation also contribute to its demise. In California at the time, unclaimed deceased in selected public institutions are "awarded" to medical colleges for "scientific purposes." There is an unadvertised twenty-four-hour window for a private rescue. Those institutions include prisons and youth reformatories, orphanages, mental asylums, hospitals, and military installations. Anyone who would be buried at public expense is required by law to be turned over to the state for dispersal. The law is elitist, a slap in the face to the most vulnerable members of society. Or is it a rational, progressive effort to advance science for the benefit of all, making the dead, even a convicted murderer, an integral part of human progress?

The official dead trade is highly regulated, at least on paper. The law designates that those entities entitled to receive bodies must post bonds. Other entities entitled to deliver bodies must obtain receipts. It is a lucrative, abundant, and competitive carrier business as undertakers and private companies vie for the public fees. But there is still a private demand. A doctor is caught in possession of an renegade cadaver in 1883. The *Alta California* poses the question and the answer. "If the practice of body snatching is to be stopped, we must have a law that will not permit the escape of the guilty party by the simple device of swearing that they know nothing about the manner in which the body was obtained. Nobody will ever confess himself guilty, either as a principal or accessory, of the odious offense of body snatching unless caught in the act, and nobody will ever be convicted." The solution is simple: Make the mere possession of a body analogous to the law stating that it is an offense to have burglary tools.

"Odious" is not too strong a word to describe the public reaction to body snatching, made more reprehensible when the actual culprits—the recipients—are regarded as exemplary citizens. The *Alta California* editor minces no words: "The ghoulish work of robbing graves is so horribly repugnant to the moral sense, especially when carried out by men claiming to take rank in respectable society and making pretensions to science, that the strongest measures for its suppression are justifiable."

To be caught in the act is to be vilified, even publicly shamed. In 1894, an older gentleman trying to sell "smuggled" cigars at a downtown San Francisco hotel is identified as a person with a past. Many years ago, according to information collected by a local journalist, "that man was a respected citizen of St. Joe Mo., with a wife and two intelligent daughters, all of whom went in good society. The man himself was well-bred and educated, and although he had no visible means of support this fact causes no comment until after a sensational experience. The breaking out of a malignant smallpox among the students in a medical college at Keokuk, Iowa, led to an investigation as to where this disease originated, and it was found that it had developed from a body furnished the college by a professional 'resurrectionist.'" The exposure causes his wife and daughters to leave him and ultimately drives the culprit from the area.

It is not uncommon to find the "ghastly remains" of college dissections at or near medical school dumps. One might assume that without medical colleges begging for specimens, there would be no traffic in bodies. That was the considered assessment of Fresno County (150 miles from San Francisco) in 1895, when it confronts the grave robbery of August Modenbach, who had been dispatched by a Southern Pacific train. A sexton of the Adventist church digging a nearby grave notices that the Modenbach plot seems longer than the one he had dug just a couple of days ago. On inspection, the remains are gone. It is the first recorded snatching in the county, according to authorities, who downplay public talk that the body was taken by students looking for a subject, explaining that there are no medical schools in the area and only a few doctors.

San Francisco hosts the largest medical school in the region and provides adequate cadavers for research. Yet the superintendent of Calvary Cemetery in the city chances upon a grave in 1896 that is dug down to the coffin, two shovels nearby. The robbers were apparently interrupted and fled or had gone to get a vehicle to transport the loot. A long police stakeout produces no results. The body might have been intended for a private group, such as the Cadaver Club of Oakland ten miles across the bay, composed of eight doctors that the *San Francisco Examiner* reports "hold secret conclaves at night over cadavers in the interest of science." On one occasion, a member has secured the remains of a "Japanese," and the club is "delighted at the prospect" of an exotic specimen. But internal squabbling among the physicians prompts an undertaker to expose that escapade, leading to public consternation and threats of prosecutions. In 1907, a story breaks in Los Angeles, "Trade in Dead Human Bodies," revealing the "wholesale and horrible traffic of human bodies." The four medical schools in the city had stated that forty cadavers per year will meet their needs, but investigators find that more than 400 bodies are taken in annually, and many of these corpses are "believed to be bartered by mercenaries," a scandal that "may involve physicians and undertakers. . . . It was intimated that there lie at one undertaking establishment more than fifty bodies 'in pickle,' ready for disposition and they are not used for legitimate anatomical research." Authorities promise to start a new regime of corpse disposition and begin charging bonds to participants in ensure proper handling.

Other jurisdictions can have the opposite problem. The University of California, just across the bay from San Francisco, complains in 1916 about the scarcity of cadavers and blames it squarely on the current county infirmary superintendent, who has instituted a policy that those who die at the infirmary will be buried in the county cemetery if they simply leave the name of a friend or relative, even if no claim has been made.

YERBA BUENA CEMETERY: A SHORT STORY

Amid the grisly chaos of unregulated burials in San Francisco, it is hardly surprising that understaffed local authorities fail to conduct thorough inquests or keep records of the deceased. A fledgling coroner's office opens in April 1850. It will take some years before it is effectively operational. A young man voluntarily and privately steps into the early void. He tallies what he can: 963 burials for the last half of 1850, which is surely less than reality but still high. Nathaniel Gray is partner in a New York City funeral establishment that dispatches him to California to open a branch office. He travels by way of the Isthmus of Panama and disembarks after a six-month journey. Funeral supplies, shipped around Africa's Cape Horn, arrive before him but are immediately consumed in one of the early San Francisco fires. With only his trunk of personal items and a few hundred dollars, he purchases the one city undertaking business, consisting of two mules, a wagon fitted up to be a hearse, twelve coffins, some lumber, carpenters' tools, and a canvas tent. From this inauspicious start, N. Gray Undertakers begins, prospers, and operates to this day. He serves as the second city coroner.

Waves of immigrants are gnawing at what usable land still exists, worsening an already dire "dead" situation, especially in North Beach. City fathers scramble to find a solution. The result is the first official city cemetery, situated between historic Mission Dolores and the nascent central city—a sixteen-acre triangular sand dune outlined by Market, McAllister, and Larkin streets.

The city has carefully inspected the site and found it both accessible and practical to accommodate a cemetery that will be sufficient to house the dead for the next half-century, according to the *Alta California*, reporting on the opinion of one Mr. Eddy, the surveyor, whom the editors tout as an expert in this field. There are already some fifty unofficial interments there, so the government is prudently co-opting an evolving situation before it spirals out of control. The *Alta California* pleads for other unofficial burial grounds scattered about the city to be relocated to the new "endowed" site—without offering any practical means to accomplish the goal.

At the time, few raise concerns that this patch of land might be in demand for the living. The proposed area is inhospitable and practically inaccessible from the hub of commerce. And something bold must be done to alleviate the ever-growing dead dilemma. Dedicated in July 1850, the cemetery experiences a brisk business, facilitated by an uptick in fatal diseases.

Some 50,000 pioneers poured into San Francisco by that time. Those who perish have no official cemetery other than Catholic Mission Dolores. Yerba Buena is a municipal facility open to all—fees are modest for those that can afford the cost, free for those who cannot.

The situation at North Beach grows worse. The owner is continuing to cut roads through the property—with gruesome consequences: City excavations for Powell Street are uncovering more graves. The sheep pen grows larger. Robbers plunder the terrain for precious wood coffins and memorials—a resource not available locally. And since you are already there, some local "doctors" have a standing offer of an ounce of gold for a warm cadaver.

The authorities have had quite enough. In the fall of 1852, they hire a contractor who hires a subcontractor named Fitzgerald to move the North Beach Cemetery to Yerba Buena. "This Irishman, or perhaps Australian, was currently free on bail on an assault charge," writes North Beach historian Richard Dillon. "He dug up the corpses and callously piled them in carts like logs and either burned the coffins or broke them up and sold the wood for kindling." Half the bones are stolen or dumped willy-nilly. But by the end of 1853, the North Beach dead are gone. Gradually, some bodies from other makeshift burial grounds are relocated to Yerba Buena, without ceremony or documentation.

It takes a year and half from the earliest wave of émigrés to establish the first official city cemetery. In the long meantime, countless die in San Francisco and the goldfields without traditional care or burial rites. Survivors thank their lucky stars that it is not them. But it *is* them. They are witness to an unprecedented situation. Except for war, when has there been such an ignominious disposition of bodies of this magnitude? The experience will shadow the young pioneers.

Yerba Buena brings a sense of regulation, but physically, it is hardly more than a technical upgrade. The *Annals* describes the land in 1855 "as among the most dreary and melancholy spots that surround the city ... a hollow among miserable-looking sand hills, which are scantily covered with stunted tress, worthless shrubs, and tufted weeds." Individual markers are typically makeshift. Wind gales blow off topsoil to expose shallow-dug graves. Vandalism, cadaver harvesting, and grave robbers in search of loot disrupt the enclave. In its early days, the grounds could draw praise for the picturesque starkness or the handful of ornamented memorials. But deterioration comes quickly when the city denies any maintenance funds. It is by intention and default a cemetery for the indigent, although with scant alternatives, non-Catholic souls of worth might land there.

The Board of Supervisors believes that Yerba Buena, if not the final solution to the city's burial problem, will be *the* location for the foreseeable future. But how does one read the coffee grounds in a sandstorm of immigration and volatile change? As San Francisco civilization creeps ever faster toward the now hallowed ground, commercial interests begin salivating for the property. The *Alta California*, waxing poetic in the journalistic lexicon of the day, declares that the time for reclamation has arrived: "Houses peopled with living tenants already cast their shadows down on these subterranean cabins of the dead. The opening of the Market Street Railway has given a wonderful impetus to improvements hereabouts, to remove these remains as the busy hand of enterprise invades the sacred precincts of the tomb."

Soon, there are even bigger plans for the property—nothing less than a city hall and civic administration buildings. Yerba Buena is officially closed to further burials in 1860. In that year, a baby born when it opened has not yet reached puberty. A new "City Cemetery," larger and farther from the population center, is on the drawing board.

Legalities delay until 1866 the Yerba Buena exhumation order to the new city burial ground, whose grand opening is not slated for a few years hence. Between closure and actual relocation—eleven years—the city designates Yerba Buena a public park, but with no funds to landscape or provide facilities, the grounds continue to deteriorate. A final stumbling block is local resistance to a state law stripping Yerba Buena of "cemetery" status. The state supreme court declares that "progress" overrides such sentiment. Some of the now coveted property is sold for commercial frontage on Market Street.

In soliciting bids for the Yerba Buena removal, the city declares, "The work to be done in a good and workman-like manner, and to the entire satisfaction of the Committee on Health and Police." When the deceased are transferred to just-opened City Cemetery in 1870, the project is executed in a typically indelicate manner. Michael Svanevik describes the scene: "Hundreds of graves, obliterated by shifting sands, cannot be found. Searchers probe for them with long iron rods. When remains are located, they are dried in the sun to 'prevent offensive odor' and then 'cast into a common receptacle' for removal."

Every effort at civic improvement in the old Yerba Buena Cemetery grounds exposes more evidence of those left behind. The *San Francisco Call* reports in September 1889 that "many bones were discovered" in excavating the foundation for a new city hall. "Now its massive foundations stand as tombstones over the bits of skeletons that were left in the early seventies." So obscure had Yerba Buena Cemetery become in just a generation that the *Call* is compelled to add, "No one knows just when it was established, but it was a recognized cemetery when the surrounding country was sand dunes and the city was a village on the shoreline at Montgomery St." Six months later, ten bodies, including "several" Chinese, are exhumed in the excavation for a city hall western wing, bringing the grand total to seventy. The *Joaquin Valley Times* reminds readers that the land had been previously used as a cemetery.

Sixteen More Graves Discovered on Site of Yerba Buena Cemetery
—*SAN FRANCISCO CHRONICLE*, APRIL 9, 1908

Word of the spectacle spreads fast, and crowds gather. The construction foreman immediately orders all remains be placed in special containers for the coroner, but no one from the office is dispatched that day. The work crew arrives the next morning to discover that all the skulls have vanished. "It is presumed that they were taken by medical students, or ghouls," the reporter comments.

In 1934, excavation for a new federal building near city hall unearths more than twenty bodies. All the remains are left where found and built over. During construction of a new main library and the Asian Art Museum in the late 1990s, skeletons keep popping up. On this occasion, the city does its historical homework and hires a forensic pathologist. He cannot definitively identify any of the dead. As remodeling for the Asian Art Museum starts in 2001, eighteen skeletons are discovered. The *San Francisco Chronicle* reports they had "lay hidden in the earth for well over a century as the city built over them—twice—at long last being sent to their final resting place." A total of ninety-seven "pioneers," many Chinese, uncovered during these digs are reinterred in Cypress Lawn Cemetery in Colma. Local political power broker Rose Pak suggests that such generosity is prudent to appease agitated ancestors.

The dead can materialize anywhere. In 1894, the *San Francisco Examiner* headlines "Ten Crumbling Skeletons" that appear during excavation work on Second Street in "the old cemetery of Happy Valley." An illustration of an open coffin *macabre* punctuates the story. Crowds quickly gather amid speculation that once a "House of Horrors stood upon the lot, wherein dark deeds were done." This is quickly dispelled by Robert Gunn, an "old pioneer" who told of an informal burial ground used "by the settlers who came here in the forties." Some were sick when they arrived and died within hours, he recalled, which explains why so many garments and shoes are discovered in the remains. Mr. Gunn reports that skeletons have been periodically uncovered: "Several years ago a small boy saw a bootleg protruding from the earth there. He tugged at it as he pulled it out. But he brought a skeleton leg with it and abruptly abandoned his search." The *Examiner* concludes, "Strangely enough, when the city authorities shifted the public burying-ground from First street to Yerba Buena no effort to remove the bodies was made."

Another news story reveals "A Neglected Graveyard" in 1899: "Seven-year-old Willie Elsie of 2722 Golden Gate avenue was playing Klondike yesterday with some little fellows of his own age at the junction of Golden Gate avenue and Stanyan street, and in digging for gold unearthed some human bones and fragments of a coffin. Pieces of the shroud and a pair of boots were also found. The gruesome relics were taken to the Morgue, but neither inquest nor autopsy will be held. The site of which the bones were found was a cemetery many years ago and when the bodies were exhumed some were forgotten."

More than bones are unearthed. During the 1930s federal building excavations, three skeletons produce a trove of loot: two $10 gold pieces dated 1843 and 1847 and five rare silver Spanish coins from the early 1700s. Such finds are not unusual and reflect the burial practices of a bygone generation. A lady speaking of her experiences as a seventeen-year-old in 1940 remarked, "I had a boyfriend, a nice Irish boy . . . he was so happy he got a job digging up graves over at

Laurel Hill, but he was upset about the security—police here, police there, and they were watching that the boys wouldn't open the graves and steal jewelry and rings, you know that in those days the old timers used to take their jewelry with them when they died." Countless people from the Great Earthquake of 1906 are buried "as is" and might provide a treasure trove when unearthed.

Even buried tombstones attract interest. An 1898 skeleton lode reveals a handsome example inscribed "Sacred to the Memory of Michael O'Leary, late of the City of Cork, Ireland, Who Departed this Life October 22, 1851. Aged 32 Years. Requiescat in Pace." Both Irish Societies and the Society of California Pioneers claim the prize. A long and nasty public quarrel ensues for possession of the sacred relic.

How many are buried in Yerba Buena? We will never know because virtually all birth, death, and burial documents from those years are destroyed in the 1906 earthquake. John Blackett posits a figure of 5,000 to 9,000. Most estimates fall in this range. Two years after the cemetery closure in 1860, the *Alta California* conjectures that 7,000 to 9,000 burials had occurred.

Just how many of those are moved to the new City Cemetery? It is a hard question with soft answers. A San Francisco Library environmental impact study concludes that "most" Yerba Buena remains are reinterred to City Cemetery. The *San Francisco Chronicle* notes that the city had a mandate to move the Yerba Buena bodies to City Cemetery: "It's unclear whether officials shirked their duty or simply didn't find the deep graves, but 'plenty' of people were left behind." Michael Svanevik says that "many" were never disinterred; the same word is used by other historians. The online *Encyclopedia of San Francisco* states that it is "unknown" exactly how many remains were transported.

History is not an exact discipline: witness "most," "many," "some," "unknown," "probably," and "plenty." We have semantics in place of statistics.

Instant city madness distorts judgment. Lacking a stable population or prospects for civic development, how can you envision a
community much less plan it? Harsh reality demands a laser focus
that shuns future-based thinking. There is no "there" there. The paucity of women and family life compounds the problem. Traditional
respect for the dead is so disregarded in these early years that it
discourages the sentiment for following generations. Pioneers who
experience this altered reality are spawning California. The gradual
withdrawal from time-honored death and funeral rituals across the
nation in the twentieth century begins in the American West. San
Francisco cemetery issues are unique because of its birth and geography, and common because all American cities grapple with dynamic
and unpredictable growth. How to treat your buried and soon-to-be
ancestors becomes a national issue. The embrace of pragmatism at
the expense of sentiment and tradition turns California into a general laboratory of innovation, the cutting edge of modernization. The
cemeteries will be overwhelmed.

———

What if there had been no gold rush? Mid-nineteenth-century
Seattle or Portland seem equally opportune as a great West Coast
port. Gold anoints San Francisco early and abundantly. Even lacking such fortune, it would be a thriving Pacific metropolis. Set in a
more traditional foundation with reduced but vibrant immigration,
one can imagine San Francisco as a world-class city nestled around
its historic and well-cared-for burial grounds.

CHAPTER 5

A SEMBLANCE OF ORDER

A PLACE FOR EVERY SOUL AND EVERY SOUL IN ITS PLACE

*By this time [1860s], the haste, the despair, and the loneliness
that characterized the burials of a transient and disparate population had given way to a more standard attitude toward death.*
—DORIS MUSGRAVE, *OLD SAN FRANCISCO*

YERBA BUENA CEMETERY IS THE FIRST EFFORT TO BRING ORDER
to the cemetery chaos. Burials are intended primarily for the
indigent—a VIP would not be caught dead there. The grand project
is obsolete a decade later.

Since the earliest days, Mission Dolores is the gold standard of
burial—for Catholics. Now the elite and aspiring can aspire to Lone
Mountain. A cabal of investors purchase 320 acres from the city to
develop the much-needed private cemetery land. It promptly sells
half the allotted spread for commercial speculation, convinced that
the smaller acreage will prove more than sufficient to bury the city
dead well into the next century. The cemetery is inaugurated in 1853
to fanfare and invocations.

A journey to the grounds is formidable, requiring a circuitous
route of four footprint miles. Grading and planking the muddy
Bush Street "thoroughfare" cuts the distance by half, but a trip still
extracts a full day for plodding funeral processions to traverse the
wilderness and return.

The expense of cemetery maintenance quickly leads the owners
to sell off parts of the property. Lone Mountain is subdivided into
separate cemeteries for Masons (1854), Odd Fellows (1854), and the

Catholic Church (1860). The remaining fifty acres are sold in 1867 to an association that changes the name to "Laurel Hill" after the now famous Philadelphia "garden" cemetery built a generation earlier. The Lone Mountain moniker is regarded as too sad and forlorn. Laurel Hill is the only "nonsectarian" grounds. More than any of the Lone Mountain cemeteries, it is conceived and funded to be a resting spot for the elite. "Many of the incorporators," the *Alta California* notes at its inauguration, "have built expensive tombs in these grounds under the impression that the Cemetery would forever remain sacred to the dead." Those eight incorporators are heavy hitters indeed. Half will have San Francisco streets named in their honor. Eleven U.S. senators are at rest in Laurel Hill when burials stop in 1901.

At Lone Mountain's gala founding, there are abundant congratulatory pats on the back: The grounds elevate San Francisco to a dignified and respected level of care. It is regarded as the final solution to the private cemetery problem.

The "Big Four" endeavor to be "garden cemeteries," an evolving national movement to replace traditional burial grounds—located in congested, dilapidated churchyards—with expansive spaces offering a tranquil oasis in which to pay proper respects. It is a radical idea: Cemeteries are for the living and for healing. Each deceased has an eternal spot in a pleasant setting. On the surface, this is a democratic gesture—one person, one grave—but in practice serves the wealthy and middle class rather than the poor and "indigent" that usually encompass the majority in any given locale. However, the movement is more inclusive and egalitarian in the United States than in Europe, where "rural" burial grounds are priced solely for the economic elite.

"Graveyard" is replaced by "cemetery"—a revival of the Greek word meaning "a place to sleep." Visitations become family communions. Pere-Lachaise, built by Napoleon in 1804, and Mount Auburn, established near Boston a generation later, serve as models for this revolution. It is an idea whose time had come. By 1800, in Europe and parts of America, conventional burial infrastructures are overwhelmed by dramatic population increases, especially in concentrated and burgeoning industrial areas. The dead are piling up, creating a gritty, hideous, and—widely believed at the time—unsanitary habitat that threatens public health by contaminating water and emitting noxious pathogens.

It is the age of the grand garden cemetery. To the end of the century, inspirations of Mount Auburn are conceived in Brooklyn, Buffalo, Rochester, Philadelphia, Cincinnati, Chicago, Lexington, Louisville, St. Louis, Savannah, and San Francisco, among other places. The private San Francisco cemeteries serve vital religious and cultural needs. The ambiance invites personal visits to the dearly departed—leaving flowers, offering prayers, and commiserating with family and friends over repast.

The grounds inspire local pride as a civic asset. San Francisco in the 1850s is a dreary frontier outpost with nary a patch of green, and this paucity persists into the 1870s. But a haven beckons. Featuring ornamental shrubs and plants and statuary with open community spaces, Lone Mountain lures San Franciscans to romp with their children, promenade, picnic, go for evening carriage rides, and even have weddings and celebrations while gazing from mountaintop perches at the glistening bay five miles distant. Cemeteries serve as the public park before Golden Gate Park, providing a place for ordinary people to enjoy fine outdoor recreation previously available only to the wealthy. Early garden cemeteries on the East Coast and fast-growing Midwest cities serve a similar public purpose before the construction of their large civic parks. San Francisco's Laurel Hill Cemetery seeks to capture the arboreal settings of eastern garden cemeteries, but it will take the founding of Cypress Lawn Cemetery in 1892 at nearby Colma to fulfill this vision. Not coincidentally, the dead relocated from Laurel Hill in the mid-twentieth century are placed at nonsectarian Cypress Lawn.

As inviting as it is, Lone Mountain falls short of a grand garden cemetery. The most renowned landscape architect of the era, Frederick Olmsted—who will design Central Park in New York City—describes the area as "scourged by wind" and dotted with "stunted greenery." It impressed nineteenth-century historian Theodore Hittel only because he regards anything there as an improvement on the endless sand dunes undulating to the ocean. Over time, the mausoleums and private landscaping of the well-to-do provide a more formal and regal appearance, especially in Laurel Hill, which boasts twenty miles of avenues and is prominently mentioned in tourist guidebooks of the 1880s. A newspaper could sing its praises: "It is elaborately beautified in floral design and contains many handsome monuments. The park-like atmosphere and elegant nineteenth-century statuary produces an oasis of calm amidst the hustle and bustle of urban San Francisco life."

The elegant San Francisco cemeteries of the 1850s—an atonement for the neglect of previous years—give formal recognition to the sacred nature of burial rituals in the life of a community. The unsettled environment that encourages a blasé attitude toward death serves to make the old ways more attractive and urgent for others. At Lone Mountain's inaugural, which a newspaper describes as "the most pleasing and interesting public cemetery we have ever witnessed in California," women make up almost half of the attendees, yet perhaps 5 percent of the city population. It is testament to the nascent "female" influence on far western culture. By this time, the critique of the rough-and-tumble male psyche, from manners and morals to family and public decorum, is acknowledged by civic leaders. The fixes are superficial and symbolic: more elegant entertainment venues, cleaner streets, effective policing, and a new park-like "rural" burial grounds. Lone Mountain is more than a gesture but less than a commitment. San Francisco will embrace the anti-cemetery sentiment gaining traction at the turn of the century and lead the nation into a secular new world.

———

A large burial complex funded and administered by the city is expected to accommodate public cemetery needs in a manner and dignity that the first city cemetery had not. Yerba Buena is a postage stamp, a mere thirteen acres. The new City Cemetery will remedy that with a tract of desert fifteen times the size, this largesse due to its far-flung location: "Lands End" at Golden Gate strait, a hardy trek from the city proper through sand dunes and howling winds. There is a cursory effort to make the forlorn sandy land look "rural" with plants and shrubs, but there are no trees on or around the grounds to protect graves from the nasty Pacific winds that blow everything everywhere. So distant from what is envisioned as a possible developed area, most regard the five-miles-from-downtown spot as a permanent fix to the public cemetery problem. Out of sight, out of mind.

Early San Francisco has as many exotic ingredients in the cultural melting pot as any East Coast city. It establishes dedicated burial areas in City Cemetery for Germans, French, Italians, Jews, and Chinese—all managed by ethnic benevolent associations. A smorgasbord of groups quickly emerges. The dedicated sections of City Cemetery include the following:

Beth Olam (Jewish)

Caledonian

Chinese, five subsections in addition to a larger section

Colored Masons

Grand Army of the Republic

Greco Russia

Japanese

Knights of Pythias

Master Mariners

Old Friends

Independent Order of Red Men

Italian

Russian

Salem (Jewish)

Scandinavian

Seamen

Slavonic-Illyric

St. Andrew

Orthodox Easter Greek Church

Grand Army of the Republic

Ladies' Seaman Society

Old Friend's Society

Colored Odd Fellows

Chinese Christians

The largest area of the cemetery is set aside for the Pauper's section; more than half the bodies will be placed there.

The first City Cemetery internments arrive in July 1871, when deceased from Yerba Buena are finally relocated there after protracted court battles. Less than a generation later, the sprawling far-flung terrain is declared off-limits to new burials. By that time, the San Francisco population is lurching west as terrain is gobbled up by a new breed of pioneer whose journey to the promised land consists of two miles rather than 2,000, although the adventure still demands traversing rough terrain. This restless movement unfolds in all major urban areas—the daring and the desperate pushing practical city limits. Cemeteries get in the way.

———

Even the gambling tables languished. People invested all they had, all they could borrow, beg, pawn, or steal, in silver stock. No one talked of anything else; and many women, known as Mud-hens, sold stock on the curb. Everybody assumed that one spot of earth at least had enough for all, and on this day one year he be

handling money by the bushel and proclaimed that never in this
life would he do another stroke of work.
—Gertrude Atherton, *California:*
An Intimate History, 1914

There are great expectations for gold rush San Francisco. The
Annals prophesies in 1855 that it will become "the most magnificent,
wealthy and powerful maritime city in the Pacific—a city which is
destined, one day, to be, in riches, grandeur and influence like Tyre or
Carthage of the olden time, or like Liverpool or New York of modern days." San Francisco does become just that, but it needs another
tonic mineral shot in the arm.

It is never certain that the blessings of gold will turn the city
into a mega-metropolis. How long will the bonanza last? Some contemporaries openly worry what might happen to the port should
the goldfields be depleted. At that time, the port *is* the city, and in
less than a decade, gold output plummets. Still extracted for many
years, the fabled "rush" slows to an amble. Businessmen remain in
denial despite a dramatic drop in immigration and the exodus of
eager beavers who had arrived just a few years earlier. Other pioneers
stay but shift to farming or manufacturing. These developments will
prove beneficial in the long run. But as imported goods now become
available locally, it deepens the downturn in San Francisco, where
the major import houses are located. As revenues quickly decline,
the port that has looked so promising suddenly appears at risk. And
what is there that could replace gold as the engine of prosperity?
Michael Svanevik characterizes San Francisco in 1859 as "still little
more than an awkward, overgrown gold town."

The city is rescued by another manna from heaven, specifically,
a small swath of land on the eastern slope of Mount Davidson in
the Nevada Territory. The Comstock silver lode is five times the distance to the old Sacramento goldfields, but its umbilical cord proves
just as enriching. Like gold, the game is completely controlled in
San Francisco. "By the boldness in which she invested her capital,"

writes John Hittel in 1878, "San Francisco became the owner of nearly everything worth owning in the silver mines, which were then worked mainly for her benefit."

Silver invigorates San Francisco beyond imagination. It instantly propels an aging instant city from "wannabe" to "contender"—the equivalent of a modern tech boom, attracting money and talent and sparking huge accumulations of wealth. Silver enterprises produce the first genuine crop of millionaires. A breathtaking city expansion ensues. Great downtown buildings and Nob Hill mansions are financed by silver money, as are a slew of restaurants, theaters, hotels, and retail stores. The influx of capital dramatically transforms the business district, where more than 1,000 new structures are constructed in and around the burgeoning area.

Lone Mountain cemeteries are born of gold. They are killed by silver. Nourished by a new bonanza, the city's population doubles to 300,000 by the mid-1880s. Some dare to predict a million inhabitants by the turn of the century. The Outside Lands, regarded as indigestible excess, suddenly look inviting. Confined to seven square miles, where else could the bulging, waterlocked city expand? The Pacific Ocean becomes San Francisco's manifest destiny at the same time the nation itself is marching to the spot.

The fate of that nearby "desert" and the cemeteries become inextricably linked in an existential struggle—as the fortunes of the Outside Lands increase, those of the cemeteries decline. Lone Mountain cemeteries sit on the western flank of an urban army moving inexorably to the Pacific. The dead lands are expansive, in the way, out of place, an anachronism. A civic mania to "catch up" to the great cities of America will butt heads with a kinder and gentler vision to temper this dynamism with heritage. It is the same quandary played out in other cities: how to preserve the past as you create the future. The physical foundation of San Francisco rests on seismic faults and landfills. Its cultural foundation rests on an equally shifting and shallow sense of tradition. Survival is adaptation. Settlers create a city ex nihilo and a corresponding mentality—one that compels a fast resolution to complex problems without sentimental or practical attachment to tradition. This will affect an array of issues, from divorce to death. Later, as a civic wealth-building impulse feeds a relentless anti-cemetery drumbeat, the army will arrive at the gates of the dead. What ensues is an epic and nasty tug-of-war—a battle for the ages.

———

What if there had been no silver rush? San Francisco continues to grow and prosper but hardly at such a pace and intensity. City development west to the ocean is more gradual and organic. Certainly, San Francisco becomes a critically important commercial harbor dominating the region. The gold rush did not generate the city's land rush to the Pacific Ocean, only to the desert near it. The silver money makes the Outside Lands indispensable to expansion, as it provides the resources to conquer that desert. Even without this impetus, there is a steady migration to "Lands End." But one can conjure up a map of twenty-first-century San Francisco accented by historic old burial grounds—albeit reduced and tastefully commercialized—where tourists revel in the past as they spend dollars in the present.

CHAPTER 6

THE CEMETERY WARS

DON'T FENCE ME OUT

They have seized and hold in mortmain the best building land
in the city. . . . The development of the city is stopped short by
these tyrants. . . . From their cemeteries—the dead look down
with grinning jaws upon the city below. . . . The invisible effluvia
that rise in the air from cities of the dead contain gaseous poi-
sons of the most deadly character. At present they are absorbed by
the vegetation of the cemeteries in question. But, as they become
crowded, what must become the fate of little children and delicate
wives when the San Francisco of the future is split in two by this
death dealing cemetery ridge, and every wind that blows carries
anguish and desolation to some home, withers some lovely child-
flower, and widows some fond heart?
—Speaking of the four Lone Mountain cemeteries,
San Francisco Post, 1878

Must we declare the opening salvo of the war between the living and the dead, let it be this poetic public provocation titled "The Tyranny of the Dead." Anti-cemetery forces are fighting on two fronts. One is private Lone Mountain, an unwelcome neighbor occupying 160 acres in the middle of thriving if nascent communities. City Cemetery, claiming an even bigger swath on the magnificent Pacific coastline, is an unwelcome squatter.

A mere sixteen years after the first City Cemetery burial in 1871, newly elected Board of Supervisors member Aaron Burns is trolling for a major change. He offers a resolution that dutifully praises the then much-needed public cemetery grounds but in the same breath requests a special committee to examine how City Cemetery could be used for the *current* public good, especially the large "pauper" section. In typical long-winded bureaucratic patter, the official resolution concludes,

> *Whereas Golden Gate Cemetery is a most eligible site for recreation purposes, and if connected with our public park would be a most valuable adjunct thereto as a healthy resort for our people . . . to consider further interments therein; also if in their judgment further interments should be prohibited, to examine and report as to the interments made, the character and value of improvements made in plats or lots in said cemetery, and whether, if deemed proper that the remains therein interred should be removed to and reinterred in other cemeteries, what probable expense, if any, would be installed upon or should be borne by the city and county; also whether the plats or lots, wherein interments have been made, could be improved and allowed to remain without detriment of the use of said tract of land as a public park; also whether there exists any necessity for the city and county to acquire lands for cemetery purposes; also whether the said reservation should be placed under the care and control of the Board of Park Commissioners to improve and beautify it for the uses and purpose of the public and whether the Increased appropriation authorized to be made by the last session of the Legislature for the improvement of the public parks will afford said board the means to carry out such systems of improvements.*

In unvarnished smoke-filled-room candor, Mr. Burns might have said,

> *Gentlemen, we suffer a sprawling domain of the dead—forlorn and ignominious—that sits adjacent to our noble enterprise for a grand public park in our beloved city that sorely lacks such amenities—a park that will soon rival . . . dare we think . . . New York City? A splendid oasis that can draw thousands to play and construct new neighborhoods around it. But will we follow our fortune? City Cemetery is a blight that could forever discourage even the hardiest of pioneers*

*to plant roots near there. We must incorporate this dead space into our
living space! [cheers and hosannahs] I know the language of my resolution will appear to be many things to many people. This is by intention.
We must get the engine of progress rolling. To appease the less progressive and more tradition-bound, let us proceed with due decorum and
respect. But! Let us never permit the past to dictate the future. It is not
enough to contain the cemeteries; we must occupy the cemeteries. The
land belongs to the living! [cheers and hosannahs]*

"A free round for all!" the barkeep shouts.

"BOOSTERS"

Chicago is regarded as a boomtown, surpassing San Francisco in
population by 1860. Mankind had required a million years to produce its first city of a million people, Gunter Barth notes, while Chicago accomplishes the feat in less than a century. But that growth
is tentative and uneven. At incorporation in 1833, there are 350
residents; by 1850, it is still less than 30,000. Then the population
surges. Chicago is not an "instant city" in Barth's formula, yet its
growth is dramatic enough in Daniel Boorstin's view to qualify as an
"upstart"—a vibrant urban center spawned by westward migration.
St. Louis and Cincinnati are other examples.

It is at this time that the concept of the "businessman" appears
in popular culture—uniquely American and more dynamic than
the European "merchant." Alexis De Tocqueville, a French aristo-
crat traveling America in the 1830s, is one of the first to journal
the phenomenon in his widely read work *Democracy in America*. As
defined by Boorstin, that businessman is a peculiar breed of "hustler"
and community builder who blends public and private prosperity.
They become "boosters," gauging success by the rate of growth in
their adopted homes. He characterizes those newcomers as young
and bold with tenuous ties to their origins—perfectly suited to a
mad dash into a new world where they "pieced together a mosaic of
practices ... reflecting in their immediacy and usefulness the creativ-
ity of the new cities" that literally have no past. Booster loyalties are

"intense, native, optimistic and quickly transferrable." Once settled in the new environment, boosters are steadfast as long as the venture remains profitable.

If Chicago is an "upstart" compared to Boston and New York, how should we characterize San Francisco, an urban cauldron perhaps never to be witnessed again? The "upstart" psyche—weak respect for tradition, ends-justify-means impatience, and belief in growth as an overriding good—is even more intense in California. The dead have a feeble voice in this dynamic, especially when resting on prime property.

In ordinary cities, Barth observes, "customs and tradition reinforced the staid pattern of life, supported by time-honored laws upholding previous accomplishment . . . change came slowly and almost imperceptibly." The strength of an ancient metropolis rests on the inability or reticence of people to leave. New World cities thrive on recently formed loyalties and enthusiasm, which are easily transplanted. San Francisco, in particular, "bred a state of mind that worshipped the useful and elevated the practical to a culture."

Boosters are not necessarily enemies of cemeteries—at least when the grounds are superfluous or serve a perceived civic purpose. But should they interfere with "progress," citizens have the right, even duty, to act in the best interests of the "people." Boosters mean bulldozers. Vibrant, growing Midwest cities have similarities to California at the time, but the heartland displays more balanced and traditional civic personalities. In the mid-nineteenth century, the Midwest is the mid-psyche of the nation—the mild West, mediating between the Wild West and the staid East.

The bedrock of boosterism is pragmatism. Practitioners are both ignorant of its principles and fully engaged in the practice well before it becomes an academic doctrine, which is regarded as the most important and unique American contribution to philosophy, more specifically, epistemology—the study of how we acquire knowledge and discern "truth." The proposition is articulated in an outburst of intellectual and popular literature beginning in the

1870s. In the words of William James, "Consider the practical effects of the objects of your conception. Then, your conception of those effects is the whole of your conception of the object." Translated into action, it means that if a behavior works to benefit you and mankind in a tangible, measurable way, it is true—judge an idea by its consequences. Practice becomes theory, and as reality changes, truth changes, which means that thought can alter—indeed create— truth, even if that truth is transitory. This is the frontier mindset; it is also the heart of early twentieth-century American Progressivism, a movement nurtured in American cities but born on the frontier. From William James to Thomas Dewey, public thinkers provide an intellectual framework for what is already happening on the ground. Those gritty participants are people of action, not ideas. The philosophers stand on the shoulders of trailblazers.

The expanding, seemingly endless American frontier is the perfect laboratory for fresh ideas, turning California into what Wallace Stegner calls an "experimental society." Common sense is elevated to a system of thought. In Europe, there is little perceived hope for a new and better life—it lacks a frontier, literally or spiritually. All is stuck in time and space. In America, the world is turned on its head. Pragmatism encourages a willingness to reconsider and, if necessary, abandon long cherished ideas and passions—social tradition, Victorian virtue, or even Christianity. Caste and class, love and marriage, birth and death should be subject only to the test of outcomes— "radical empiricism." Pioneers likely experience the behavior as a basic survival instinct rather than a reasoned choice; to some extent, everyone who steps into the New World is converted to pragmatism. For the most daring, it can be an unexpected and rude baptism. Even when you struggle beyond survival, the mindset remains as an embedded impulse of thought and action.

Pragmatism is the most simple and radical idea in philosophy— the anti-philosophy, a provocateur, the ultimate disrupter that leaves confusion and hope in its wake. Boosters are pioneers with bowties. They are one step ahead of the masses because they nurture both a social and personal agenda honed to coalescence and obsession. William James quips that the worth of an idea is its "cash value"—how well the vision plays out in practice. Who else but an American would define the apex of his thought in such terms? Mundane and brilliant. Metaphysics distilled to social physics.

TAMING THE OUTSIDE LANDS

San Francisco expansion into territory once regarded as uninhabitable leads to the demise of the cemeteries. The appropriately dubbed "Outside Lands" is the marshy, desolate tundra west of the emerging city that extends to the Pacific Ocean. An 1870 San Francisco map labels the area—today, the densely populated Richmond and Sunset districts—"The Land of Fog—Uninhabitable." Another map dubs it the "Great Sand Bank." The vast area is regarded as suitable for small farms, light industry, warehouses, orphanages, horse racing tracks, and cemeteries, all of which require substantial property at low cost. Whatever residential potential the area promises is a gamble at best, and few developers are willing to roll the dice.

Hearty "Kit Carsons" pioneer the forsaken and largely unknown terrain. Always the enterprising pathfinder, Sam Brannan opens the "Cliff House" in 1863, an appropriate name for a restaurant perched on a precipice overlooking the Pacific Ocean. Immediately, the Mount Lobos Toll Road for horses and buggies—the present Geary Boulevard—is cut through the sand dunes to deliver the wealthy and powerful to hobnob far from the madding crowds. Three U.S. presidents sip Napoleonic brandy in its luxurious setting. But those madding crowds are soon beating a path there, spawning roadhouses and little shops along the route. Trekking to Lands End to watch the frolicking sea lions becomes a popular weekend retreat. The beaches flourish with a jumble of vendors and adventurous entrepreneurs like Captain Jack Williams. who cavorts with the wild creatures and swims around Seal Rock with his extremities tied. The captain can attract as many as 10,000 spectators in a single day.

The undeveloped sand dune terrain desert between civilization and "Lands End" at the Pacific Ocean. Fleishhaker Pool (at bottom, middle left), then one of the largest outdoor public swimming facilities in the world, is opened in 1925. The residential city is inching its way there. *Virtual Museum of the City of San Francisco*

It takes Adolph Sutro to turn the spot into a citizen's retreat in 1890, when he opens the largest and most famous public bathhouse in the world, located just below his palatial mansion overlooking the Cliff House. Build it, and they will come, especially when you establish reliable and inexpensive railcar service.

This development of the Pacific coastline, however impressive, is hardly the taming of the Outside Lands. The terrain between Lone Mountain cemeteries and the coastline remains unpopulated sand dunes.

There is a gradual encroachment of "civilization." Electric streetcars introduced along Geary and California streets in 1877 stimulate expansion. The earliest residents are modest businesses and small farmers huddled near the lines. More prosperous working-class people and some professionals trickle into the new single-family cottage neighborhoods dotting the still-inexpensive land. Neighborhood improvement clubs spring up.

Soon come upbeat booster assessments of the area. When Lone Mountain cemeteries opened, the *San Francisco Evening Bulletin* comments twenty-four years later that "they were considered to have been located out of the world as it were, and the most farseeing of the people in those days would have thought the ideas of the city's growing up to that far away spot too ridiculous to mention. But facts are stubborn things."

As always, the proof is in the pudding—the hobgoblin of urban planners. Civic chefs concoct recipes based on available ingredients and tastes, but time can sour the dish in what seems like yesterday. "The citizens are reaching out even beyond all of the cemeteries and have built up homes to enshrine therein their lares and panates," the *Bulletin* declares. "Nearly every block of land beyond those would-be barriers to the city's growth has been bought up by speculators, who are holding the same for the time which will ultimately come when they will receive good, round prices for their town lots. But a few years ago scarcely a residence was located to the westward of the first Point Lobos road tollgate, and not an avenue existed besides the Cliff House road. Now, that road is being rapidly built up with dwellings of all descriptions, and innumerable groceries, haberdasheries, bakeries and other branches of business line the thoroughfare. To the north and south, broad avenues have been laid out, lots sold, and many of them have also been built upon, the whole forming a miniature city of itself."

GOLDEN GATE PARK

A grand Park within the reach of every citizen would do more in preventing dissipation and vice than half the sermons preached, half the moral lectures and teachings given to children and to men.
—*SAN FRANCISCO CHRONICLE*, 1855

Today, San Francisco is praised for its abundance of public parks. They were a long time coming. The *Annals of San Francisco* in 1855 laments the absence of any vision for civic recreational space—"the true lungs of a city. . . . Not only is there no public park or garden, but there is not even a circus, oval, open terrace, board avenue, or an ornamental street or building or verdant space of any kind." Portsmouth Square in city center, Washington Square in North Beach, and Union Square to the west are the only open spaces where a soul might meander in relative calm without fear of sinking into quicksand.

The much-heralded and prosperous San Francisco harbor was, in the words of Charles Lockwood, "chilly and desolate." One could feel that they were "thousands of miles from civilization in a land unique, grim, desolate, sufficient unto itself, shut off by sea and mountains from the great world." City fathers are too overwhelmed with digging sewers and altering street grades to address quality-of-life infrastructure. The city is virtually bereft of trees. Some outdoor playgrounds and amusements do come in the 1860s, most notably Woodward Gardens, but until further development of Golden Gate Park, the "instant" city remains a ramshackle urban jungle of warehouses, smoky factories, and boxy structures with little in the way of civic buildings or museums to offset the grim overtone.

"People have forgotten," Mark Twain opines in 1868, "that San Francisco is not a ranch, or rather, that it ought not properly to be a ranch. It has all the disagreeable features of a ranch, though. Every citizen keeps from ten to five hundred chickens, and these cackle all day and all night: They stand watches, and the watch on duty makes a racket while the off-watch sleeps. Let a stranger get outside of Montgomery and Kearny from Pacific to 2nd Street and close his eyes, and he can imagine himself on a well-stocked farm, without any effort, for his ears will be assailed by such a vile din of gobbling of turkeys, and crowing of hoarse voiced roosters, and cackling of hens, and howling of cows, and whinnying of horses, and braying of jackasses, and yowling of cats, that he will be driven to frenzy."

Frederick Law Olmsted, the nation's anointed urban planner, pontificates that "a park gives a city a soul." He has souled New York City with Central Park. San Francisco boosters yearn to create their own celebrated public playground. No city can dare claim to be great without such a civic centerpiece. New York City is regarded as the standard. But when Mr. Olmsted is hired to replicate his eastern gem, he declares the "outside lands" so barren and sandy that a park as the city envisions there is impossible. Instead, he proposes three smaller parks in three other locations.

Boosters will have none of this practical, narrow-minded thinking. Visionary city planners, spurred on by residents bordering the cemeteries, convince the Board of Supervisors in 1871 to begin a single, expansive park in the Outside Lands, one that will stretch to the shores of the Pacific.

Over the next twenty years, the 1,013-acre tract is developed at the speed of a tortoise. Before a hoe can dig, the city must deal with the land's "residents": squatters who know well the old Spanish pueblo law of boundaries and land transfers. They also know how to negotiate. The purchase price eventually rises to a lofty $800,000 ($25 million today) for what is widely regarded as a swath of desert.

The project is hardly met with general approval. Those lands are widely ridiculed as a "joke" or "not worth a button." One newspaper sneers, "Of all the elephants the city of San Francisco ever owned, they now own the largest in Golden Gate Park, a dreary waste of shifting sand hills where a blade of grass cannot be raised without four posts to keep it from blowing away."

In its fledgling days, Golden Gate Park is more promise than reality, but soon, an elegant city road (The Panhandle) leads to an arboreal paradise in the easternmost section of the land expanse. Immediately, the spot becomes a recreation retreat for the rich and the aspirational. In the 1870s, as many as 600 carriages enter the park on weekdays and twice that on weekends—the favorite place for the hoity-toity to see and be seen.

Still, progress for the vast acreage remains stuck in the sand. Will the city ever see the fulfillment of that grand vision of a park that will rival New York? "The Outside Lands are sand and lupin, lupin and sand, and nothing else until the cliff's hanging over the ocean for the most part," the *San Francisco Examiner* complains just five years before the 1894 California Midwinter International Exposition, which officially proclaims Golden Gate Park open to the world. The much-maligned "lupin" is one of the few plants that can take hold and survive in the inhospitable terrain. Although much more work needs to be done to reach the Pacific, the exposition demonstrates that a determined elite garnering public support can overcome seemingly impossible obstacles. The destiny of that long-held dream is harnessed by an eccentric bulldog of a genius who builds the playground; in doing so, he builds the city and sets in motion the demise of the cemeteries. Landscaper to the stars, John McLaren enters the scene in 1887. Previous administrators are engineers and politicians lacking the perspective, practical skills, and political muscle to move "mission impossible" forward. With McLaren, that spectacular dream bears fruit or, more literally, vegetation. He is a miracle worker—a man with the right skills at the right time at the right place. Historians describe his reign "as spectacular years when Nature was brought under control," a time when a champion "tamed the unleashed power of the wind and the sea." His most important miracle is to tame his city bosses. By virtue of ingenuity, experimentation, and tenacity, McLaren transforms windswept sand dunes into grass, trees, gardens, and lakes.

Common folks do find their way to early Golden Gate Park, but Lone Mountain cemeteries remain the popular recreational getaway. Since its founding in 1854, city leaders are keen to promote Lone Mountain as an urban park, which relieves public pressure to provide open spaces on more valuable real estate. Development of Golden Gate Park gradually changes that equation. The potential to conquer and use all the land to the Pacific makes the cemeteries not only obsolete but also obstacles. Those historic sanctuaries come to be redefined as dilapidated, health-threatening nuisances that should be reimagined as homes, schools, businesses, and, of course, tax revenue.

As original planners hoped, Golden Gate Park, however slowly, draws San Franciscans westward just as Central Park is nudging Manhattanites northward. It takes determination and vision to get there. "Something spectacular was needed," Gray Brechin observes, "to overcome the notorious disadvantages of heavy fog and drifting sand in the bleakly named Outside Lands. Early plans for public parks in the Outside Lands spoke to the cultural ambitions of San Francisco's city planners, who sought to emulate the urban landscape of established metropolises like New York and Boston."

Richmond District residents interpret the funding of Golden Gate Park in 1871 as a signal that the Board of Supervisors will support neighborhood action against the cemeteries. It is touted as a historic moment that heralds a "real" park, one without neglected monuments, macabre settings, funeral processions, and lurking health risks.

Pioneers are swarming around the Lone Mountain cemeteries. Neighborhood property owners—aptly designated the Richmond District Improvement Association—initiate a campaign to bring in street construction, fire stations, water mains, and schools. Funding for the lobby draws from private citizens, typically businessmen and professionals. Once the city begins to provide infrastructure, it must by legal and moral necessity also assume responsibility for urban planning, a consequence well understood and leveraged by expansion activists. It is a conspiracy but one with wide participation and virtually transparent machinations. The marching orders: support sympathizers in the city administration and infiltrate pockets of power there, control interest groups that influence civic decisions, and convince local neighborhood improvement associations spread out over the city to work in hand in hand with wealthy boosters to lobby the government.

The Richmond District Improvement Association wages a long, unrelenting anti-cemetery campaign. It is always ahead of the curve because it is creating the curve. As early as the 1880s, it calls for total eviction. "A blur on our fair city's face," bemoans the *Richmond Banner* in 1895 on behalf of the now estimated 3,000 pioneers of the area. At 1 percent of the city's population, the tail is wagging the dog, but it can generate powerful winds when movers and shakers like banker William H. Crocker and entrepreneur Gustav Sutro join the parade, even if that nobility is calling only for a cessation of cemetery sales at that time. The Midwinter Exposition promotes the city as a delightful destination at that time of year—opening on January 27 as the East and the Midwest descend into their annual deep freezes. The event is widely hailed as a success. A million and a half attend the exhibits on 200 acres in the park. Superintendent John McLaren fights hard against staging the extravaganza in his domain, warning that "the damage to the natural setting would take decades to reverse." It was one of the few battles he lost.

"METROPOLITANISM"

The "City Beautiful" crusade flourishes at the turn of the century, inaugurated at the 1893 World's Columbian Exposition in Chicago to celebrate the 400th anniversary of Columbus's discovery of America. Smitten by the national Progressive movement, urban planners across America propose "beautification" and public pomp to inspire a sense of moral and public virtue. Citizens of all classes will share a common heritage and space—a lofty Progressive notion that civic improvements per se contribute to social reform. It promotes the beaux arts style implemented by Napoleon III: long boulevards accented by spectacular structures and monuments. The movement results in the grand and grandiose makeover of cities à la Paris.

The frontier booster bug that bites Chicago and St. Louis infects San Francisco—but more intensely. The East Coast cities are already great and established centers of culture and commerce. With all its prestige and urban building, San Francisco is still a "wannabe" caught in a frantic catch-up mode. The simple boosterism of the 1870s will not do. San Francisco needs a makeover; even more, the city's destiny begs expansion. The Outside Lands may be the impossible dream, but it is the only dream in town.

The 1894 Midwinter Exposition comes from the booster playbook. Designed specifically to advertise San Francisco and California to the world, it is arranged by Michael de Young, editor of the *San Francisco Chronicle*, and underwritten by local businessmen aided by significant donations from ordinary citizens. Civic leaders want the city to be "The City"—not just Queen of the West but a crown jewel of the nation. To achieve that status, you must attract eager newcomers—the magnet is growth, building, jobs, opportunity, and wealth, all in a wonderful climate. Can Chicago say that? The timing is fortuitous. The nation is mired in depression; might not the exposition be a tonic for the times? It does not take a seer to realize that significant immigration to San Francisco will lead to and likely through the Lone Mountain cemeteries.

James Phelan serves as mayor from 1897 to 1902. After making a fortune in real estate, he uses his political power to orchestrate a "city beautifying" project that expands public transportation and utility services to stimulate growth, including his own. This is the epitome of boosterism—the blending of personal and public wealth for the benefit of the city and its citizens.

Former mayor Phelan is president of the Association for the Improvement and Adornment of San Francisco—a cabal of elites determined to complete the transformation of the city from its rough Barbary Coast image into a "Paris of the West," San Francisco's new anointed nickname. He invites Daniel Burnham, a distinguished urban designer and prominent developer of the 1893 World's Columbian Exposition, to draw up plans for a reenvisioning of the city. It is time, Phelan declares, for San Francisco to become "a great and wondrous city or wander aimlessly to an uncertain end."

Planners consider various urban designs. All agree on one action: The cemeteries must go. Golden Gate Park has sparked the dream of a vibrant city extending to the Pacific Ocean shores. Cemeteries stand directly in the path of expansion—not just the dead land itself but also the land around them as it is gobbled up by speculators, which makes development more complicated. These run-down, ramshackle enclaves of the past with little hope of restoration are a civic embarrassment—and a glaring contradiction to beaux arts.

In 1918, Phelan recalls the earthquake as a pivotal event in the abandonment of the grand Burnham vision: "[The people] dropped the plan in order to house themselves and rehabilitate their affairs. It was the worst time to talk about beautification. The people were thrown back to a consideration as to how again they would live and thrive." The main Burnham beaux arts plans that materialize and endure are the Civic Center Plaza and the widening of 19th Avenue and Geary Boulevard.

The "opening" of Golden Gate Park at the Midwinter Expo unleashes a reinvigorated anti-cemetery assault emphasizing the thousands of out-of-town visitors—potential residents and investors, not to mention gabbing journalists from everywhere. What might guests see and report back to the world when they behold the deteriorating, unhealthy lands of the dead in the center of a thriving metropolis? Our future demands better.

What the world thinks of San Francisco is an obsession among local politicians and businessmen. Other cities are building, expanding, creating wealth, and solving problems. San Francisco can do no less. The *Richmond Banner* declares, "Where homes and mansions should rear their pinnacles to the western sky, cold tombstones and clammy vaults stand, a silent menace to the living, a mockery to progress and the advancement of civilization." Chicago is offered as a model for how neighborhood improvement clubs might work with municipal government to achieve urban progress—defined as space for more homes and businesses. By failing to implement more dynamic planning, the editors warn, San Francisco diminishes its potential and fails to meet the standards set by other American cities. The world will notice.

Business and civic leaders are in full embrace of "metropolitanism," defined by Gunter Barth as a mission to "inaugurate and maintain a style of life characteristic of a great city." The cemeteries thwart this vision. "No progressive citizen can afford to ignore so important a movement," the *Banner* warns.

CITY CEMETERY BITES THE DUST

In familiar San Francisco fashion, the future arrives ahead of time. A city newspaper sends out a clarion call in 1887, along with a financial balance sheet: "The public burial grounds, established a mere 16 years earlier at the edge of the local universe, must go.... It transpires that 200 acres, covering a most suitable site, can be obtained for $22,500. The removal of bodies can be effected for $30,000, making a total cost of $52,500. The present site would then be available for building purposes, and would readily sell for $2,500 an acre, leaving a profit on the transaction of $447,500. Besides, a nuisance would be got out of the way, and room made for a very desirable addition to the city."

On January 1, 1898, the Board of Supervisors hangs a "No Vacancy" sign at City Cemetery. There is land left for burials but no political will to preserve it. The grounds hold some 18,000 to 20,000—no one then or now can provide an accurate count. Chinese subsections total as many as 5,000 remains. The numerous "ethnic" portions comprise perhaps 3,000. Some 12,000 "paupers" occupy the remainder.

The city edict is a stop order, not an eviction. City Cemetery is dead, but, as always, politics and legalities delay the funeral. In 1908, the board drops the other shoe: Service organizations overseeing official ethnic areas are ordered to remove all remains and monuments for the establishment of a new "Lincoln Park." They are granted six months for the rescue.

By this time, the decision to reclaim City Cemetery is an easy call. Neglect has exacted its toll; so-called vandals and grave robbers have ravaged the most vulnerable parts of the cemetery at Potter's Field. A *San Francisco Examiner* investigation describes City Cemetery as "desolate and forsaken." The Jewish and some fraternal and ethnic sections are judged to be in decent condition, but there is "a land of graves, uncared for and seemingly forgotten. Here lie the city's pauper dead. The dry grass tangles thick and long, and here and there are bunches of scraggly brush—skeletons of dead bushes. But there is not a tree in the whole place."

The reporter grapples to describe the scene. He asks the superintendent where the paupers come from:

From the Morgue, mostly. Some come from the City Hospital, some from the Poor House, and some from the Foundling Asylum. Some were tramps, anonymous, and fatal victims of crimes.

The neglected graves stretch out row after row. At the head of each was once a board numbered with the number of its silent owner. There are no names upon these headboards, and wind and weather have worked hard to obliterate even this simple mark of identity. . . . It behooves a curious wanderer in this city of the silent to watch his footsteps carefully, for the sodden ground is treacherous and full of holes.

The old footboards lean tipsily over the graves or fall in decayed forlornness on the ground. Toward the end of the rows the boards are only charred sticks, burned out of all resemblance to what they once imitated. There are a few scattered single graves, which are fenced in alone and lettered with the names of the sleepers. The fences are crazy and dilapidated, and the earth within looks little cared for.

The grass is littered with rubbish. Old shoes, old hats, rusty tin cans and bits of paper lie scattered about.

Upon one lonely mound, set a little way apart by a rotting railing, there lay a broken cup that once held a plant. It was the only evidence of human thought or care in the whole dreary place, and that had evidently lain broken and forgotten for many months. . . .

The Chinese section is very crowded . . . when the Chinese burn the clothes of the dead, as is their custom, they often toss them into the city plot and set them afire there. Yesterday the ground was strewn with garments so sodden with damp decay that they refused to burn. So they lay flapping gaudily above the sleeping citizens in the plot below, like some flaunting mockery of their low estate.

Once started in 1908, the work of reclamation goes as fast as a bull-dozer. A mere year after the eviction order, 150 acres are formally transferred to the City Park Commission and fifty assigned to the U.S. Army stationed at nearby Fort Miley. City Cemetery is transformed into a vacant lot—a vast, rough-hewn tabula rasa. The Board of Supervisors Health Committee declares, "The best use which may be made of the magnificent site of the cemetery, overlooking as it does the Golden Gate, the bay, and ocean, is to turn it into a permanent park in line with the Presidio and the Gold Gate Pleasure Ground." This is just what Board of Supervisors member Aaron Burns recommended in his resolution twenty years earlier: to consider if City Cemetery "should be placed under the care and control of the Board of Park Commissioners to improve and beautify it for the uses and purpose of the public." The objective in those earlier years is to kill City Cemetery any way possible—the lure of an urban pleasure ground is the most logical and effective line of attack. It is widely believed that only when the public and investors know for certain that the 200-acre "dead spread" is to be transformed will they invest blood, sweat, and money in the land around it.

———

Golfing on heaven's door. The first invasion of the Golden Gate deadlands is a golf shot. A pair of gentlemen in 1902 approach John McLaren, San Francisco's dictator of public parks, with an idea whose time had come. National amateur champion Jack Neville is a member of the recently formed Claremont Country Club in Oakland. Vincent Whitney owns the Whitney Building in San Francisco and hobnobs at the exclusive Olympic Club. San Francisco must build a municipal golf course, they submit.

John McLaren is quick to suggest the Potter's Field section of Golden Gate Park as a fine location, instructing Neville and Whitney to construct a design. Burials have been banned there for three years, and the remains remain; it will be eight years before the official exhumation order is issued. Golf is regarded best played as near as possible to the Pacific Ocean. Potter's Field is a dream site. By the end of 1902, a three-hole layout is established on a hilly, windswept, almost treeless land. Some sneer: It is only an "experimental" course and not even the first one—a small three-hole link had been planted by "rogue fans" in the same general area. The new semiofficial course proves popular—too popular. Free to the public, by 1909 the loop looks like rush hour at the Ferry Terminal. The City requests that three more holes be added, which are located where the fourteenth, fifteenth, and sixteenth holes presently sit in Lincoln Park Golf Course. Devotees organize a full-fledged municipal club, culminating in an August 1918 inauguration of a resplendent eighteen-hole layout. The eighteenth hole lands in the old Italian section of City Cemetery, which, by lucky geography, is temporarily spared in the old removal. When finally claimed, the city allocates funds for the disinterment of 8,000 deceased. Superintendent of Parks John McLaren oversees the project, and Italian societies cover the cost of relocation at the Italian cemetery in Colma.

The official Lincoln Park Golf Clubs History describes the evolution of the recreational project, noting that by the turn of the century, golf associations managing courses are a national trend, and San Francisco was lagging behind. No booster could tolerate such a liability, especially in a progressive, everything's-up-to-date city.

THE NUMBERS GAME

How many deceased are moved from City Cemetery? At the time, San Franciscans think that the Golden Gate Cemetery dead are relocated by city government and benevolent associations. Actually, at the time, San Franciscans do not think about the dead at all. The jarring truth does pop up here and there, especially in 1921. But it is the grisly discoveries at the 1989–1993 Legion of Honor retrofit and expansion that finally disrupt the popular view, forcing a painful revision of city history.

Old ideas or, in some cases, just old copy persist: The National Park Service's page on the Golden Gate Cemetery website states, "The graves of Golden Gate Cemetery were exhumed and moved to Colma." However, its Palace of the Legion of Honor page notes that the "cemetery board was ordered to exhume the burials and reinter them in cemeteries in Colma ... but hundreds of burials were unearthed during construction of the Legion of Honor in 1921 and again during the expansion activities in 1993. It is clear that many remains were not exhumed as the City ordered, and more are likely still buried beneath the museum."

Researchers are confounded by the lack of City Cemetery removal records. Without such, Michael Svanevik points out, a determination is impossible: "I am not aware that any of them were exhumed." Perhaps it is to be expected that the "Potter's Field" indigent would be disrespected, but what about the benevolent society sections? That effort has been characterized by a San Francisco supervisor whose district sits on the land as "scattered and disorganized." The Daly City History Guild concludes, "City cemetery plots were sold to twenty-five individual 'societies' of the time including The Improved Order of Red Men. They moved some, but for the rest—they just shoveled dirt right over them."

The Lincoln Park Golf Course is a focus of criticism. The official website states, "What is presently the eighteenth fairway of the golf course was a burial ground, primarily for the city's Italian community. That which now constitutes the first and thirteenth fairway was the Chinese section of the cemetery, and the high terrain of the fifteenth fairway and thirteenth tee was a Serbian resting place." The site does not reveal that with the exception of the eighteenth fairway, most of the bodies are likely still there.

So how many remains remain in larger Lincoln Park? "Unknown" according to the *Encyclopedia of San Francisco*. There is a rough consensus: at least 10,000, likely more. San Francisco historian Woody LeBounty believes that a serious intention to relocate Potters Field never existed. "The City and County did not feel it was necessary to move the thousands of bodies the county itself had buried over the years, deciding to leave these individuals under the ground at the new park. Mostly economically disadvantaged, these people, still there, never had more than a simple wooden cross as a marker. The ruling attitude is reflected in newspaper headlines, such as *The Dead Must Not Be Permitted to Injure the Living.*"

As with Yerba Buena, we may not know how many are moved, but we have evidence of those who are not. Two days before Christmas 1921, a reporter from the *Daily News* discovers work crews pulling up bodies and coffins from Lincoln Park grounds, where the city is building a World War I veterans memorial as part of the Legion of Honor. "Just as I arrived one large and two small skeletons were ripped out of one grave. In the grave were household utensils. Besides the skeletons lay the coffin boards. Wrapped about them were the shrouds. Workmen steered clear of the mess. 'It's horrible,' the foreman said. 'We've taken up about 1500. We've uncovered all of them now, I think. It's clear sailing now. . . . The men don't like them. Won't touch the bones. All we can do is to scrape them [move by machine] over and cover them up again.'"

Two reporters return later in the day. They are shocked. The headline did not mince words: "Coffin Sticks Out from Bluff." Neither did the story: "There were piles of bones not completely covered by the dirt. Along the ledge just where the hill drops abruptly were many coffins—cut in half by the steel teeth of the excavating machines.... Here was the bottom end of a coffin sticking out of the sand bluff. Further along the bluff the head of the coffin. A skull there. The coffins poked out all along that cliff. At night, after the workmen have gone, small boys of the neighborhood kick their toes into the dirt. Why? One said that $35 had been found in one of the coffins. An expensive ring in another, he said. And the skulls—sometimes students at the Affiliated colleges bought them."

The hubbub attracts the attention and ire of attorney W. C. Eastin, representing Mary E. Bush, whose family is buried in the affected area. Eastin insists that the city attorney had signed a document eight months earlier that stipulated that no bodies would be removed from City Cemetery without a public thirty-day notice. The plaintiff is prepared to seek an injunction preventing the further removal or disturbance of any bodies and to reintroduce an earlier injunction that he withdrew calling the action illegal based on a U.S. grant of the land to the city with the express purpose of using the land for burials. "The city's action is nothing less than a felony and those responsible should go to the state penitentiary." Mr. Eastin does not prevail.

The California Palace of the Legion of Honor, a museum gift from the Spreckels family, is constructed on part of the old City Cemetery's pauper section. In the exploration for a new subterranean Legion of Honor gallery, contractors in the late 1980s stumble on what is described initially as "isolated bone scatter." It turns out to be more. About 800 burials are eventually exhumed and "many more left in place." There is evidence, the *San Francisco Weekly* concludes, that the original contractors "just plowed through burial sites, and plumbers laid pipes right through bodies and skeletons. . . . They threw headstones off the cliff into the ocean."

In response to the 1989 Loma Prieta earthquake, the Legion of Honor undergoes seismic renovation as well as expansion. In the summer of 1993, the *Los Angeles Times* reports that "about 300 corpses from the Gold Rush era—two of them still clutching rosaries, others were wearing dentures and Levi's—were unearthed from what appears to be an old pauper's graveyard. Some experts say another 11,000 bodies might lie underneath the museum grounds." About 800 remains are uncovered in this part of the work, including 700 coffins. Research identifies the departed as "poor, working-class people of European ancestry" as well as Chinese, interred between 1868 and 1906. On this occasion, there is due respect for these dead, who are conveyed to the coroner's office to be buried at Skylawn Cemetery in San Mateo. The artifacts are donated to the City Museum.

Colma Historical Association

The overall effort to accommodate the dead is highly criticized. The Legion of Honor hires archaeological photographer Richard Barnes to document the retrofit and expansion in the early 1990s. "When they were digging trenches, they would come across a body that was half in the trench and half out of the trench, and they were told at the end that they would have to speed things up, and in order to speed things up you need to take half the burial out and leave the other half in the trench.... You begin to see the care that was being taken of the artwork. Some of it was near life-sized statuary and the care in terms of the crating and the padding that was going on, and then what was happening on the outside in terms of the burials being thrown into cardboard boxes. To me it was quite jarring, the juxtaposition, to find out what was more important."

The Legion of Honor turns down a proposal by the archaeological firm for a more extensive excavation, stating that such a project is beyond the scope of its mandate.

As the twentieth century begins, San Francisco cemetery wars reach a boiling point. It is the future snipping at the past, boosters confronting sentimentalists, justice for the living versus justice for the dead. Plebiscites set up speed bumps to eviction. How the issue is resolved becomes a clinic in unruly politics, proving once again that democracy is not the ideal system, only the best.

There are anti-cemetery movements in all major urban areas, but few are as strident, well organized, and persistent. Most American cities will celebrate their past with dedicated cemetery spaces and public memorials. Not so in San Francisco. The battle over cemetery lands lasts almost a century, divides families and politicians, spawns contentious referendums and litigation that shapes national jurisprudence, and, in the end, leaves no significant memorials to its ancestors.

CHAPTER 7

A NECROPOLIS ARISES

THE 1901 BURIAL BAN IN THE CITY AND COUNTY OF SAN FRAN-
cisco is total and revolutionary. It declares cemeteries "dangerous
to life and detrimental to health." Three years earlier, the Board of
Supervisors had banned burials in public City Cemetery. The short
life of the Lone Mountain private cemeteries, established hardly a
generation earlier, hardly goes unnoticed. The *San Francisco Chronicle* comments, "Everybody will concede now that it was a mistake
to locate them where they are, but when those sites were chosen few
were sanguine enough to suppose that in a little over a quarter of a
century the city would grow beyond them. Such has, however been
the case."

The city cat has toyed with the cemetery mouse for as long as
folks can remember. When the Board of Supervisors move in for
the kill, the victim is not dispatched but moved to death row. The
new law means no burials in existing cemeteries, no further sales
of property or services, and no hope of expanding or creating new
cemeteries on any city land no matter how small or distantly located
in the Outside Lands. The city and county of San Francisco are
surrounded by water on three sides and a separate county to the
south. By 1901, the year the city bans further burials, there are six
budding cemeteries where the deceased can find true eternal peace
nestled in the agricultural pastures of San Mateo County nine miles
away. Even the "old" dead, with the help of living relatives, can rise
complete with memorial and relocate to the garden paradise of
Colma—the only American city incorporated for the sole purpose of

preserving and protecting the dead. It becomes America's first and only necropolis—a city of the dead. It currently has 1.5 million permanent residents in seventeen separate burial grounds and 1,700 living souls. The official city motto: "It's great to be alive in Colma."

Before it is a necropolis, the area is known as the "market basket" of the Bay Area, producing the vegetables, dairy, hogs, and flowers for a quickly expanding San Francisco and Northern California. Dotted by small farms and ranches, typically owned by Irish and Italian immigrants, trains and horse-drawn wagons deliver the goods. Sometimes they work in tandem. If the mud is too thick for wagons to navigate the steep hill leading to the city, it is common to place it on the San Francisco & San Mateo Railway tracks and push the burden over the hump by streetcar.

In a twenty-year period from 1887, six cemeteries are built in Colma, most of them on land under farm cultivation at the time. Archbishop William Riordan begins the process by standing in the middle of a potato field to consecrate Holy Cross Cemetery. "Colma" is the original name for a general region extending some ten miles south from the city and county line of San Francisco. On one side sits the Pacific Ocean, on the other the San Bruno Mountains, both immovable parameters. The town that is today Colma is a modest part of that area, about two square miles. Eighty percent of that land is owned by cemeteries.

The first mayor, Mattrup Jensen, touts the plan to locate all the burial grounds of a municipal area in one spot as the only one of its kind and design anywhere: "the most unique City in the World." The purpose for incorporation is simple and transparent: "It draws a line around the cemeteries . . . so as to preserve them against any future invasion, should San Francisco desire to extend its city limits in years to come."

Until after World War II, virtually all businesses in the city of Colma are related to the cemetery industry—monuments makers, flower growers and shops, metal foundries, and lodging for workers—except for a brief and bizarre juxtaposition when Colma serves as both the burial and the boxing capital of the United States.

Boxing is a major spectator sport in early twentieth-century America, rivaling the "national pastime," baseball. Prizefighting can be gladiatorial. Twenty-one states have banned it by 1900 but not California. When San Francisco joins the ban, the get-around is simple: Step over the border to Colma and set up open-air arenas. The 1906 earthquake accelerates the effort by consigning "underground" city venues underground—literally. It inspires a new breed of entrepreneur, epitomized by "Sunny Jim" Coffroth, a flamboyant promoter who opens a venue just fifty feet south of the city limits. It quickly becomes the best-known fight pavilion in the country—a workingman's tourist attraction. Twelve thousand fans can pack in and typically do. Flatcars on nearby railroad tracks provide observation points to accommodate the overflow and freeloaders. Even with all its nouveau riche glamour, San Francisco remains an immigrant working-class town where men outnumber women two to one. Gary Kamiya calls Colma in this period "the pugilistic capital of the planet."

Celebrity fighters of the day square off at Coffroth's Sunshine Arena on Mission Street. Among the attractions are Jack Johnson (the first big-draw black heavyweight champion), James J. "Gentleman Jim" Corbett, and Robert Fitzsimmons, who held world titles in three weight divisions. For the historic 1905 lightweight title rematch between Oscar "Battling" Nelson and Jimmy Britt, Coffroth adds 3,000 seats to the arena. The scheduled forty-five-round match, which ends early in a brutal eighteenth-round knockout, is a huge financial success with ticket revenues of $2 million in today's value, breaking all national records for a non-heavyweight bout. The promoter sells the film rights to the bout for an astonishing $5 million.

The Colma boxing industry is just that. Main streets and back alleys are dotted with gyms and training quarters that attract eager fans and hangers-on with a thirst for liquid as well as visual entertainment. Enter professional gamblers, brothels, and opportunists of all sorts. Fighters typically train in small makeshift gyms built in the back rooms of saloons. Roadwork is in cabbage fields. Hotels and lodgings pop up to accommodate fighters and entourages. When California outlaws professional boxing in 1915, as many as a quarter of all businesses in Colma consist of saloons, gambling halls, and houses of ill repute—or any combination of these venues. Police at the time complain about street fights and unruly behavior, especially on fight days.

Unlicensed boxing venues emerge, lacking even the inadequate regulations of professional contests. In 1906, two aspiring young friends meet in a match. One dies in battle. There is handwringing and threats of prosecution, even predictions that this might be "the end of boxing in San Francisco." Little happens, and the beat goes on until 1915, when the state of California bans the sport as a professional endeavor—amateurs can spar, but there is no fighting for prize money. It was a great and memorable run for Colma, hardly remembered today.

———

Denied proceeds from land sales and services, cemetery associations must find revenue outside existing business operations to maintain the grounds—a costly and perpetual obligation. But what about the great fraternal orders that sponsor cemeteries? The Catholic Church, which consecrated Calvary as hallowed ground? And the Laurel Hill families of Gilded Age moguls resting in magnificent tombs? Is it unfair to ask whether, if all these well-heeled folks will not support their own, why average citizens should suffer any consequences—financial or cultural? There is added irony. Are not some of the most vociferous advocates for removal those very civic elites who have relatives buried at Lone Mountain?

There are individual families who do tend to their plots. The vast majority do not. Even when private cemeteries have a revenue stream from sales, it fails to provide more than basic care. There is no formal communal responsibility, which would equate to an endowment levy. Such is not the practice when Lone Mountain cemeteries open. By the twentieth century, it prevails, but the reform is more relevant for new cemeteries, not old ones, where most of the land is already sold.

A letter to the editor signed "Passerby" in 1924 comments, "The removal of the cemeteries is once more a public issue. . . . If those lot owners, who bitterly oppose the removal, would show some feeling and contribute to the care of these old graveyards and thereby giving proof that they have some respect for their departed ones, there would cease to be any public demand for their removal."

Cemetery associations try to raise special funds. But the effort is always too little, too late. If anyone can extract money from private pockets, it is Laurel Hill, host to some of the wealthiest families in the nation. In 1914, the cemetery association dispatches an urgent letter to all lot holders: "With the funds at the command of the Association, it is not possible to keep the Cemetery in even the state of preservation that has been maintained for the past few years." It proposes that all lot holders "enter into an agreement to pay the expense of putting his lot in good shape and keeping it so." Management will tend to the roads and communal spaces. The response is tepid. The president of the association remarks, "It is useless to say that your Board of Trustees are much chagrined at the result of this effort, as it seems to show a lack of interest or a belief that the removal question is not settled."

Had the public been polled in 1901, most would have interpreted the new ordinance to mean that cemeteries cannot grow denser or ever expand—not the implied removal of the grounds (witness the overwhelming "no" vote on that very question a dozen years later). Eviction is still a cultural taboo, especially on the scale San Francisco is contemplating—the dramatic disinterment of some 150,000 souls to who knows exactly where? At the time, such a proposition is regarded as drastic on both sides of the cemetery debate, at least publicly. For some, it is unthinkable.

The Catholic Church remains a formidable player in city and state politics. It is adamantly opposed to any mass deportation of the deceased. Some inside the anti-cemetery movement at the time believe that removal is not a viable option, certainly not in the short run. After all, the populations of Lone Mountain are Catholics, Odd Fellows, and Masons—still large and powerful parts of the city electorate. Nonsectarian Laurel Hill Cemetery hosts some of the most powerful families of California.

For others, the time is ripe and overripe. An 1880 *San Francisco Examiner* editorial summed up the impatience: "Since It Is to Be Done It Should Be Done at Once." The campaign increases in numbers and intensity. By 1901, the newspaper heralds the burial ban as "the initial step toward the ultimate removal of the cemeteries."

Those who want it sooner will have to bide their time.

The intrepid but prudent supervisor Aaron Burns might have consoled them with this perspective:

> *Gentlemen, this ban will starve out the cemeteries. It is a siege. It cuts off their revenue. They cannot sell or service what they have, and they cannot expand beyond their deathtraps. Already, the cemeteries are up to their necks—literally—with basic maintenance. Have you seen the violent vegetation? The grounds will get worse, and so will the health hazards. And who will rush to their aid? The Catholic Church, as cheap as it isn't holy, will not lift a hoe. For the other cemeteries, it will not be, mark my words, the plot holders—as parsimonious as they are rich— and not the city, because . . . we are the city! [hosannahs] The public will soon demand: remove the dead and embrace the future! There are now verdant cemeteries in San Mateo County mere minutes by public train from where we stand. I advise you, gentlemen, buy up all that beaten-down property around the city cemeteries. You'll reap a fortune. And soon, we will have that grand, noble city we all desire and deserve! [hosannahs and clapping]*

"Free drinks for all," shouts the barkeep.

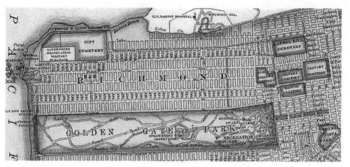

1907 San Francisco map detail showing location of the Lone Mountain cemeteries. *Colma Historical Association*

HE SAID, HE SAID

The rights of the living versus the rights of the dead are officially decided by the U.S. Supreme Court in 1908, a groundbreaking declaration that began its long journey through the court system seven years earlier. The verdict—at the time the final legal word on the subject—has direct consequences for municipalities across the nation debating the question: Under what circumstances can governments declare a cemetery a public nuisance and order its removal?

The landmark 1908 decision reseals the fate of the dead. Laurel Hill Cemetery had sued the city to overturn the 1901 ban on the basis of a violation of the Fifth and Fourteenth Amendments to the U.S. Constitution, which provide that "no person shall . . . be deprived of life, liberty, or property, without due process of law." What is due process of law? The fair administration of justice. And who ultimately is to decide if a particular administration is fair? The courts. The legal suit snakes up the judicial ladder. The Supreme Court declares that the only issue in the case is whether the ordinance violates due process.

The city's principal argument is that the health of its residents is at stake. Voluminous material is presented to the Court to support this contention, which would justify the ordinance as a fair and legal exercise of local "police powers." There is no violation of due process.

Laurel Hill counters with equally voluminous material to contradict the health argument, which would make the ordinance an arbitrary exercise of government power and thus illegal. The land granted to the cemetery in 1853 was specifically made "in perpetuity," and the value of the cemetery property was based on the expectation that it would be held exactly as written. Without such guarantees, that land might not have been purchased originally. Moreover, property owners made expensive improvements based on the trust of the original agreement.

The city contends: Previous court decisions declare that even when grants are made "in perpetuity," the contract "would have no force as against a future exercise of jurisdiction by the legislative branch of government or its police power. Such contract was based on conditions as they then existed."

Laurel Hill objects, citing a previous court case that said that a government could not exercise police power if it is "arbitrary and unreasonable, beyond the necessities of case." This is true if the possible dangers can be avoided by regulation rather than prohibition, the attorney argues, pointing out that even the California Supreme Court has declared that cemeteries per se cannot be regarded as a nuisance and must not rise to that definition unless there are legitimate health concerns. Even if properties become less valuable because of their proximity to a cemetery, however unattractive, it is not a "legal" nuisance.

The city maintains that the Board of Supervisors based its ordinance on legitimate health concerns, not on any other factors. On that criterion, due process is not violated.

The defendants respectfully submit that the health issue is at least ambiguous. The line of demarcation between a reasonable and unreasonable prohibition of burials is not the mere presence or absence of neighboring habitation but rather the presence or absence of danger to the health of the inhabitants. In fact, the question of whether cemeteries are dangerous to the health of neighboring inhabitants has never been considered or determined by any court. A mere tendency is not enough according to previous decisions. It is a question of actual necessity and not one of mere possibility or tendency to danger.

The plaintiffs respectfully disagree. The people's representatives must maintain the power to make such a health determination. In a democracy, that should be the final word. We agree with the Court that judges are not in a good position to make such an assessment and must stay out of the issue. Courts should defer to a legitimate exercise of democracy.

Laurel Hill states that the ordinance is also "unreasonable" because within the corporate boundaries of the city, there are hundreds of acres of land scattered about that are unoccupied or farmed. These lands could be utilized for burials that would be more than a mile distant from any people or public thoroughfare.

The city vigorously contests this assessment of available land. And even if true, the penal code of the state already makes it illegal to bury anyone except in an existing cemetery.

Laurel Hill retorts that a request for additional city cemetery space could be made.

The city asks why such applications were not submitted.

Laurel Hill replies because the Board of Supervisors is not amenable.

The city answers, haven't you answered your own argument?

And round and round it goes. The Court does not mince words in its decision. On the issue of whether the use of police power is legal, "Every doubt is resolved in favor of the ordinance." The justices are not rendering any assessment on the validity of the health argument. "The Court will not declare the act unconstitutional when the legislative conclusion has the support of public, common belief or scientific authority." In short, "the Court should not substitute its conclusion for that of the legislature."

It did address the argument that there is room left in the city for burials away from the population. The defendant failed to demonstrate "that such tracts are suitable for cemeteries/owners want to use them for such purpose/that they are not adjacent to dairies, etc. and water sources." The Court also agrees with the city that cemeteries not near people or only near a few can be removed even if health reasons are unproved because the Board of Supervisors can restrict the cemeteries when it believes that lands may soon be endangered in the event that people *did* move near such cemeteries. This provided additional support for the city's argument that previous grants of perpetuity are based on then-existing conditions, which, if changed, can alter the terms of the original grant.

SHAKE, RATTLE, AND ROLL—OUT TO THE HINTERLAND

Between the 1901 burial ban and its 1908 Supreme Court approval, a minute of nature's fury transforms cemetery landscapes. If laws fail to pound the final nail in cemetery coffins, the Great Earthquake of 1906 does. Whatever possibility burial grounds have to keep up appearances come tumbling down on a devastating April morning. "Darling Papa & Mama & Sisters, A terrible thing has happened," a young resident pens. "San Francisco is no more." This is hardly the time for cemeteries to beg for money.

Although sitting outside the historic downtown that suffers the brunt of seismic and fire damage, the Lone Mountain cemeteries nevertheless take a big hit. Many sections are already in poor repair, including eroding buildings and eroding soil underneath. Thoroughfares buckle; tombstones are sucked into the earth. Statues topple. Mausoleums collapse. With no endowment and prohibited by law to sell burial property, physical conditions at Lone Mountain quickly descend from bad to worse. Critics of the cemeteries increase their attacks. The Richmond District Improvement Association, never one to miss an opportunity to score anti-cemetery points, reports that recently collapsed Lone Mountain structures pose a new public nuisance. Armed with cameras to record dilapidated conditions, it warns that children, the elderly, and the infirmed might fall victim, literally, to unstable ruins should they venture there.

"Devastation in Cities of Dead," headlines the *San Francisco Chronicle*: "The damage in the cemeteries, from a monetary standpoint, seems almost beyond calculation. The keeper of one of these cemeteries ventured it as his opinion that there weren't three pieces of stone in his cemetery that hadn't been disturbed in some way or another. . . . The costs of repair and restoration will reach a figure at which even the superintendents of the various places will not hazard a guess."

Nine miles to the south, Colma cemeteries fare better. Reports detail considerable destruction but less than San Francisco, which sits on the epicenter. Colma monuments are of recent construction and thus better built. The still-fledgling cemetery efforts mean fewer structures to topple over onto one another. The largest Colma cemetery suffers the most damage: Holy Cross announces three-quarters of the statuary and memorials toppled or twisted on bases. Virtually all the rail lines serving Colma cemeteries are damaged, some substantially. Railroads will get fixed fast.

The first violent shaking lasts an agonizing sixty-five seconds. Then countless aftershocks rattle through the city. As structures collapse like matchstick houses, it triggers a perfect disaster—gas lines and water mains fracture simultaneously—spawning a conflagration that burns for three days. Surrounded by the bay and the ocean, there is water everywhere but nothing to spray. Stand along Van Ness Avenue and look north, east, and west toward the bay—virtually all is leveled. The Great Earthquake of 1906 hits on April 18 at 5:12 a.m., catching residents asleep. Modern science calculates a massive 8.3 trembler, the epicenter a mere two Pacific Ocean miles from San Francisco. Up to that point in history, no major city had been hit so close and directly by a high-magnitude earthquake.

An enumeration of the dead will never be made. All vestiges of them were destroyed by the flames. The number of victims of the earthquake will never be known.

—Jack London, 1906

The belief is firm that San Francisco will be totally destroyed.
—The special combined *San Francisco Call-Chronicle-Examiner* newspaper the day after the earthquake

The event is regarded as the largest natural disaster in the nation's history until Hurricane Katrina in 2005. Quakes and fires destroy or severely damage some 28,000 buildings—more than 80 percent of the entire city. An astonishing 250,000 of the city's 400,000 residents are instant homeless refugees. It is also regarded as the largest natural disaster cover-up in the nation's history. The Board of Supervisors quickly fixes the fatality count at 478. Despite widespread skepticism at the figure, it is generally accepted, even as contradictory stories emerge detailing countless victims impossible to recover under debris, makeshift graves, and reports of many more fatalities. The official figure remains unchallenged until one day in 1964 when Gladys Hansen, a research librarian at the San Francisco Public Library's Special Collections, is asked by a patron for an official list of the dead. She discovers that such a record does not exist. The revelation spurs a lifelong dedication. One journalist describes her effort as "doing detective work for the bureau of missing persons." Hansen's exhaustive research eventually produces a dramatic revision of the death toll: at least 3,000—and counting. It is projected to climb to more than 6,000. On the centennial of the Great Earthquake, the San Francisco Board of Supervisors revises the official 1906 fatality figure of 478 by declaring the dead at "over 3,000." The occasion is commemorated at Cypress Lawn Cemetery with a special memorial dedicated by Gladys Hansen to the thousands of uncounted souls. To this day, it is the only formal tribute to those victims. A personal Gladys Hansen memorial is added to the spot in 2017 on her passing.

"I shall never forget the scenes at the ferry-house," recalled theatrical producer George Musgrove. "It was bedlam, pandemonium and hell rolled into one. There must have been 10,000 people trying to get on that boat. Men fought like wild cats to push their way aboard. . . . Women fainted, and there was no water at hand with which to revive them." The removal of San Francisco residents to safe locations across the bay is the largest evacuation of people over water until the withdrawal of British troops from Dunkirk during World War II. As crowds frantically jostle at the Ferry Building to escape amid a citywide collapse of civil order that threatens looting and mayhem, Brigadier General Frederick Funston orders troops stationed at the Presidio army base to march into San Francisco— the only occasion those troops ever leave the enclave to enter civilian territory. Technically, it takes one step. Army and navy forces are joined the next day by city police and the California National Guard as well as motley bands of armed civilians to prevent disorder. There is little coordination of effort. Without organized control, various groups issue and follow contrasting orders, the most important of which comes from the mayor's office: "The Federal Troops, the members of the Regular Police Force and all Special Police Officers have been authorized by me to KILL any and all persons found engaged in Looting or in the Commission of Any Other Crime."

Some who are not part of official law enforcement enthusiastically embrace both the letter and the spirit of the order. More disturbing, continual reports of official military misconduct circulate, especially in the early, hectic trigger-happy days. Residents complain of unnecessary and arbitrary evacuations and careless implementation of the official order to shoot criminals and looters. The army denies any involvement by its troops in illegal or violent actions, attributing the activity to other military or civilian armed units. This collateral damage has never figured prominently in any assessment of earthquake fatalities, at least not explicitly. But Richard Hansen and David Fowler have documented, based on U.S. Army records, at least 514 people classified as "looters" and "criminals" killed. This is a far larger number than has been estimated by most historians. We will never know how many deaths occur as a person is rescuing their own possessions or, helping a friend, is mistaken for a looter.

Despite the meticulous effort of Gladys and Richard Hansen, we are left with Jack London's haunting eyewitness words: "An enumeration of the dead will never be made."

The firefighting practice of the time encourages firewalls to eliminate natural fuel that flames need to survive. In forests, you destroy living trees and brush in advance of the moving flames. In cities, the fuel is structures, and dynamite is the tool of choice. In 1906, this approach is less tested than in forests, and there are problems peculiar to urban applications. Defiant owners stand in front of properties with weapons, questioning the law or an official's judgment. Dynamiters, a few reported as inebriated, blow up the wrong buildings. Some explosions are larger than expected and take down nontargeted property. One enthusiastic contractor under explicit orders from Mayor Schmitz to concentrate on Chinatown is arrested for reckless mayhem; the mayor is spared the indignity. High winds in fires near water spawn a cyclone effect that blows embers every which way and start countless unintended blazes. In the chaos and later assessment, the decision to create firewalls is not officially debated. There is no evidence that the operation did more good than harm, and there is considerable evidence to the contrary.

The earthquake is no respecter of class. All "big four" transcontinental railroad barons' mansions on Nob Hill are destroyed. Chinatown is completely leveled.

How do you calculate the number of dead in such a widespread and complicated disaster, especially under pressure to deliver the figure quickly? There is mass dislocation and disrupted communication. Many bodies cannot be counted much less rescued from the rubble of burned-out buildings, especially in Chinatown and the crowded South of Market hotels and boardinghouses. Adding to the confusion are unsettling reports, such as one in the *San Jose Mercury and Herald* that estimates that more than 150 fire victims in the vicinity of Telegraph Hill and Union Street are cut off from escape. This figure alone is almost one-third of the final estimate, and no one knows if those who compile the official list have any knowledge of the claim. Throughout the city, some victims are quickly buried in nearby open spaces. Countless folks are whisked to cemeteries and placed in improvised graves. Still others remain unnoticed or neglected in hasty and undocumented cleanups. Due to the lack of city hospitals to absorb such an emergency, many of the injured are triaged in place and put on available railroad transportation to the nearest town with facilities to take them; most rescued in this way are unrecorded at the point of origin or arrival, and there is no way to determine if they were moved again, survived, or died.

Among the most serious flaws in the fatality count is the lack of any official effort to ascertain Chinatown casualties. The vast overcrowding and reluctance of the Chinese to interact with local officials has made an accurate census impossible. As a result of anti-Chinese immigration laws and popular prejudice, that population is decreasing after 1890. At the time of the earthquake, there are estimated to be as many as 25,000 residents in a sardine-packed twelve-block region that suffers utter destruction. As late as 1984, Gladys Hansen can document only twenty-two Chinese deaths in an area that is dramatically less seismically sound than the rest of the city. Yong Chen estimates 435 dead in Chinatown, 3,500 injured, and 20,000 escaping to Oakland in the disaster. James Dalessandro believes that at least as many as the official count of 478 perished in Chinatown alone.

In general, the uncounted are more recent immigrants and poor—Italian longshoremen, Irish nannies, and Asian laborers—concentrated in South of Market tenements and Chinatown.

Accurately accessing the casualties is a herculean task that demands patience and painstaking dedication, virtues that rattled city fathers cannot muster. Instead, there is a stampede to judgment orchestrated by civic and business leaders—a deliberate effort to manage the news. Today, we call this "spin control." The city must protect its civic reputation and formidable resources invested there. The Great Earthquake is regarded by local leaders as nothing less than an existential threat. There is an urgent need to reassure potential developers and future settlers that San Francisco remains a thriving urban area dedicated and able to sustain dynamic growth. Will the disaster trigger an exodus, reducing the great city to a shadow of its former self? For boosters, this is the stuff of sweat-filled nightmares. Generations of growth and marketing, not to mention personal investment, might swirl down the drain. The first line of defense is to deny the extent of the disaster. Next, create a smoke screen of obfuscation and optimism until the impossible recovery. Finally, somehow make that impossible recovery possible.

The campaign aims to reduce negative publicity by controlling how and what information is disseminated. Before radio and television, out-of-town news arrives by telegraph wire to publications. Manipulation of information from San Francisco is all too easy. In 1906, as a confidence-boosting project, the city hires writers to craft positive stories, sometimes ignoring claims of human death and minimizing the connection between the earthquake and the fire. Due to its vast landholdings and hauling business in California and San Francisco, the Southern Pacific Railroad has a strong vested interest in softening public perceptions of the crisis. *Sunset*, its monthly magazine, runs optimistic and misleading stories about the fire and recovery with hardly a mention of the earthquake itself.

Photography at the time was not the province of average people, so original pictures of the disaster and immediate aftermath are rare commodities. Insurance companies, newspapers, the Southern Pacific Railroad, and private citizens—mostly owners of damaged property—acquire earthquake photos in order to destroy them. Some pictures are "photoshopped" to reveal less structural damage by hiring artists accomplished at retouching portrait photographs. There was another reason, both immediate and compelling, for the suppression of photographic evidence. Insurance companies generally compensated arson but not earthquakes. The first 2,000 insurance claims are fire damage, a statistically unlikely result and prima facie evidence of fraud. Partially destroyed structures are sometimes finished off with a match. In 1906, the Board of Supervisors sets total property loss at $300 million (in today's dollars)—a drastic underestimation as part of a larger effort to downplay the public perception of damage. Insurance is far less purchased than it is today, and even among those who held coverage, it is common for an owner with multiple buildings not to insure all of them. The official city property loss statistic is likely based on insurance claims paid, which are only a portion of the actual filings.

Journalists are implored to describe the disaster as a fire. Banks and insurance companies will invest in a city that suffers a citywide conflagration, such as Chicago in 1871, but an earthquake is regarded as a different beast of nature—a capricious act of God that cannot be guarded against or controlled much less understood. It will surely scare off investors and immigrants. This begs a disturbing question asked at the time: What if San Francisco is an earthquakeprone region?

The Great Earthquake should not have come as a complete shock. The geological history of Northern California is unsettling—some 250 episodes strong enough to be recorded in newspaper and other accounts. In the 1860s, two such events open eyes.

New York–based *Harper's Weekly Illustrated* characterizes the 1865 Northern California earthquake as "the most severe shock of the kind ever known in that city." The *San Francisco Chronicle* echoes the sentiment: "It stands quite by itself, and all previous earthquakes felt in the city must take back seats. Indeed, when compared with appalling manifestation of yesterday, the preceding slight disturbances scarcely seem worthy of the name of earthquakes at all." The following day brings a more sober and balanced analysis. It could have been worse, the *Alta California* submits: "The earthquake has come and gone, and San Francisco still stands with her people, her enterprise, her skill, her knowledge, her wealth, and her houses of brick."

A bigger jolt will soon test its mettle. A boy digging potatoes near what will later become Holy Cross Cemetery describes that October day in 1868: "We felt no earthquake, but the mountain seem to bob up and down. A freight train was going north. Shortly after we observed the mountain apparently moving, the earthquake reached the railroad track and the freight train appeared to gyrate like a snake. The next instant we felt it. The shock was very severe, throwing us to the ground and knocking over the sacks of potatoes. A band of loose horses . . . ran around the field at great speed, utterly panic stricken."

The 1868 earthquake is called the "Big One" prior to 1906. The mighty 7.0 shock kills five, injures forty, and causes about $16 million in property damage (in current value). Both the physical size of the city and its population are much smaller then, about 150,000.

The Greatest Calamity That Ever Befell San Francisco.
Great Excitement—The People Filled With Terror.
Business Suspended & the Whole Population in the Streets
       —*SAN FRANCISCO CHRONICLE*, OCTOBER 9, 1868

The city has grown rapidly in the years leading up to the first "Big One." A resident recalls that "many people were so frightened by the shocks that they were ill for days afterward" and decided to leave San Francisco forever. After all, there was a bad one just a few years earlier, and might this auger an earthquake age out West? Although substantial earthquakes hit largely unpopulated Missouri in 1811–1812, states in the East and Midwest are not regarded as earthquake country; it is understandable that a newcomer from there might be convinced to leave California for the familiar comforts of hurricanes and snowstorms. In general, earthquakes have little effect on the hearty constitutions of western pioneers. Life goes on and gets more crowded, creating the conditions for the "Big One."

One dramatic result of 1906 is the acceleration of the population west into the Richmond and Sunset districts. Thousands of citizens displaced from historic areas, especially south of Market Street, settle into refugee camps along today's Park Presidio Boulevard and adjacent grounds. Literally forced into the Outside Lands, people start to rethink their future, at least for the short term. Soon, many

Earthquake "shacks" for refugees. More than 16,000 San Franciscans are housed in 5,610 tiny cottages spread out in eleven designated camps. When camps begin to close in 1907, refugees sometimes transport the structures to private lots and even cobble them together to form expanded "estate" residences. Of the 5,343 moved from the camps, only a few are certified to still be standing. *Virtual Museum of the City of San Francisco*

put down roots, building permanent homes to replace tents and temporary cottages. This movement of population is a game changer or at least a game advancer. It accelerates the gradual shift west of a population into territory that had been regarded as hinterland. The siege of the cemeteries is complete.

The Great Earthquake cover-up is facilitated and driven by California's still-vigorous "frontier" tradition that downplays and, when necessary, ignores death and burial rituals. The year 1906 creates a

1125   After the Fire, April, 1906
(From Fairmont Hotel)

A Portion of the New San Francisco, 1909
(Same view point)

Virtual Museum of the City of San Francisco

Virtual Museum of the City of San Francisco

challenging new frontier calling for the same grit as the old one. Do we still have the "right stuff"? Deeply rooted lessons are conjured up. It is time for a new instant city! People are fleeing San Francisco in the tens of thousands. We must stop the exodus and rebuild. One cannot be too attached to the past if devoted to the future.

The city is booming as people tuck into bed on April 17, 1906. High hopes to host the grand 1915 Panama–Pacific International Exhibition abound. Then calamity strikes. The city lays in ruins, and boosters pretend that "it" never happened. There is an urgent need to reassure potential developers as well as fleeing citizens that San Francisco will remain a thriving urban mecca dedicated and able to sustain dynamic growth. Instead of suppressing boosterism, the earthquake reinforces it. A mere three years from near annihilation, San Francisco officially enters the twelve-city sweepstakes. There is an instinctive reaction to circle the wagons when in crisis. In old cities of the East or expanding cities of the Midwest, such as Chicago and St. Louis, the threat to business and prestige from disasters is regarded as manageable. In San Francisco, a penchant for existential crisis meets the perfect storm. The booster mentality inflamed by a chronic inferiority complex assumes a life of its own—a mixture of paranoia and illusions of grandeur with old gold dust fairies dancing in new expo dreams.

San Francisco will not just rebuild. The new booster mantra becomes bigger and better than ever. Defy the pundits. Spit into the wind.

On April 18, 1906, we unwittingly pulled off the greatest advertising stunt ever before attempted. The world thought we had received our deathblow. They thought that at the least it would take a quarter of century to recover. It was predicted that it would take five years to remove the debris. And then the world was staggered by the heroic determination with which we commenced rebuilding before the bricks were cold. Ye Gods, what an

advertising opportunity. What glorious and convincing copy that never appeared. Men of San Francisco, it is up to you. What are you going to do about it?
—WILLIAM WOODHEAD, PRESIDENT OF THE ASSOCIATED
ADVERTISING CLUBS OF AMERICA, 1909, URGING THE CITY
TO KEEP THE WHIP TO THE HORSE AS IT PURSUES THE 1915
PANAMA–PACIFIC INTERNATIONAL EXPOSITION

One year after winning the national sweepstakes in 1911, the Board of Supervisors votes the unthinkable—a "notice of intent" to evict the Lone Mountain cemeteries. The battle line is drawn. Citizen armies, backed by newsprint and agitators in high and low places, engage.

CHAPTER 8

WHOSE CITY IS THIS, ANYWAY?

Editor "Chronicle"—Sir: I am the owner of a lot in one of the cemeteries of San Francisco and since 1900 I have occupied a seat on a mental seesaw in regard to the matter. At one epoch: "There will be no necessity of removing your dead": a little later, "by order of the etc. etc. the cemeteries must be removed within such and such a limit." I need quote no more of that. . . . The first of this year, supposing the matter to have been decided, I bought a lot and removed my dead to San Mateo County. With a week there have been two letters in your paper that the matter is to be decided at an election in November. Truly, in justice to the living, I think the city of San Francisco should be compelled to compensate lot owners for the wear and tear in regard to this elusive subject.
    —"A DAUGHTER OF A PIONEER," MAY 22, 1914

THERE ARE APPROXIMATELY 150,000 BURIED IN SAN FRANCISCO cemeteries at this time, all on private property situated around Lone Mountain in the Richmond district. The "dead lands" occupy some 160 acres, the equivalent of seventy city blocks that could house as many as 50,000. San Francisco has a small domain (forty-nine square miles) located at the tip of a peninsula with no room to expand. But all cities face challenging and changing physical restrictions and limits. For a generation after San Francisco's founding, there is little concern about insufficient land for the dead, much less that the deceased would ever have to be evicted. San Francisco declines an opportunity to claim swaths of potential new urban territory in adjacent San Mateo lands to the south when it formally incorporates as the City and County of San Francisco in 1856. It reasons, does it make sense to suffer the costs of developing and servicing and litigating new expanses of rural property at a time when the smartest people think the city has all the territory it could need and afford to handle?

Sentiment and Progress Do Not March Together
—*SAN FRANCISCO CHRONICLE*, 1924

This is not a city where we recognize death.
—GLADYS HANSEN,
LATE CHIEF ARCHIVIST OF SAN FRANCISCO

The guillotine falls. City Cemetery was dispatched a few years earlier. The Board of Supervisors votes a "notice of intention" in March 1912 to declare the removal of all remaining (private) cemeteries on January 1, 1914: "The Masonic, Laurel Hill, Odd Fellows, and Calvary Cemeteries have been declared to be and constitute a public nuisance and a menace and detriment to the public health and welfare." The city envisions plot owners fairly compensated by sale of their lands. If they fail to comply, authorities will order the cemetery associations to conduct a removal and charge individual lot holders for the cost. There is a fourteen-month window of compliance.

In 1914 and 1924, citizens of San Francisco vote on the eviction of the "Lone Mountain four." The Richmond district, which comprises most of this area, has jumped from 3,000 at the turn of the century to 66,000 by 1920. Over the next ten years, it will double from that. In elections, the technical question is, should the people reject the board's eviction? Both produce a "yes" vote, but the margins narrow dramatically:

1914   68,918 to retain cemeteries

            43,433 to remove

1924	71,065 to retain cemeteries
	64,063 to remove

There are some 20,000 more total votes in 1924. Most of those favor removal. The ten-year interval between elections exacts a toll on both old cemeteries and old sentimentalists. Some connected personally to the dead die. The additional voters are largely new residents and those coming of civic age—hardly the demographic of cemetery devotion. City population jumps more than 100,000 in that period.

There are perplexing cemetery removal issues that every city must face.

We organized under the rural cemetery act of California, and that gives us the right for all time to a cemetery. So where can a local Board of Supervisors come in and control us in any?
—A. J. Gunnison, president of
Laurel Hill Cemetery Association, 1896

Who Owns the Land? Many cemetery plot owners do not realize today and did not then that you are not the owner of the lot in the same sense as when building a house or a business on land that you purchase. Legal ownership remains with cemetery associations, which are sued frequently in this period by individual lot holders who disagree with management decisions. But even that generic property right is hardly absolute. The actual owner has technically acquired an "easement" that permits the property to be used as a burial ground. If in the future there is a compelling public need to reuse the land for another purpose, that easement can be superseded. Such arcane and open-to-interpretation legalities are seldom discussed publicly during the cemetery wars. The lawyers struggle to interpret the law; would the average person even listen? Some actions muddy the already muddy waters. In divine indifference to worldly concerns, Calvary Cemetery grants purchasers in the late nineteenth century a "deed" authorizing occupation of a particular spot until 2000. Some deeds permit the owner to renew for 300 years.

To Endow or Not to Endow. There is no formal endowment system at any of the four cemeteries or for virtually any burial grounds in the United States. Endowment typically consists of an initial one-time assessment on land purchases to be devoted specifically for maintenance, usually through an invested fund from which only the interest may be spent. This becomes standard procedure for the new Colma burial grounds and is eventually made mandatory by state governments. When Lone Mountain cemeteries are undertaken in the 1850s, endowment is neither the theory nor the practice; the task of preservation falls to cemetery associations, which can barely meet the need, and, ultimately, to individual plot holders. According to George Skaller, a prominent anti-cemetery spokesman, only 1 percent of all cemetery properties in Lone Mountain are under "endowment" care in 1914, that is, private trust funds to cover maintenance for specific plots.

It is a flawed business model. Certainly, some families do keep up appearances, dispatching gardeners from their Peninsula estates. Others in more modest circumstances have relatives who visit regularly and tend to loved ones. But the majority are less cared for and most not at all. As long as cemetery associations are selling property (and services) and generating income, some revenue can be devoted to maintenance. But what happens if the cemetery runs out of land and cannot buy more or is forbidden to sell or use what land it still has for burials and services? The disposable income for maintenance shrivels. And over time, fewer relatives are left who still care. There is a common but misguided nineteenth-century assumption that the Catholic Church, grand fraternal organizations, and wealthy families would voluntarily provide upkeep and maintenance. Surely, such folks and institutions will not abide having their kin and brethren surrounded by decay. But when further city burials are prohibited in 1901, the cemetery lands around Lone Mountain are in a state of unkempt grandeur verging on eyesore. It will get worse.

What Is a Public Nuisance? As in other American cities, removal of the dead requires the cemetery property to be officially designated a "public nuisance." When declared, it transfers "police power" to politicians. Courts have declared such acts as valid government restrictions of activity—without compensation—to ensure the health, safety, and sanitation of the community, even its morality, as in the case of prostitution, usually under the rubric of public health. Municipal police power has the legal authority to override the Fourteenth Amendment if the property is declared a "public nuisance." Of course, any municipal decision can be challenged and overturned, but there is a general right to exercise such broad power.

When land is declared a public nuisance, it can theoretically be confiscated without payment. The government is regarded as exercising its lawful power of zoning, nuisance abatement, conservation, business regulations, and other functions and has the right to include prohibition of a business, even one that has been allowed to operate previously. Courts have typically decided that any economic loss suffered by private citizens is an incidental consequence of the lawful exercise of police power and not compensable.

In 1900, there is ambiguity over the extent of police powers regarding cemeteries. Cities try different approaches. The 1901 San Francisco ban takes a safe and established position, asserting that such burials are "dangerous to life and detrimental to the public health."

The legal definition and scope of an urban "nuisance" subject to local police powers is changing dramatically in the early twentieth century. The U.S. Supreme Court decision on the 1901 burial ban declares that it will base a decision solely on whether the ordinance violates the due process clause of the Fourteenth Amendment. It decrees that Laurel Hill fails to prove both that it is unlawfully denied rights and that its land poses no health hazard. But the Court goes on to suggest in general commentary the possibility of an enhanced definition of a "public nuisance" for cemeteries by stating that the ordinance might still be proper in "the interest of future growth and prosperity of the city."

In 1914, the first official removal ordinances justify use of police powers by declaring cemeteries "a public nuisance and a menace and detriment to the public health and welfare." The addition of "welfare" is an escalation of words from the 1901 no-burial ban. "Health" is a restricted and theoretically determinable fact. A danger to "welfare" is as ambiguous as it is subjective.

The San Francisco Health Code that serves as the basis for subsequent removal ordinances incorporates almost verbatim California's 1923 Morris Act permitting local police power when the existence of an entity threatens the "health, safety, comfort, or welfare of the public." It is a new, wider "nuisance" net. The idea that a cemetery could be declared a public nuisance only for health reasons becomes a relic of the past.

Why Not Exercise Eminent Domain? Eminent domain is the right of local governments to acquire property for the public good—such as building a road or a dam—and requires a financial buyout to satisfy the constitutional prohibition against confiscation of private property without compensation. That exercise of power exists everywhere in the United States, but its interpretation and execution vary widely. Eminent domain is seldom mentioned directly in the San Francisco eviction battle. It is more relevant to specific projects, such as cutting roads through cemeteries for traffic convenience. Various ideas of this nature are declined by cemetery associations that plead a lack of legal authority to grant permission. Government has the power through eminent domain to declare that this or that street be altered for the public good and execute the provision—but in conjunction with government compensation. The costs for any specific proposed project could vary widely. In 1896, the estimates to condemn and acquire a part of Sutter Street that runs through Laurel Hill is as high as $1,000,000 ($30 million today), but the president of the Richmond District Improvement Association claims that it can be accomplished for a mere $70,000.

However sweeping in theory and needing only an act of government, eminent domain has its limitations in practice. To use it against cemeteries for complete removal is regarded by most as unwise, unprecedented, and fraught with legal difficulties. The government, not cemetery property owners, will have to bear the full cost of removal. Just what would be a fair price for the property? It must be arbitrated and then adjudicated; only the lawyers prosper. Next comes the complex and agonizing issue of removing the dead, then the problem of a government selling property to private parties. In a typical eminent domain case, it has a narrow purpose, such as building a bridge or constructing a highway, but in this case, the development of 160 acres of prime private land could take many directions with many interested parties. Government is not well equipped to handle such a conversion in a free market economy, not to mention the opportunity for graft and corruption it provides. Any effort to remove the cemeteries by this means will inevitably involve the courts. "Courts" is a synonym for "delay," which also serves as a synonym for "kill." The city decides that this path is not eminent and not in its domain.

Calvary Cemetery footprint in late 1930s. *Colma Historical Association*

Two definitions of urban progress competed for a place in the modern landscape, one emphasizing urban growth that made communities prosperous, the other cultural and historical places that bound communities together. The debate captured an early twentieth century moment when San Franciscans questioned what kind of city they wanted to live in and what role its past might play in their future.

—TAMARA VENIT SHELTON

At the turn of the twentieth century, cemetery debates intensify across the country in legislatures, courts, newspapers, and around kitchen tables. The controversy in San Francisco, over a generation of political wrangling, serves as a bellwether for other municipalities.

The Health Card. Cemetery "health" issues had been bandied about in American cities since the 1870s. Fear of burial grounds as a public health menace is a powerful argument, especially when "science" on the issue is tentative and incomplete. There is pro-cemetery pushback. A San Francisco disinterment inspector's report in 1890 refutes the claim that cemeteries spread disease, instead suggesting that the real risk may lay in exposing and spreading disease during removal of the dead. This argument keeps surfacing even as late as the 1924 election, when a speaker informs the Board of Supervisors that "terrible epidemics of disease" invariably follow mass disinterment.

Written more than two decades before the Board of Supervisors bans burials in 1901, the *San Francisco Daily Evening Post* publishes an essay, "Effect of the Proximity of the Cemeteries upon the Health of Cities." Beginning with the statement "Authorities Differ," it concludes that the preponderance of evidence refutes all health hazard "hysteria" as bad science: Is there an "indefinable, almost unnoticeable gas" rising from these graveyards that poisons the living? Cemeteries have been in populated areas for centuries with no record of significantly more deaths around them. Could they be any worse than the sewers that produce "miasmatic effluvia through manholes?" The editors declare that several cemeteries combined could not affect the health of San Francisco citizens "to the extent that but one of its Chinese quarters is capable of doing!!!" Cemetery workers do not appear to suffer, either. And belief that city water and private wells are contaminated by burial grounds is not supported by evidence or facts. The issue of the removal of the dead "is not likely ever to hinge on the fact that their presence in injurious to public health but will turn more directly on the question of the vast benefits that will eventually accrue to San Francisco by having more space for development."

Such a frank assessment is a minority view at that time and remains so for many years. In the 1914 election, a *San Francisco Chronicle* editorial states the standard anti-cemetery position: There is "nothing sacrilegious" in its removal position because scientific evidence of the negative health effects of cemeteries in populous areas is "well documented" and "virtually irrefutable." This "standing menace to public health" must take precedence over the "sensibilities of some people who are controlled by sentiment." The editorial ends on an ominous note. The very lives of the citizens are at stake because "every year's delay in discontinuing burials in these cemeteries has been aggravating the evil that spring from them."

Here is the primary legal and moral anti-cemetery argument, at least publicly and officially, in the 1914 election debates, perhaps because at the time it is the only appeal that will fly with a public still too conservative to evict the dead. Lurid news stories during the referendum campaign add to the health paranoia, especially when two young children drown in stagnant cemetery pools. A newspaper editor posits a "compelling need" to remove such "death traps" that are characterized as the breeding grounds of mosquitoes and rats. Residents are still reeling from the rat-delivered bubonic plague that struck the city a decade earlier. Gradually, the health issue loses credibility and effectiveness. By the 1924 election, the argument comes to focus on the nitty-gritty: money and power. The problem begins to be defined as a battle more of land and progress than of science and health. Headlines like "Cemeteries Held Obstacle to San Francisco Growth" become common.

The Civic Pride Card. Despite earthquake devastation, San Francisco defies pundits in 1911 by beating out a dozen entries, most prominently New Orleans, in a national competition to host the 1915 Panama–Pacific International Exposition—an extravaganza that promises throngs of visitors to the chosen land. Skeptics say that such a gargantuan San Francisco rebuilding effort in such an impossibly small time is chutzpah and madness. Few of the skeptics are from San Francisco. "The prophecy was freely made that it would be decades, if ever, before San Francisco would rebuild to her former strength," notes the publicity director for the just-opened 1915 exposition. "Those who came to look upon these miles of twisted steel and broken brick could see little hope for the city." Less than a year after the earthquake, the official city organization to lobby for the event is incorporated.

The exposition is yet another catalyst for anti-cemetery sentiment. The "instant city" rebuilding of the "instant city" takes place around the enclaves of the dead, not in them. Further damaged by the earthquake, the cemeteries are regarded as an urban eyesore. There are concerted but futile efforts in the years leading up to the exposition to cut streets through their lands, some of the proposals promoted to facilitate streetcar and auto traffic for the event.

When in January 1914 the Board of Supervisors posts the official notice of removal to be completed in fourteen months, there is little chance this date can be met. Even if Mayor Rolph does not call a plebiscite, court battles would have postponed its execution well beyond the exposition's opening on February 20, 1915. But city boosters could at least tell visitors that those ancient ruins will soon be gone.

After the pro-cemetery 1914 election result, the Outdoor Art League of the California Club proposes an ambitious plan for cemetery associations: Sell the unoccupied sections of the grounds, which are already off-limits to burials, and use the proceeds to beautify the remainder of the cemetery. The Art League also floats the idea of transforming Laurel Hill Cemetery into a memorial park. The grounds would be donated by the cemetery association to the city, which will then construct streets through some properties but refurbish and maintain the rest as an official public park. Laurel Hill quickly rejects the problem-laden project, citing lack of legal authority to authorize the construction of streets through the cemetery or to donate its lands to the city.

The Civic League of Improvement Clubs is the poster child of metropolitanism. In the first election campaign, it distributes anti-cemetery resolutions to every abode within half a mile of the cemeteries, declaring those grounds not merely a health hazard but also a civic embarrassment. A 1924 election statement minces no words: "The voters are asked to remove unsightly burying places from the gaze of visitors [read: tourists who will report conditions to their hometowns] and to take them away from congested residential sections" [read: prospective residents and commercial interests cannot build where they want, dampening immigration and investment]. Calling attention to the "moss-covered, decaying walls, the fallen tombstones and years growth of rank vegetation," the ladies describe the scene as "one of ignominy and humiliation for a city that dares to term itself progressive" [read: San Francisco is still a wannabe; let's put our money where our mouth is!].

The Civic League is loaded with prominent business and civic leaders, many of whom identify as "Progressives." That political impulse, especially as administered in cities, is not the same as the modern connotation—social and economic justice. In fact, the turn-of-the-century movement could in practice resemble its opposite. It is driven by "booster" pride, the promotion of business, an emphasis on government efficiency, and the active recruitment of new capital and residents—all of which will in the process transform the slums, end government corruption, and uplift the working class. Certainly, this program includes better working conditions, sanitation, public education, and aid to the poor, but by modern standards, it might be regarded as unashamedly elitist, capitalistic, and patronizing. One fact is certain: There is no place for deteriorating cemeteries in this forward-looking vision.

Traditionalists retort that cemeteries *are* progressive. Real progress acknowledges the past. Surely, there is room for compassion and respect for ancestors in the future prosperity and growth that all citizens covet. "In New York, Boston, and New Orleans," the Cemetery Defense League asserts, "the old cemeteries lie in the very heart of the business districts and are never disturbed by ruthless greed, but are the treasured landmarks of the cities. . . . Are we San Franciscans more deficient in sentiment and honor for our forefathers than our Eastern brethren?" Here again is a favorite and spirited defense of cemeteries—San Francisco falls short of the great eastern cities.

Cemetery defenders see their chief antagonist as a character type with well-defined attitudes and behavior. He is dedicated to expanding wealth and power with little regard for tradition. Some are dismissed as simple "schemers" and "grifters." The more insidious—often publicly perceived as prominent and worthy citizens—are those who talk of social prosperity and grand civic life but whose actions serve to undermine the deepest bonds of human nature and civil society. The word "desecration" is liberally hurled by churches and cemetery associations. The drive for "progress" comes at the expense of compassion, they say; advocates of progress are prepared to ignore, even mock, what they disdain as "sentimentality." Our ancestors, our family ties, and our time-honored rituals are mere inconveniences. "Progress" is the new god, and his servant cares little what or whom he tramples on to build, expand, and conquer. The lure of prosperity and modernity seduces the people.

This is the classic negative critique of the nineteenth-century "booster" businessmen who follow the frontier, building great Midwest cities. California breeds a more intense version.

As it stands, the grounds are a blistering disgrace to every decent minded person . . . unknown persons have been decorating the stones, principally those of women, with literature of unspeakable vulgarity and equally vulgar pictures. That behind all this desecration there is a fixed motive is a fact of common knowledge. The Masonic Cemetery occupies one of the most beautiful sites in San Francisco and its position has long been desired, it is said, by interests that would not stop short of anything to accomplish their ends.
—SAN FRANCISCO BULLETIN, 1921

The "eyesore" issue is a talking point in the 1914 election; by 1924, it is a focal point. With no funds to improve cemetery grounds, the passage of ten years between referendums renders such conditions worse. A typical comment in 1914 referring to "loitering and suspicious characters, which constitute an abiding menace to pedestrians and residents," has escalated in 1924 to reports "concerning the removal of human skulls by young boys from some of the vaults in the abandoned burial places" and to "orgies and desecrations of the dead committed by the criminal element." The city health officer complains in 1924 that "dangerous characters have inhabited the burial grounds. Drug addicts and generally dissolute people have been known to congregate and are a menace to the safety of the neighborhood." Residents report eerie sounds and cries coming from the cemeteries. Criminals evading Prohibition laws are said to hide out and transact business in dark corners of the dead lands. These habitats dwell in the midst of residential communities.

A well-publicized Board of Supervisors personal inspection of cemeteries in 1924 reports on the "deplorable" conditions in Masonic Cemetery, where "some bodies had already been carelessly removed as the land and memorials were left to nature's wrath, including fallen trees. Where graves have been opened, no attempt to conceal this fact has been made, and the plots have been strewn with debris." The other fraternal resting place also gets a failing grade: "Miscreants and neglect have ruined Odd Fellows' Cemetery." The Church fares no better: "Calvary Cemetery has become a scene of 'wreckage and ruin.'" Laurel Hill receives the highest marks: It presented a "fairly good appearance in spots," but in many areas, there was "the same evidence of abandonment of graves as are in the others, and the weeds and wreckage are strewn about the vicinity."

As time passes, it grows harder to defend deteriorating cemeteries. Of course, the deterioration is due largely to the ban on selling land and services or to expand to other parts of the city. But this is a complicated and boring debate point, so cemeteries in the 1920s gradually duck the "condition" issue or make promises to ameliorate, relying instead on an appeal that critics label "sentimentality."

That sentimentality could carry a sting. Archbishop Hanna warned in a 1924 election letter sent to diocese clergymen that the "homes of the dead are no longer holy places, no longer safe, from the ruthless hand of those who believe not in a future life, or the still more ruthless hand of those who would coin money on the very bones of our beloved ones." A lawyer representing Calvary declares before the Board of Supervisors, "We do not believe in making merchandise out of the homes of the dead."

Archbishop Riordan fends off critics by pledging to improve Calvary, especially around election times. After the 1914 cemetery victory, the *San Francisco Chronicle* reports that proposed work had commenced on the Geary Street boundary of Calvary with the removal of a row of overgrown cypress trees and a dilapidated fence. The cemetery officials promise that the grounds would be "generally cleaned up and improved, so that there will be no cause for complaint about its appearance."

The complaints do continue. The archbishop admits just before the 1924 election that Calvary is "not in good condition, far from it, and as it stands is a blot upon us." But he promises again "to put it in order no matter what may be the cost." Then, celebrating the 1924 election victory, the archbishop touts a new plan for "beautifying" Calvary Cemetery, including roads and pathways. The 15,000 pauper graves in Calvary that have "few living to care for them" will be kept in "decent order." His inspiration for overall change would be "the old and beautiful burial places of the East." Of course, this transformation would require considerable expenditure, and he counsels the public to be patient and the faithful to fork up. He prays that this second public rejection of removal will "settle the question for all time."

Clearly, by this time, the business community and most politicians want the cemeteries gone. The many Board of Supervisors votes, from bans on burials to expulsion orders, are lopsided in favor of eviction. Civic self-improvement and neighborhood associations are vociferous and consistent in advocating for removal. In the 1924 election, the cause of the dead has little ammunition left other than timeworn platitudes and epithets, such as "sentiment" and "desecration," words that the Cemetery Protective Association likes to fling, remarking at one point, "The grave-digging scene from Hamlet would be a solemn procedure compared to such removal."

Removal advocates try to turn the "sentiment and desecration" argument on its head: How can we dare disturb the dead, our critics ask? But the question should be, how can we dare let the world see this disgrace to our city? Is not keeping these dilapidated cemeteries more of an insult and sacrilege to the dead than removing them?

Two of the Lone Mountain cemeteries are created by the most prominent fraternal organizations in the city—the Odd Fellows and the Masons—who could presumably afford to contribute to upkeep. Laurel Hill hosted some of the most prominent and wealthy families of San Francisco, many also members of the fraternal organizations. Calvary is hallowed Catholic grounds. Is it unfair to ask, if all these well-heeled citizens will not come forward to support their own families and cemetery, why should average citizens suffer any consequences—financial or cultural?

Of course, some families do take care of their plots. Other than the wealthy, countless next of kin dutifully tend grave sites by hand, then order such behavior from reluctant children. But the chain of responsibility grows weaker with each generation. There is no communal responsibility, which would involve the establishment of a private endowment fund. According to George Skaller, a prominent anti-cemetery spokesman, only 1 percent of all cemetery properties in Lone Mountain were under "endowment" care in 1914, that is, private trust funds to cover maintenance.

There are efforts to think outside the box. As early as 1893, the Odd Fellows propose a plan for the city to take over the cemetery and offered to fund an endowment:

WILL DEED TO THE CITY. Plan for Perpetuating the Odd Fellow's Cemetery. George T. Baker, president of the board of directors of the Odd Fellow's Cemetery Association, is agitating a proposition to deed the cemetery to the State or city authorities, to be maintained forever as a public park. It is part of the plan to give $100,000 with the deed of gift, the interest on this sum to be used in keeping the cemetery in good condition.

The plat of land now used as a burying ground was purchased by the association in 1865, and was paid by an issue of bonds taken up by the different lodges of Odd Fellows throughout the city. These bonds have been redeemed long since, and the property consequently belongs to the association. As each individual plat-owner has an absolute right to the property he purchased, the association has not the power to divert the land from its present purpose and it therefore must remain as the city may see fit to condemn it. It is for the purpose of preventing this latter alternative and to secure for the plat-owners a perpetuation of their rights that the association is making the present move. It is estimated that two years will be required to dispose of the burial plats yet unsold, and nothing definite will be done until this has been accomplished.

As the association exists under the rural cemetery act, a special act of the Legislature will probably be necessary to ensure the perpetuation of the burying ground as proposed.

The Economic Card. Civic pride is the stalking horse for the economy. The earliest anti-cemetery agitators bemoan lost development opportunities. By the twentieth century, the argument is more obvious and relevant: An increasingly important expanse of land that can house 50,000 "living" citizens is being held hostage by impassable dead lands. Eager new immigrant blood will locate somewhere else, lost forever to the city. Imagine instead the general prosperity and tax revenue. During the 1914 referendum, the Downtown Association envisions jobs for 10,000 of the "building trades." The Civic League of Improvement Clubs estimates Lone Mountain cemetery land to be worth $10 million ($300 million today)—all untaxed. Subject to its fair share, that is $500,000 in city coffers. To add insult to injury, these grounds no longer bury people and thus serve no civic purpose. The revenue deficiency, which is "now being carelessly presented to private corporations . . . is unjustly shouldered on to the private citizen."

Property value increases around the cemeteries will provide fair compensation for cemetery plot owners plus pay for relocation. So say the removalists. But what if lands fall short of the prices that city officials predict and fail to cover moving and reinterment costs? Would the "ever-burdened" taxpayers be stuck with the bill?

All these arguments are speculation. No one knows what such a gigantic transfer of properties and monies would produce, including collateral damage and unintended consequences. To complicate matters, time is money. The longer you wait to solve a problem, the more expensive it grows.

The 1923 Morris Act, which forms the basis of the 1924 removal ordinance, allows "reservation of sufficient grounds of the original cemetery site for the erection of a mausoleum or columbarium, and/or preservation of monuments or vaults of historical interest, and preservation of remains in the mausoleum or columbarium where it is desired that they not be removed from the cemetery location." Removal proponents argue that with this provision, cemeteries have more leeway to preserve at least a part of their grounds and that they should take it as a consolation prize.

Some dare to take aim at the Catholic Church, willing to confront a sacred cow. In 1914, the Divisadero Improvement Association states that in contrast to the private cemeteries at Lone Mountain—whose lot owners would pocket the money from land sales—sale of property in Calvary, which is legally leased, will go directly to the Church and provide a $2 million windfall even after the cost of removal. This revenue, the association recommends, should go to some "charitable purpose that will help the present generation."

The Church hotly disputes such assessments. Just before the 1924 election, Archbishop Hanna estimates that reinterment of the Calvary population to Holy Cross in Colma would cost more than $3 million, while the sale of all the property would fall short of $1 million. "By what right by what law," he demands, "dare our lawmakers impose this impossible burden upon our people?"

Clearly, the cemeteries disrupt traffic and organic neighborhoods. The Richmond District is typically described as a hodgepodge of broken streets, bottled-up enclaves, and mad, circuitous routes. In 1910, the *San Francisco Chronicle* counts nine "important thoroughfares" running east and west plus a "large number" north and south that are blocked by the cemeteries. Some improvement clubs push for an extension of Sutter Street through Laurel Hill to provide a direct line of travel downtown through the main business district on Clement Street.

The dead lands create a headache for streetcars forced into zigzag routes that lead to extra commute and shopping time. Residents near the cemetery complain that they are "trapped" and "cut off" from downtown. Local areas are described by the *San Francisco Call* in 1912 as "crazy, irregular, non-rational neighborhoods, non-natural neighborhoods that cause traffic congestion, lack of development, and hurt to business." The automobile is becoming ubiquitous, pushing traffic problems from bad to worse. The car is the mortal enemy of the cemeteries.

Campaigns abound in the 1930s to build streets through Laurel Hill Cemetery: "Break the bottleneck!" There are now ten times more cars on city streets than there were twenty years earlier. New public transportation is hobbled by the dead lands. But Laurel Hill "improvement" campaigns are constantly stymied. The cemetery is

opposed to a major disruption of its sanctuary. The city attorney submits his own deal-breaker when he decides that the consent of all
cemetery plot owners will be necessary to provide rights-of-way.

Grand civic wealth is a formidable vision. "Sentiment" faces an
adversary offering the Promised Land—the final step San Francisco
must take to become a world-class city dominating the American
West. Eager new pioneers will build homes and businesses in our
neighborhoods instead of in East Bay or the Peninsula. Riches will
flow.

*The opening of these graves will recall old wounds, while sorrow
in our hearts remember the past. This city shall not behold the
daily spectacle of endless funeral processions, while the countless
thousands of our dead are carried off wholesale, to satisfy private
greed and land shark speculators. The commercialized removal of
these bodies is abhorrent to sentiment and decency.*
            —CEMETERY DEFENSE LEAGUE, 1924

In both elections, "land schemers" are accused of going every
which way to leverage the situation. They wax pro-cemetery when
scooping up devalued property around burial grounds. But should
such speculators sniff political winds that auger removal, they could
turn anti-cemetery to inflate land values, even in cahoots with some
cemetery lot owners, the Daughters of California Pioneers allege.
The Cemetery Defense League calls real estate investors "wolves in
sheep's clothing."

Speculating on cemetery land is an old issue. In 1878, the *San
Francisco Daily Evening Post* reports a scheme to buy 400 areas in
San Francisco and then lobby the state legislature to prohibit burials within the existing city cemeteries because their location allows
breezes to carry various "odors peculiar to places of sepulture." The
effort is met with skepticism. "This bill from its nature was to a certain extent a selfish scheme engineered for the enrichment of the

parties who had bought the Visitacion valley property, with the intention of locating a cemetery there just as soon as the law had been passed."

Author of the Morris Acts of 1921 and 1923, Assemblyman Clarence Morris, characterizes as "all bosh" the accusations that "landgrabbers" are behind cemetery removal.

The new San Mateo cemeteries are regarded with particular suspicion. Those rival burial grounds have an obvious vested interest in the city cemetery battle. The president of Laurel Hill publicly accuses Hamden Noble, founder of Cypress Lawn Cemetery in Colma, of surreptitiously funding San Francisco removal while "scheming" with other San Mateo cemetery owners to get the Board of Supervisors to ban city burials.

Noble does publicly promote San Francisco cemetery removal, usually in conjunction with promotion of his new burial grounds. An early Cypress Lawn brochure asks, "Does it not make you heart-sick to go through the city cemeteries and see the neglected graves overgrown with weeds, the tottering monuments and headstones, the cracked and crumbling coping? Go through CYPRESS LAWN, with its beautiful lawns, shady trees, peaceful lake and magnificent buildings, stately mausoleums and ever-blooming flowers, and see if you do leave it with a quiet and peaceful feeling that death is not so bad after all if only one can be buried in such a beautiful place."

San Francisco evictionists welcome the San Mateo cemeteries. City residents now have an inviting place to bury (and relocate) their loved ones. In 1896, the *San Francisco Call* advocates going south, waxing poetic on the grand new cemeteries there—Calvary, Mount Olivet, and especially Cypress Lawn, "where it would be difficult to find a spot where nature has more lavishing disposed of her gifts. . . . No expense has been spared to make this cemetery one of the finest in all the country, which has been laid out on the lawn or park plan now so popular in the East." A stampede of important people, the travelogue concludes, are making reservations in the new San Mateo cemeteries.

THE PARADISE EXPRESS

Busy Mission Street/El Camino Real is the one main thorough-fare from San Francisco to Colma—a dusty nine miles by horse and buggy. The automobile as common transportation is a generation away. Passenger rail service cannot accommodate transporting a casket and funeral goers. This is changing.

The Southern Pacific adds funeral service to its regular lines, which traverse Colma in the 1890s on the way to other destinations. There are two scheduled funeral trains daily. Just before Cypress Lawn's opening in 1892, the San Francisco & San Mateo Railway inaugurates an electric trolley line every fifteen minutes to Colma cemeteries from Fifth and Market streets in downtown San Francisco. It is a ribbon-cutting event. The much-ballyhooed and celebrity-attended "Electric Road" travels from the Ferry Building to Holy Cross Cemetery, stopping along the way for a guided tour of the "magnificent power station" running the train. "On the outward and return trips the city streets were crowded with people, and windows of each house had ladies and children who waved their hands and handkerchiefs as the cars passed." Although the area from the city limits to Colma is only nine miles, the *San Francisco Call* article describes it "as going through a country that is comparatively unknown."

This new venture is a direct challenge to the Southern Pacific business—and cheaper. The San Francisco & San Mateo Railway sets the price of transporting a casket to any of four existing cemeteries at $10, beating the competition by a dollar. Funeral guests can ride in special cars for the standard ten-cent fare. A year and a half later, the service accommodates official funeral parties, offering a handsomely equipped car with dedicated compartments for the casket and immediate family plus special mourning cars for guests at the standard fare.

City-owned streetcar lines glide into the business. The first funeral customer for the "electric hearse"—as dubbed by the *San Francisco Examiner*—is Napoleon Lazard, a prominent member of the Knights of Pythias, many members of whom are in the party. "The novel sight draws a curious crowd along the route," but the editor is less than impressed, referring to the funeral car's "lifeless burden," chiding the handkerchief-waving enthusiasm "as if it were a gala occasion of some sort," and lamenting public jostling around the funeral car itself "with the morbid eagerness that a crowd always possesses to get a glimpse of a coffin." In fact, there is no need to celebrate this so-called progress: "It was as if we had indeed reached the age of electricity and the dead must be rushed along to their last abiding place with all possible speed, so the living could hasten back to their frantic race for existence." The inaugural run takes one hour to reach Cypress Lawn, where it switches to a side spur into the grounds.

"United Railroads of San Francisco Funeral Cars. An effective service affording comfort, courtesy, and quickness to the cemeteries of San Mateo County. We operate three specially constructed funeral cars, each divided into three compartments: one for the casket, one for the exclusive use of the mourners, and one for the accommodation of friends attending the funeral. Each car has a seating capacity of forty persons, and is further provided for the accommodation of extra seats." *Colma Historical Association*

Going in style. Southern Pacific funeral car. *Colma Historical Association*

Southern Pacific will not be outdone for the luxury trade. A popular accommodation for twenty-plus passengers is an upgrade to the company's *El Descanso* or *Greenwood*, both with magnificently furnished funeral parlor coaches adorned with draperies, plush carpeting, wood paneling, velvet-cushioned wicker furnishings, and separate "apartments" for men and women. Groups desiring even greater flexibility can charter an entire train for $50 in addition to the standard mourner and casket fees. By 1905, the Southern Pacific is serving Mount Olivet, Masonic, Odd Fellows, Eternal Home, Sholom, Emanuel, Cypress Lawn, Italian, and Holy Cross cemeteries.

The United Railroads Company establishes a five-car fleet of specialized trains painted deep green with brick red–colored roofs. "Funeral Car" in gold letters identifies the mission. The cars have three sections—one to carry the coffin, a lavishly furnished suite for the family with heavy drapery and blinds to provide privacy, and, for the general mourners, a well-appointed larger compartment that includes special attention to detail, such as polished brass spittoons. All the cars feature lead inserts in the wheels and gears to provide a softer and quieter ride. As autos gain a foothold and roads to grave-yards improve, income from funeral service trains declines. By 1926, the last three cars of this line are scrapped.

Railroads use feeder lines to reach the cemetery gates and return to the main track. At Holy Cross, one rings a special bell at the gate to summon a priest who places the deceased on a wagon and leads parishioners to the burial spot.

Convenient public transportation is a critical part of the enter-prise to establish "rural" burial grounds in American cities. Their success in Colma is not a sure bet. A major drawback is the dis-tance. Well into the nineteenth century, without automobiles and convenient rail transport, it remains the custom to be physically near, even walking distance, from your dearly departed—a psychological as much as a physical measure. Garden cemeteries, even if just a few miles from city centers, are initially resisted. "People thought he was crazy at the time," remarks Michael Svanevik, referring to San Francisco archbishop William Riordon's decision to establish a new cemetery in Colma. "Who in the world would ever bury their dead that far from the center of the city?" In fact, it proved a challenge to sell the new San Francisco Yerba Buena Cemetery in the 1850s—a mere one mile from downtown, which is fine as the crow flies. But a family with young and old must navigate makeshift streets, howling winds, and sinkhole sand dunes to reach the grounds. Imagine the consternation when the Lone Mountain cemeteries—established at about the same more than two miles from the most populated areas—demand a full day's trek to pay proper respects and return home by moonlight and oil lamps.

Removal sentiment in Northern California feeds the emerging Colma cemeteries, which are receiving new "dead" business as well as voluntary relocations from private city cemeteries, the latter averag-ing about 300 a month by 1903, including a trickle of VIP families.

Lone Mountain burial grounds, however deteriorated, are still a veritable museum of grand classical structures, statuary, and stained glass. The upstart Colma cemeteries boast beautiful new landscapes but little else in terms of adornment. It will take years to assume the appearance of properly populated resting grounds that attract customers to a place others wished to be. This is a particular problem for Cypress Lawn. Sectarian cemeteries have a captive audience. Cypress Lawn, like Laurel Hill before it, does claim Catholics, Jews, Odd Fellows, Masons, and the dubious. But most such groups are inclined to the tribal fraternal grounds. Hamden Noble's grand project at Cypress Lawn is a privately funded business that depends on enticing a religious and lodge-oriented public to try nonsectarian eternity. The aggressive entrepreneur is making money while serving the public good—the textbook example of "booster." This can include "poaching," of which he is accused. Noble boldly predicts that as soon as San Francisco adopts a proposed new charter, "everyone owning a lot in the cemeteries within this city will be compelled to buy another lot elsewhere." Andrew Jackson Pope, the deceased owner of the most successful and celebrated lumber company in the American West, has built a magnificent family mausoleum at Laurel Hill Cemetery where he is placed in 1878. Noble has deep connections to the San Francisco elite. He can assure the Pope family and the world of, as he states in his *Advantages of Buying a Burial Lot in Cypress Lawn*, "first, permanency. It is sufficiently far from the city to ensure that there is absolutely no danger of it ever being removed, even were it not in the center of a long line of cemeteries. This makes it permanent beyond the question of a doubt."

The family is persuaded by his offer to fund removal of its mausoleum at Laurel Hill and its reinstallation as the first such private structure at Cypress Lawn. The Greco-Roman pillared granite temple must be meticulously disassembled piece by piece, transported along with the human remains, and meticulously reassembled. Set prominently near the imposing Cypress Lawn entrance gate, a dramatic stained-glass angel rises to life in the mausoleum at sunrise each morning within sight of the main road. It is an advertising jewel for the new cemetery and a new prominence for the lumber baron, who had arrived in San Francisco as a penniless lad.

Other prominent families see the writing on the tombstone and decide, some with Noble's friendly persuasion, to switch sites. James Flood practically owns the Nevada Comstock silver lode when he dies four years prior to Cypress Lawn's founding. Noble is one of Flood's stockbrokers. In 1906, the family relocates from Laurel Hill to Cypress Lawn its eighteen-columned Parthenon burial palace—to this day the largest private structure on the property. Thus, scattered about Cypress Lawn and other Colma burial grounds are memorials where the first recorded death date precedes that cemetery's opening. Most of these relocations come from Lone Mountain cemeteries. People are voting with their souls. An 1898 advertising brochure informs the public, "Even if you have already purchased a lot elsewhere, you can have the remains of your loved one removed to Cypress Lawn before the first five days allowed by law after the interment expires. If you delay beyond that time a period of one year must elapse before this can be done."

The golden age of private mausoleums stretches from the Civil War to World War I. They represent the art and pretentions of the age, both of which are changing rapidly in the 1920s. At the turn of the century, a prominent private mausoleum runs about $5 million in current value: The land is the most expensive per-square-inch real estate on earth, but half the cost goes to the structure itself—magnificent looking but only a few hundred square feet of "living" space that lacks separate rooms, attics or basements, plumbing, or lighting.

Why so expensive? The building, with all its parts and adornments, consists of handmade, once-executed fabrications crafted from the finest granite and marble available. A heavy, articulated bronze entry door will be cast, and then the mold will be broken. But before anything is executed, you must hire an architect and surveyor. Not just any architect will do. You need someone accomplished and well known. You also fancy a dramatic piece of stained glass, so you retain Louis Comfort Tiffany, who has already done a piece for your mansion study. Then, on a trip to Italy, you fall in love with a marble angel statue by a renowned sculptor; it is shipped home for the mausoleum's interior. Your death memorial is truly unique, one of a kind in every manner, including the cost. It is typical for the buyer to complete these plans while alive so that the dwelling is ready when he is. A mogul might live longer than expected and witness interments of younger relatives in the family mansion before he is laid to overdue rest.

Who would indulge such extravagance? The new pharaohs. Many of the richest and best-known personalities of the era reenact textbook tales of rags to (great) riches and (great) power in a single generation. Has there ever been such a phenomenon on this scale in so short a time? Hubris is unavoidable. Humble origins breed grand exits. And it is a perfect historical moment for grandiose ambitions and grandiose rewards. For 200 years in the United States, new entrepreneurial vacuums travel west. Fresh frontiers create unprecedented personal and family wealth. Cemeteries across the country reflect this national bonanza as aging wunderkinder build tributes to themselves, usually in the form of grand Greco-Roman structures. One at Cypress Lawn in Colma, constructed by the "Potato Chip King of California," is a down-to-detail all-marble scaled reproduction of the Temple of Poseidon. Hamden Noble is such a story right up to the end (but not including it). He rests beneath a nondescript gray slab sarcophagus that rises a mere twelve inches from the ground. The inscription consists only of names and dates. Noble is not a particularly modest man in life, but apparently, he needed no more in death. Perhaps he felt that his monument was Cypress Lawn itself.

HERE COMES THE SUN

Why are San Francisco cemeteries not removed sooner? They have an unlikely and reluctant champion. "Sunny" Jim Rolph serves as mayor from 1912 to 1931, masterfully strolling the thin line between warring cemetery armies as he extracts at least the grudging approval of both. It demonstrates how a single individual can influence and guide historical events.

The mayoralty oversees a civic building spree, including a grand new Civic Center to replace the rubble of 1906. The 1915 Panama–Pacific International Exposition, which promises a visitor avalanche into a city proudly "rising like a Phoenix from the ashes," serves as a tailwind for multitudes of projects, and Rolph seldom misses an opportunity to be on hand for openings. He earns and relishes his title as the "Builder," proud to lead the "metropolis" parade. Although the public face of boosterism, he is also a pragmatic politician with an apparent streak of Jeffersonian democracy. This permits the cemetery death march to prevail with a measure of decency.

When the Board of Supervisors passes an official resolution of eviction in January 1914 with a fourteen-month deadline, most business and political leaders believe that Rolph will immediately sign the document and that the issue will finally be resolved. After all, he is on public record throughout his career in support of cemetery removal: "If we must provide for the expansion of our city, it must be a city of homes. To this end sentiment must yield to progress. It is conceded by all that these cemeteries must be removed. All the ground within San Francisco is required for living inhabitants."

But when faced with that reality, the mayor unexpectedly announces that he needs a bit of time to consult "all the interested parties" on whether he should allow the measure to become law without a public vote of approval. That decision does not come overnight, which causes days of public and private indigestion as the cliffhanger unfolds. He is lobbied, sometimes intensely, by both sides. Rolph does more than listen, often asking pointed questions or seeking clarifications. Just before the anticipated big decision, a delegation "packed" his office, urging the eviction ordinance to become law immediately. Those expecting a definitive answer are disappointed.

Mayor in Doubt on Cemetery Bill
—SAN FRANCISCO CHRONICLE, JANUARY 16, 1914

His public statement on that day feeds the confusion as it offers a whisk of comfort to anti-cemetery stalwarts: "I realize that the majority must rule at all times and the minority must submit to the majority. I know that you have your homes in the district in which cemeteries are situated and I appreciate the conditions surrounding the cemeteries. I have until next Saturday night to act upon the measure."

If clear that the "majority" must rule, why the indecision? A Board of Supervisors spokesman announces its annoyance with His Honor continuing to meet with opposing sides and apparently in a quandary. The elected representatives voted fourteen to one. What need is there for any other vote?

Had Rolph signed the bill without calling a referendum, the cemeteries would have to go. Certainly, legal slings and arrows would delay that process for years, but the path to removal is greatly facilitated.

The mayor's position is shaped by political realities as well as what constitutional philosophy he embraces. Rolph senses the significant disconnect between the elected elite and the citizenry. He is an Odd Fellow, as are many of the leading citizens—its Lone Mountain Cemetery is one of the four in danger of removal. The mayor is also Catholic and keenly aware of the influence wielded by the Church. Catholics are perhaps one-third of the city's population, more religious than today and more inclined to vote as instructed by the Church on relevant issues. In the 1924 election, Archbishop Hanna sends a letter to his clergy "exhorting" them to preach a "yes" vote from the pulpit at the two Sunday masses preceding the referendum. Those who support removal, the archbishop declares, have committed an act against "the whole Catholic population." He praises Mayor Rolph's "high sense of justice that has always marked his rule."

When in 1924 the Board of Supervisors votes in favor of removal, there is little doubt that Rolph will call a popular election. "One of the basic principles of popular government is to give the people a voice which directly affects them," he states, defending his action by citing the city charter's provision that any matter of policy may, on the discretion of the mayor, be given to the electorate for a decision. Removal advocates again fume.

Perhaps Rolph is indulging in elaborate political theater to appear as impartial and judicious as possible. By advocating for removal and letting the people decide, he could have his political cake and eat it too. The vote in the first election with its large "no removal" margin may have surprised most but probably not Rolph, and it seems to embolden him. A much smaller margin of victory in 1924 still does not harm him politically; after the plebiscite, he serves six more years as mayor before sailing on to the governor's mansion. Few are in a better position, as an elite booster, to constrain the anti-cemetery momentum. It is akin to Richard Nixon going to China or Ronald Reagan leading a nuclear disarmament pact.

In 1914, most politicians and pundits regard the Board of Supervisors' vote as putting the law into effect immediately—to be challenged in court, no doubt—but it is the law until a judge says it is not. Supervisor James Hayden contends that the only way to order a popular referendum on the issue would be for the board to pass another ordinance repealing the first one. Such a repeal ordinance could be proposed by the mayor, six supervisors, or an initiative petition of registered voters. That legal assessment does not prevail.

There are still differences of opinion in 1924 if a popular vote can automatically override the law, which will, according to some experts, go into effect immediately unless vetoed by the mayor. The Western Addition Improvement Association characterizes the election as "merely to get an expression of the voters' view of the subject." A league of four improvement clubs concurs, declaring that the ordinance is in full force; the referendum ordered by Rolph is so that "the people might express their views." Would that vote legally override the law? The league offers no definitive opinion but fears that referendum is "threatening the entire [removal] project and will undo the work of two decades ... forever perpetuating the cemeteries in our midst."

The Board of Supervisors is vocally upset at the mayor. In 1914, its vote was fourteen to one. Ten years later, it was seventeen to one. Are not the Board of Supervisors the elected representatives of the people, entitled to make decisions on their behalf? A "city official" informs the *San Francisco Chronicle* that should the public vote against removal in the upcoming 1924 election, the board would have the discretion to repeal the removal ordinances or "otherwise take cognizance of the vote.... The ordinances are now law, and the vote of the people would not repeal them. A vote of the board would be necessary to repeal them."

Contrast that legal assessment with Archbishop Hanna, who asserts that the mayor's decision to put the 1924 ordinance to a popular vote "had taken the matter out of the hands of lawgivers and put it into the hands of the people ... who will have an opportunity of nullifying by their votes against action of the Board of Supervisors."

The only person who might fathom the law on this matter is Sunny Jim. He is concocting the law.

Contemporaries describe the cemetery issue as a "war." As in most public policy disputes, the majority of citizens likely remain oblivious or indifferent to these nasty skirmishes, but for those on the front lines, it is a do-or-die issue.

A *San Francisco Chronicle* report on a 1914 election debate euphemistically calls the confrontations "spirited arguments," but a gathering can resemble, as one gentleman there put it, "a good old-fashioned ward meeting." At a North Beach Promotion Association function, speakers for and against are "frequently interrupted and hissed, the debaters themselves indulging generously in personalities to such a degree as to threaten several times to disrupt the meeting." The Daughters of Pioneers pleads to all sides for more decorum, referring to the "personal bickering" of opponents and the hurling of epithets such as "grafter and miser." A Chamber of Commerce spokesman there labeled the 1914 ordinance an "evil law" and "most vicious."

There are a variety of stakeholders in the disposition of cemetery lands, as illustrated in this dramatic account.

Gravediggers from the Cemeteries Attempt to Break Up Meeting, but in Vain.
—*San Francisco Call*, May 22, 1897

Citizens, led by "property owners" of the Richmond District Improvement Association, hold a well-attended meeting to push for cemetery removal. Such gatherings are becoming common, as are the agendas: Speakers condemn the cemetery blight, report a new health warning, bemoan stagnant property values, and wax poetic on the opportunities for prosperity once the land is reclaimed. Letters of support are read from outgoing mayor Sutro and incoming mayor Phelan. Then come resolutions addressed to the Board of Supervisors and the Health Department.

The gathering is attended by fifty "unfriendly persons bent upon raising a row" before resolutions could be passed, the *Call* reports. "The disturbers are not property owners in the District," declares the chairman, who urges to no avail that a police officer present arrest one of the unruly speakers. The meeting continues to unravel. "The confusion became so great, and the language used by the rough element who packed the meeting became so foul nearly all the women left the hall in terror and disgust." Another police officer arrives and makes an arrest that restores a veneer of order. The chairman is astonished that persons "who sold their manhood for a drink" should invade a meeting of "order-loving citizens" and frighten away numerous lady property owners. A young woman who has retreated to the exit door exhorts the chairman, "That's right! Give it to them!" He announces that in the future, no one will be admitted to meetings without an invitation card from the association. "We will send cards only to gentlemen."

What transpires after two elections can best be characterized as a decade of limbo. The bold "instant" city that forges a great polis overnight, that conjures up a pastoral oasis from desert sands, that overcomes the greatest natural disaster in American history, and whose motto is taken from President Taft's declaration: "San Francisco is the city that knows how," remains mired in a nasty cemetery war. The dead will die by a thousand cuts.

CHAPTER 9

NO COUNTY FOR OLD MEN

*In 1937 was begun what was perhaps the greatest mass removal
of the dead in human history: the disinterment and relocation of
all the graves from Calvary and Laurel Hill cemeteries.*
—KEVIN STARR, CALIFORNIA HISTORIAN
AND LATE STATE LIBRARIAN

THE "BIG FOUR" PRIVATE BURIAL GROUNDS IN THE CITY AND
County of San Francisco—containing some 150,000 remains—are
eventually and in stages removed to Colma. The task is not fully
completed until 1940. The cemeteries offer families an opportunity
to rescue loved ones and memorials before the public execution.
Otherwise, remains will be collected by contractors and placed in
designated mass locations at their respective Colma cemeteries. All
the monuments are slated for demolition.

The 1924 election saves the cemeteries—but barely. There is a
sigh of relief but little joy; another ballot battle will surely mean
defeat. The election spawns a tangled legal limbo. It will take thirteen years and another election to decide the fate of the dead. The
two vote tallies reveal a dramatic shift in anti-cemetery sentiment.
In part, this represents raw numbers: The Richmond District surrounding the cemeteries has mushroomed from 3,000 in 1895 to
66,000 by 1920. There are some 20,000 more total votes in 1924
than 1914—largely coming-of-age or new residents with less passion to preserve the past at the expense of the present.

For Odd Fellows and Masons, the 1924 skin-of-your-teeth victory is especially hollow. Both had their hearts, if not their feet, out

the San Francisco door even before the first election. Those cemeteries lack the grandeur of the Catholic Church or the pioneer gravitas of Laurel Hill. Fraternal cemetery lands are also smaller—almost by half. And even with member donations, always disappointing, there will never be sufficient funds for proper large-scale removal to Greenlawn (Odd Fellows) and Woodlawn (Masonic) cemeteries in Colma until city cemetery lands are sold.

From the summer of 1912, when the San Francisco Board of Supervisors files a public "notice of intention" for cemetery eviction, to November 1914, when the ordinance is rejected, cemeteries are living under a relentless and seemingly inevitable eviction drumbeat. It is no wonder that Odd Fellows and Masons treat the 1914 victory as little more than a reprieve and continue to advise removal of remains in anticipation of property sales and mass relocation. Masons begin to court buyers, raising a thorny issue. What if there is no plot holder's consensus on the right course of action? Did cemetery associations have the authority to make decisions in the face of such disagreement? The law and ethics surrounding this matter are vague in San Francisco and the rest of the country.

The California legislature eventually enters the battlefield of the dead with the 1921 Morris Act—a "soft glove" approach that encourages cemetery associations to voluntarily vacate and dispose of their land. A cemetery will now have the right to remove its dead and transfer the property if a majority of plot owners consent. This sale will presumably provide the income required for large-scale removal.

Under the provision, the Masons continue the still-modest effort to relocate individual remains to Greenlawn Cemetery in preparation for an eventual sale of the San Francisco land and mass removal. But seventeen dissenting families toss a legal monkey wrench into the works. The 1923 case *Hornblower v. Masonic Cemetery Association* strikes down the 1921 Morris Act, citing an unconstitutional use of local police power that violates the rights of individual plot owners in a dedicated cemetery, even when a majority votes otherwise.

The court enjoins the Masonic Cemetery Association from further removal where such action is not desired by all plot owners.

State legislators are miffed. The purpose of the Morris Act is to motivate cemetery associations to act on their own, avoiding any complicated showdowns with local government. In a quick reaction to the court decision, the California legislature passes a new and improved 1923 Morris Act that renders the previous act moot. The gloves come off. Now the law authorizes all municipalities of more than 100,000, if they so desire, to *require* the removal of remains where burials have been prohibited by law for fifteen years. To mitigate the edict's apparent hard-heartedness, it lays out various ground rules for removals designed to ensure "dignity" for the dead and "fair notice" to the living, even permitting that "sufficient" land may be set aside by any cemetery for a memorial/columbarium/park subject, of course, to local government approval. The San Francisco orders are jolted by the news but hardly surprised. The Odd Fellows immediately closes its San Francisco cemetery in preparation for a sale and removal.

The Board of Supervisors quickly passes updated eviction ordinances in 1924 based on the new Morris Act, and predictably, these are again put to plebiscite by the mayor despite his continued public advocacy for cemetery removal. Ten percent each of the then-existing four cemetery lands can be devoted to memorials. For Laurel Hill and Calvary, this constitutes five acres; for Masons and Odd Fellows, about two. The election delivers, however thin, another reprieve for the cemeteries. Masons and Odd Fellows view the hollow 1924 victory as a slow-falling guillotine, making removal and relocation more urgent. It is a stark reality for the orders: The grounds are in ruins, there are no funds for improvement, and public opinion is turning against you. Suddenly, any such removal plans are halted in their tracks, again, as the issue tumbles down a legal rabbit hole that interrupts large-scale relocation for the rest of the decade.

The election unleashes another storm of litigation, most significantly an arcane but significant challenge by pro-cemetery lawyers who argue that the Board of Supervisors' ordinance pertaining to Odd Fellows and Masons must be declared unconstitutional because it covers only those cemeteries, not Calvary and Laurel Hill, which are addressed in a second and separate ordinance with different provisions and is therefore discriminatory and illegal.

The 1920s is the "lost decade" of cemetery removal. Whatever intention fraternal orders have for relocation is stymied as this lawsuit and others inch up the judicial ladder. While legal issues are mired in litigation, no one dares to take any practical action. "The living battled advocates of the dead," notes a legal historian, "in a series of 'bare-knuckle no-holds-barred' legal fights waged in state and federal courts." The wheels of justice turn slowly, especially when oiled by well-paid attorneys on both sides. Finally, a federal court rules in 1930 (*Masonic Cemetery v. Gamage*) that municipalities can abate nuisances one at a time and each in its own way if so desired and if the degree of "nuisance value" requires more immediate action in one case than in another. The verdict explodes a legal logjam, enabling the Masonic and Odd Fellows relocation efforts to continue in earnest—this time leading to the complete removal of their San Francisco cemetery properties soon thereafter.

TALE OF TWO ORDERS

The Orders, whose dead find rest in these graveyards, are numerously represented in San Francisco, and are powerful and wealthy. The bond of brotherhood that holds the living in such harmonious unity, is not broken by death, but is even more manifest to the world at the grave than in any of the ordinary circumstance.
—B. E. LLOYD, *LIGHTS AND SHADES IN SAN FRANCISCO*, 1876

The "bond of brotherhood" stretches thinner and thinner over time. By the 1930s, older children of those buried at Odd Fellows and Masonic cemeteries (before the 1901 ban) may be deceased or too old to act, so it passes to grandchildren or others to rescue a person they may have not met, liked, or remembered. Devotion to the dead cannot rest solely on personal ancestral connections; to endure, this impulse needs an explicit civic dedication to those ancestors. In the end, San Francisco could not come up with enough of either.

Masons responded to the 1901 San Francisco burial ban by dedicating a new fraternal cemetery in Colma three years later. Recent Mason deceased are buried there, while residents of the San Francisco Masonic Cemetery remain largely in place for almost three decades. In December 1931, the *San Francisco Chronicle* announces,

> *Deadline Set for Cemetery Evacuations*
> *Masonic Association Extends Time for Removals Thirty Days.*
> *Another month will be allowed for removal of bodies by relatives from the Masonic Cemetery, it was announced yesterday by George Skaller, president of the cemetery association. To inform those who cannot be reached by letter or otherwise, the cemetery directors have ordered a thirty-day campaign.*
>
> *Already 5600 bodies have been placed in other cemeteries by relatives, mostly in Woodlawn, according to Mr. Skaller. About 14,300 are left.*
>
> *Under the removal ordinance, which has been upheld in the United States Supreme Court, the cemetery association is obligated to transfer the bodies. Those not cared for by relatives will be placed in a special section of Woodlawn Cemetery.*
>
> *Of 5000 letters notifying family that could be designated of the removal conditions, about 2500 have been returned by the post office, which has been unable to find the addresses.*

The family bears expenses for a private removal and reinterment. Would the response have been better if the economy were not mired in a long depression? Of the approximately 25,000 fraternal family members in San Francisco Masonic Cemetery, some one-quarter are claimed, most of those being moved to Woodlawn in specific grave sites. The rest are transported to a restricted mass burial area there dedicated by the Mason Cemetery Association in April 1933 under a monument inscribed "In perpetual memory of Masonic Cemetery pioneers." A pair of guardian lions flank the steps. Soon after incorporation in 1904, the Colma "Masonic Cemetery" had been forced to accept nonmembers to survive economically, and the designation is officially changed to "Woodlawn." Part of the old city Masonic Cemetery land is transformed into the "Laurel Heights" neighborhood.

The rest is purchased by the University of San Francisco (formerly St. Ignatius College) in 1928. "They missed a lot of the bodies," notes Alan Ziajka, official historian of the University of San Francisco. "No one knew that until 1950, when we put up our first major building after the Depression." That would be the Gleesen Library. A backhoe churns up an entire mausoleum containing at least 200 bodies. Since then, relics of the past pop up at every major campus excavation; witness the next major construction project: Hayes-Heal residence hall in 1966, forced to halt temporarily when an excavation crew "came upon so many bones and skulls that they refused to continue until the humans remains were removed from the site," Ziajka reports. During early excavations to build the John Lo Schiavo Center for Science and Innovation in 2011, fifty-five coffins, twenty-nine skeletons, and several skulls are unearthed.

The San Francisco Odd Fellows' grounds is the resting place of "Miranda," discovered in 2016 and discussed in chapter 1. The founding of its Colma cemetery more than a half-century earlier is a poignant and scandalous story. Reacting to the Board of Supervisors' burial ban, Odd Fellows directors inaugurate a San Mateo location in 1904 by establishing a new cemetery association for fraternal members and families. According to the Grand Lodge, $50,000 ($2 million today) raised for a San Mateo cemetery maintenance endowment is embezzled in 1903 by two Odd Fellows on the board. The Grand Lodge immediately denies any official connection to the governing body of the Colma burial grounds and refuses to allow its name to be used. Soon after opening, Odd Fellows Cemetery officially becomes Greenwood Cemetery.

There is more turmoil and disappointment. Freed from legal restraints in the 1930 *Masonic Cemetery v. Gamage* decision and facing mounting pressure to remove its San Francisco cemetery presence, the Odd Fellows launch an advertising campaign to locate relatives of the deceased, urging families and friends to claim individual remains and memorials before mass removal. Where addresses of deceased relatives are known, families are contacted by mail. It hopes, as did the Masons, that fraternal connections will enhance blood connections. Results are substantially subpar to the subpar Mason initiative—thousands of letters are stamped "return to sender," and those pleas that are delivered do not deliver much.

The Odd Fellows Cemetery land in San Francisco has been stripped bare of monuments and trees years before the actual mass removal of bodies commenced. The contractor's plan is to place string lines in an east-to-west direction, spaced where it is assumed that most graves will intersect. Probers with hardened brass rods move along those string lines searching for a casket, a collapsed grave, ashes, or nothing below. A legion of hired workers then dig only where there are marks and only as deep as marked. The entire process is done by hand.

Rene Monie, whose great grandmother was relocated to Greenlawn, has studied the Odd Fellows' removal. He describes the effort as "anything but straightforward, organized, or professional . . . one

Workmen digging up graves at Odd Fellows Cemetery, San Francisco, 1931.
Colma Historical Association

can only assume that there were days when things became a muddle. . . . Notes and records were handwritten, labor far from professional, and oversight intended but likely minimal. With money to be made in land and reburial services, the dignity of the dead likely became a quick afterthought for many."

Some 26,000 to 28,000 unclaimed remains are found and are relocated by rented moving vans to Greenlawn and reinterred in a mass grave of parallel trenches on a sandy hill in the northwest corner of the cemetery. The removal process begun in 1930 is not fully completed until 1935. "Almost no details of their removal conditions exist," documentary historian Trinia Lopez says of both the Odd Fellows and the Masons. Occasionally, canvas sheets are installed around the sites, but privacy is more the exception than the rule, and an often-gruesome process of removal can suddenly become unwelcome street drama to passersby. The Greenlawn relocation site is memorialized by a simple shaft monument transported from the San Francisco cemetery. Since the original fund for endowment conservation has been lost and never replaced, there are no resources to maintain this dedicated section. During the 1960s, Greenlawn constructs a fence around the land that cuts it off from the cemetery proper.

A portion of the Odd Fellows' city cemetery property becomes a commercial zone, but most is subdivided for homesites, the neighborhood called "Franciscan Heights."

The Laurel Hill and Calvary removal projects are methodical and orderly; those of the fraternal orders less so. Michael Svanevik calls the accounts "sketchy at best." How precisely the fraternal remains from San Francisco are replaced at Greenlawn and Woodlawn cemeteries is difficult to determine. Trinia Lopez observes that the records for "mass gravesites" in Colma "vary greatly in their thoroughness." Whatever the intention of the Masons and Odd Fellows to remove and relocate families in exclusive containers, place at single depth, and record locations for each deceased reburied in Colma, the efforts fall short in practice. Greenlawn (the original Odd Fellows cemetery) and Woodlawn (the original Mason cemetery) do maintain lists of those reinterred.

Many of these bodies in San Francisco traveled further in death than they ever did in life.
—Michael Svanevik, *Journey of Souls*

Not only is life transitory in early San Francisco, but so is death. Remains can be relocated like chess pieces. Cemetery historian John Blackett estimates there were some 200,000 individual burials in San Francisco before the 1901 ban—some more than once in a long and winding road to a forever home. It is possible for you to be secreted in an anonymous patch of land in 1849, moved to North Beach Cemetery by a caring soul, relocated by the government to Yerba Buena Cemetery and then again to City Cemetery, rediscovered by the Legion of Honor seismic refitting crew fifty years later, and given a new memorial home at Skylawn Cemetery or Cypress Lawn—a six-timer finally resting in peace. Many are not as fortunate. It is estimated that up to 50,000 remains lie beneath San Francisco today.

The 1914 removal ordinance permits the Board of Supervisors, on request by cemetery associations or others, to grant a special memorial tribute area on the cemetery land. There is no mention of size. The 1924 removal ordinance permits 10 percent of each of the cemetery lands to be devoted to such a project. The retention of the Odd Fellows Columbarium, still operating today, is permitted under this act.

Before the 1924 election, the pro-removal *San Francisco Chronicle* reports that should eviction be upheld, Laurel Hill has a plan to build "a magnificent" three-story structure—all the bodies to be cremated and placed in crypts. The second floor would be dedicated to a memorial hall and the third floor to a historical library. This is the reinvention of a "memorial" plan that Laurel Hill first contemplated in 1915. The Odd Fellows propose to exhume and cremate all bodies on its ground and build an addition to the Columbarium for those remains. Masons and Catholics pledge to give lot holders free places in Greenlawn and Holy Cross cemeteries in San Mateo.

Laurel Hill and Calvary dig in their heels after the 1924 elections. Archbishop Hanna doubles down on his secular argument that proceeds from cemetery lands will fail to cover the cost of removal and reinterment at Holy Cross, ominously speculating that city taxpayers will foot a painful bill for the difference. Instead, he suggests that the city construct roads through Calvary to facilitate traffic flows between western neighborhoods and downtown. Laurel Hill makes no similar offer. It is the more significant player, as its land sits between the major commercial arteries—Clement and Sutter streets—and downtown; a letter to the editor bemoans the "dead land" that separates "the two best and growing parts of the city." But Laurel Hill holds the pioneers of California. Who would dare pave it over and put up a parking lot? The San Francisco Board of Supervisors in 1937. It declares still another eviction election to get rid of the stubborn holdouts. Archbishop Hanna immediately throws in the towel, announcing a Calvary relocation to Holy Cross. The Church itself legally owns the San Francisco property, which is quickly sold to property developers. The proceeds fund disinterment and removal of remains to Colma.

Laurel Hill is the last bastion standing. As long ago as the 1890s, it is being described as magnificent ruins. A few sites are immaculately maintained by private gardeners dispatched from wealthy estates. Some spots are attended to on occasion. Most are neglected. Laurel Hill has a particular reputation. Loren Rhodes calls it "the last refuge of single men." San Francisco does not achieve gender parity until the 1920s. In the latter half of the nineteenth century, the city has a larger proportion of unmarried men than any other major city. It will take more than a generation removed from the gold rush before folks begin to regard San Francisco as a "family town." Laurel Hill Cemetery is nonsectarian and the only one of the "Big Four" without a "benefactor." If bonds of venerable secret societies—Masons, Odd Fellows, and the Church—cannot entice (or find) living families to rescue dead ones, Laurel Hill could do no better.

Those not claimed in Laurel Hill become part of the mass removal and relocation project in 1940. One would think that prominent people who leave estates would be rescued by descendants. This is not always the case. Among the luminaries who lost their private graves and now rest anonymously in a public memorial space at Cypress Lawn include the following:

- James Van Ness, mayor of San Francisco (1855–1856)
- Andrew Jackson Bryant, mayor of San Francisco (1875–1879)
- David Broderick, U.S. senator from California
- John McDougal, governor of California
- Joseph Folsom, San Francisco port collector
- Lorenzo Sawyer and Silas W. Sanderson, California Supreme Court chief justices
- Charles Nahl, acclaimed gold rush painter
- Arthur Page Brown, prominent civic architect
- Andrew Hallidie, cable car inventor
- Elias S. Cooper, founder of the first medical school in California
- Peder Sather, philanthropist who funded the University of California's Campanile and Sather Gate
- Kate Kennedy, prominent San Francisco educator
- George Gordon, builder of the first San Francisco urban park neighborhood
- Charles Kimball, compiler of the first *San Francisco City Directory* in 1850
- Edward Gilbert, publisher of the *San Francisco Alta* newspaper
- Theodore Barry and Benjamin Pattern, proprietors of the city's elite Montgomery Street drinking emporium
- Robert B. Woodward, proprietor of San Francisco's first amusement park, the famed Woodward Gardens
- David Scannel, legendary chief of the San Francisco Fire Department, placed in a special section of the Mound reserved for firefighters

- Phineas Gage, sans head, which is awarded to his Harvard University doctor (Gage survives a severe industrial explosive accident to the skull that earns him national fame and a place in medical textbooks of the day. There is no request from Cambridge to reunite the corpse in one location.)

How could such illustrious people be abandoned? Laurel Hill burials stop in 1901 by law. It received its first burials almost fifty years earlier; by the 1940 removal, almost a century had elapsed. Great wealth seems to follow a pattern: The first generation makes the money, the second consolidates it, and the third squanders it. Throughout this process, ancestral bonds grow weaker.

In tradition-bound East Coast cities, even in "upstart" Chicago, an abandonment of ancestors in such magnitude is difficult to imagine. San Francisco cemetery history is a commentary on California's congenitally loose family connections, serial transiency, and weakness of tradition. But all cities ask these questions: Can progress and preservation coexist? Can preservation mean something other than a form of civic sacrifice, a ritual compensation to the past? Perhaps the dead ought to pull their own weight as a tourist attraction. In an ideal world, the dead would need no inspiration—they would be the inspiration.

Selling Laurel Hill as historical tourism was the last effort to make the cemetery matter to San Francisco.
—TAMARA VENIT SHELTON

The idea is bandied about in various forms at various times. Most plans will cost the city a pretty penny. Certainly, if it buys the land, but even if donated, consider the ongoing bills to construct streets, fix damaged sections, build new structures, and provide upkeep in perpetuity (for the park and the attorneys). The longer the city waits, the higher the costs. By the 1930s, it is a hard public sell in the Great Depression.

Here is a unique civic issue, different from other government underwriting, such as education or roads. Most people drive and

Laurel Hill Cemetery, San Francisco, circa 1937. *Cypress Lawn Memorial Park*

have children, and society clearly benefits from public schooling. To make a "Save Laurel Hill" argument, the taxpayer needs a personal connection to the cemetery or to perceive some clear social contribution. One benefit is a public park, but given Laurel Hill's condition, it was hard to imagine. Besides, Golden Gate and Lincoln parks have satisfied the need for urban recreation areas. As time passes, cemetery defenders increasingly play the civic patriotism card—the last line of defense: Disturbing venerable San Francisco pioneers in Laurel Hill is akin to secular sacrilege, not to mention the perhaps more egregious sin—a failure to conjure up imaginative solutions like the great progressive eastern cities. San Francisco is supposed to be "the city that knows how." The tweaking of the progressive nose is a last-ditch default argument that falls on deaf ears, but efforts never stop, right up to the 1937 referendum and beyond.

There is momentary focus on a proposal for the city to take over Laurel Hill as a public park and remove all but the most notable monuments, the land itself to become a public recreational space under which the dead remain. The City Planning Commission is receptive but not most city officials, who prefer complete removal to open the land for residential subdivisions and businesses. It is moot in the end—the Laurel Hill Cemetery Association is opposed. It is worth noting that such an idea—to build over bodies, even if it is a commemoration to those dead—would likely never have floated a generation earlier.

Another idea is proposed: Remove bodies and monuments in the cemetery while preserving about five acres (allowed in official cemetery removal plans). A mausoleum and the Pioneers Memorial Museum would be constructed on this land with selected bodies to be placed in crypts or vaults. The five-acre park is donated to the city to be administered and maintained.

Facing eviction in 1937—with the headaches of removal and relocation—Laurel Hill tosses a Hail Mary to donate all its land to the city for a memorial park/tourist attraction. This is similar to an earlier Odd Fellows proposal in 1893 but without an endowment. The Laurel Hill plan assumes that remains, if not most monuments, will be left intact. Some proponents envision the park generating significant revenues. Entry fees and special attractions will create a family-friendly destination as tourism spills into adjacent neighborhoods. A supporter implores in the *Richmond Banner*, "A memorial park would be a far greater asset to the Richmond district than another subdivision of modern dwellings. If once known, every tourist to San Francisco would want to visit it."

After the 1937 election defeat, there is a stab at still another iteration of the threadbare idea. Momentum gathers for preservation of five acres permitted by law as a civic historic space open to the public. The "Memorial Pioneers Park" is spearheaded by the Monuments Committee of the National Recreation Association and endorsed by the venerable California Pioneers Society and Native Sons of the Golden West. The proposed tract will not interfere with projected new streets to be carved through the property after body removals.

The area would contain the existing graves, vaults, and monuments of a handful of selected pioneers.

The new Laurel Hill Memorial Park Association publishes promotions extolling the aesthetic features of the site for tourists and natives alike: "What a wonderful view we get from here! I think it is the finest view in the city," a pamphlet declares. An "open" letter to the Board of Supervisors, signed "Old Timer," endorses the idea, calling attention to the less dilapidated parts of the cemetery: "Unlike the western reaches of this burial ground, the eastern part that confronts the passerby on Presidio Avenue is beautiful. It is lovingly tended . . . its tombs bear names that explain why San Francisco became a great city" and will serve as a civic-historical treasure worthy of a great city. Proponents envision a park that generates significant revenues—entry fees and special attractions will create a family-friendly destination with tourism spilling over into adjacent neighborhoods and beyond. Others extoll the benefits of historical tourism and cited examples of similar practices in New York and Boston.

The idea never gets off the ground. After a letter poll of as many plot owners as could be contacted, the Laurel Hills Board of Trustees decides in August 1940 not to retain any of the existing cemetery for a memorial park. That the proposed new park is to be maintained by the Cemetery Association, not the city, may have been a factor in the decision, especially in a depression that is persisting into its second decade. Instead, the board decides to send all disinterred bodies to a receiving vault at Cypress Lawn Cemetery in Colma and construct a Pioneers Memorial Building there that embodies the ideas proposed for a Pioneers Memorial on the original cemetery site.

A project without sense or sentiment.
—SOCIETY OF CALIFORNIA PIONEERS,
DENOUNCING CEMETERY REMOVAL, 1924

By the 1937 vote, the "eyesore" issue is widely perceived to be more serious and threatening than ever—a citywide "disgrace" of dangerous dark lands nestled amidst residential neighborhoods. "Things" are happening in there—and more than the well-reported school bonfire rallies, fraternity initiations, lover's lanes, and Halloween shenanigans of the 1920s. As Calvary Cemetery is being removed in 1939, the *San Francisco News* recalls its infamous past:

> *Here, during the cemetery's [Calvary's] abandoned years—the last burials were made in the early 1900's—ghouls held vandalish orgies.*
>
> *On moonless, foggy nights, shadowy forms have slunk into vaults. Clanking sounds, the muffled crash of a sledgehammer, have echoed forth as vandals looted the vaults of bronze flower urns, of silver coffin handles.*
>
> *Tramps piled up their pots and pans, set up their cooking utensils for a macabre type of housekeeping, even. Some say these dank vaults were hideouts for bootleggers, during the prohibition years. . . .*
>
> *Other ghouls have wreaked havoc. Bronze and iron grilled doors of ornate marble and above-ground vaults have been pried open. Inside all is shambles. Flower urns have been ripped from the wall braces, coffins hacked, bones strewn about.*

The election tally is a dramatic reversal of fortune for the dead and its defenders: 65,725 to evict Laurel Hill and Calvary against 32,449 "sentimentalists." Some of those who voted in 1924 to keep the cemeteries turn against them. The physical conditions have deteriorated, and so have the feasible alternatives to removal. Personal connections to the cemeteries are diminishing, literally day by day. The Great Depression feeds the removal juggernaut. Removal and reinterment of bodies would provide immediate and much-needed work for thousands. Then can begin the construction of a new city on 200 acres of prime land—money and jobs will flow into San Francisco. It is remarkable that one-third of voters still embrace those desolate ruins at a moment when the city is in long-suffering economic pain and bursting at the seams for expansion that could alleviate the condition.

The 1937 vote is not a choice between keeping Laurel Hill as a memorial park or removing it. The ballot is simple: Remove Laurel

Hill or keep it intact, as is. Calvary also appears on the ballot, but the Church announces a voluntary relocation before the election. The official ballot cemetery removal plans in 1924 and 1937 offer an option to keep one-tenth of cemetery land as a memorial park. No specific commitment to such a plan is on either ballot, just the formal possibility.

The Laurel Hill Cemetery Association contracts with Cypress Lawn Cemetery in 1940 to remove some 35,000 remains to Colma. Disinterment begins in February and is conducted behind six-foot-tall windscreens to block all public view. Bodies disinterred one day are transported by hearse to Cypress Lawn and placed in a receiving vault the same day. Authorities state at the time that removal can be accomplished at a rate of 2,500 per month—sixteen months in all. Individual and family remains are placed in their own redwood and other boxes, their size depending on the condition of the remains, which range from fragments to full skeletons. Each box has a metal identification tag. Laurel Hill directors promise that disinterred remains will be housed in receiving vaults to await the construction of a large memorial mausoleum. World War II intervenes. Six years later, the cost of the original plan is too expensive. Instead, a massive underground concrete structure containing thousands of individual vaults is built beneath a three-acre grassy knoll. The area is called Laurel Hill Mound, memorialized by a bronze sculpture of California's pioneers by Francis Minturn Sedgewick. A towering granite obelisk commemorating the centennial anniversary of Cypress Lawn is placed at the site in 1992.

The Catholic Archdiocese of San Francisco diligently oversees the removal of Calvary Cemetery remains to Holy Cross Cemetery in Colma. Exhumation begins March 1940 and is completed early the following year. A priest attends all phases of body removal and transport; relatives can witness the disinterment. As with Laurel Hill removals to Cypress Lawn, windscreens are erected for privacy, remains placed in various sized labeled boxes, and families kept together in a single container. Bodies disinterred on a given day are transported to Holy Cross and reinterred the same day. According to cemetery records, a total of 55,000 are disinterred from Calvary, 39,307 of which are placed at a mound near the entrance. On Memorial Day 1993, a six-foot memorial surmounted with three Latin crosses is unveiled on the 1.5-acre site.

At Laurel Hill and Calvary, there are meticulous individual records of all the deceased moved from the San Francisco cemeteries and relocated, including a plotted record map that indicates the spot where a person lays. There are no personal memorials.

In a postmortem on the Great Removal, the San Francisco City Planning Department observes in 1950, "It was realized that the entire cemetery-removal program would decrease people's faith in the sanctity of dedicated cemetery ground, and as a matter of fact, an increase in cremations was noted by officials of cemetery associations in Colma during and subsequent to the San Francisco cemetery-removal programs. Considerable 'sales-resistance' was also noted on the sale of cemetery lots, in as much as prospective purchasers would cite the cemetery-removals as an example, and say, 'What assurance do you have to give us that my plot will not, fifty years from now, be picked up and moved to make way for more densely built-up residential developments?'" Or as a gentleman asked in a letter to the editor forty years earlier, "If they are to be digging up cemeteries all the time, what good will it do for a fellow to think of his mother's grave?"

EARTH TO EARTH, QUARRY TO QUARRY

The 1937 ordinance stipulates that grave markers and monuments be left on the premises for ninety days after body removals for relevant parties to make "disposition arrangements," the cost of which is borne by individuals. The vast majority of dead are unclaimed, so the vast majority of physical memorials are unclaimed, including grand mausoleums and tombstones. The Laurel Hill Cemetery Association appeals to San Francisco historical societies to rescue the most important structures. A few are, but the response is underwhelming. Memorials, large and small, are broken up, much of it sold directly to local stone dealers. Deals are struck. The Laurel Hill-Anza Development Company hires a private contractor in 1946 to remove monuments from sections of old cemetery lands. He must have had a brother-in-law in the Parks Commission to pay eighty cents per ton to dump loads into San Francisco Bay, where they remain to this day; the going rate was $4 per ton. The city is only too pleased to take most memorials regardless of condition. Officials know exactly what to do with the rock: Create a municipal yacht harbor in the marina, line the leaky rain gutters at Buena Vista Park, and build seawalls at Aquatic Park and Ocean Beach, where pieces of the past, some inscribed, resurface at low tide. San Francisco journalist Harold Gilliam calls the physical excavations "an act of civic vandalism."

Old cemetery memorials serving as seawalls at the San Francisco Marina. *Cypress Lawn Memorial Park*

Culture and Death in the Wild West

The "big bang" of 1849 creates California. Most newcomers for the next half-century will congregate in and around San Francisco Bay, which remains remote from the nation's heartland even as the city mushrooms to a quarter of a million in 1880 and old goldfield territory become towns, most notably Sacramento, the state capital.

The Wild West officially runs out of time and space in 1890, when the national census reveals that the "frontier" is "closed": No significant tracts of land in the western United States remain unpopulated. The obituary is penned a few years later by Frederick Jackson Turner in his influential work "The Significance of the Frontier in American History." That significance is regarded as existential. Hope for a new life birthed and shaped the nation. A continuous frontier creates a safety valve, a beckoning to dare and excel, which nurtures the uniquely American virtues of self-reliance, individualism, democracy, unshackled energy, and innovation. Turner ponders the future: Can the nation continue to thrive when the physical and spiritual reality of its greatness is lost to history?

California will define and absorb the American "post-frontier" frontier. Los Angeles is the fastest growing area of the nation in the early twentieth century. After World War II, the entire Pacific coast is again the destination of a vast internal American migration. For almost two centuries, the West has been the symbol, sanctuary, and cutting edge of the American Dream, however defined. The "old" frontier had advanced gradually, clinging to distance, common purpose, and ethnicity. "No such homogeneity ever existed in California," suggests Carey McWilliams. "California has always occupied, in relation to the other regions, the same relation that America has occupied toward Europe: It is the great catch-all, the vortex at the continent's end into which elements of America's diverse population have been drawn, whirled around, mixed up, and resorted." The question persists: Has the West influenced "the states" more than the nation has influenced it? Is the Golden State, as Wallace Stegner quips, "just like America, only more so"?

During the formative California years, the idea of settling into a "normal" routine—working in the fields or at a craft, rearing a family, attending church, or building a community—seems like an implausible dream. In *The Bohemians*, Ben Tarnoff paints a picture: "What would elsewhere happen naturally becomes a ridiculous farce in the upside-down world of [Brett Harte's] Roaring Camp. The miners try to civilize themselves . . . but the most they can muster is an absurd caricature of normal society. They don't know the first thing about traditional institutions like family or religion. Luck is their only faith."

Gender imbalance and the wild rush to riches spawn a culture that lingers even when those conditions are changing. "The legacy of the gold rush," Tarnoff believes, "gave the city an unsettled feel. . . . In 1861, the *Era* noted the large number of 'nomads' who lodged in the 'vast beehives' of the city's many boardinghouses and hotels. And hotels, as Harte observed, were the Bohemians natural resting place, where he could drift with the rest of the 'living tide' perpetually passing through. The large number of unmarried lent San Francisco a loose moral tone. Fewer families meant fewer restrictions, and more freedom to crack coarse jokes or enjoy risqué entertainments." In the 1870s, the mother of the young lady who becomes the legendary "Firebell" Lillie Coit Hitchcock remarks that if single men between the ages of twenty-one and forty-five should suddenly marry, city restaurants and hotels would go insolvent overnight.

California's legendary transiency begets a willful indifference to the past. The state is growing quicker than anywhere else in late nineteenth-century America. Newcomers can arrive, as do first immigrants, on speculation. Folks who plant roots at the edge of the continent start a new life that often leaves old ones behind—both in distance and in contact; there are fewer parents or grandparents to care for and bury. Newer residents have little skin in the local cemeteries. A *San Francisco Chronicle* letter to the editor during the 1914 cemetery referendum wonders, "What would San Francisco be today had not many of the people who are buried there done what they have in the past . . . you will find that nine out of ten of those who want the cemeteries removed are people who have not been here long and also have no kin buried there and no thought of San Francisco's early settlers."

In the end, the city fails to provide even a proposed five-acre public park for the founders and builders of a great metropolis. This is not Boston, where family and community roots run deep, or nineteenth-century Chicago, where you could hop a train to Buffalo in the morning and be there for lunch. This is an end-of-the-continent boom city where the past tumbles into the future with an inbred don't-look-back attitude. It remains a "tea-pot of a town always boiling over," Lillie Coit Hitchcock's now elderly mother declares in 1890. Eventually, a family-based population stabilizes the demographic. The transition is slow, and the results are uneven, leaving San Francisco and California forever a different cut of cloth.

"It's an odd thing but anyone who disappears is said to be seen in San Francisco. It must be a delightful city and possess all the attractions of the next world." Oscar Wilde's ode suggests that those who are restless, are in identity crisis, suffer existential angst, or simply yearn to escape oppressive conditions have joined a cultural diaspora to a far-off place with a reputation for tolerance and enough back alleys to keep your anonymity and hide your secrets. Get lost in California—and find or reinvent yourself. Such a siren call encourages the nomad, the offbeat, and the visionary who, whatever their contributions to culture, tilt away from "family" norms and traditional rituals, including those for the dead.

Among the many who notice the exhilarating freedom of California is Rudyard Kipling during an 1889 visit to San Francisco forty years after the gold rush: "Recklessness is in the air. I can't explain where it comes from, but there it is. The roaring winds of the Pacific make you drunk with it." This irreverent energy continues well beyond the Bohemian movement for which California is noted. The twentieth century will witness the flaunting of Prohibition, the Beats, an explosive counterculture, "liberation" movements, and political activism—all originating or at least flourishing on the "Left Coast."

Instant-city fever is at once the mighty sword and Achilles' heel of the American West. San Francisco has spawned many "instant" cities: the gold rush, the silver rush, the phoenix-rising-from-the-earthquake rush, the counterculture rush, and tech rushes that keep on giving and disrupting. You might consider the region as the permanent home of instant cities, a unique cultural petri dish adapted to host dramatic change. Across the journey, the cemeteries become a historical footnote.

Unless San Francisco was prepared to draw a line in the sacred sand, its ancestral burial grounds were doomed. History disguises itself as fate. There dwells in any society a zeitgeist, a cultural and political momentum. But in the ticking moments, events wrought by individuals can have profound consequences. The removal of the cemeteries was a choice as much as a destiny.

BIBLIOGRAPHY

Ackley, Laura A. *San Francisco's Jewel City: The Panama Pacific International Exposition of 1915.* Berkeley, CA: Heyday, 2015.

Adams, Charles. *The Magnificent Rouges of San Francisco.* Sanger, CA: The Write Thought, 1998.

Albright, Thomas. *Art in the San Francisco Bay Area, 1945–1980: An Illustrated History.* Berkeley: University of California Press, 1985.

Allen, Terence Beckington. *San Francisco Coroner's Office: A History, 1850–1980.* San Francisco: Redactors' Press, 1999.

Asbury, Herbert. *The Barbary Coast.* New York: Alfred A. Knopf, 1933.

Atherton, Gertrude. *California: An Intimate History.* New York: Harper & Brothers Publishers, 1914.

Averbuch, Bernard. *Crab Is King: The Colorful Story of Fisherman's Wharf in San Francisco.* San Francisco: Mabuhay Publishing Company, 1973.

Bancroft, Hubert Howe. *Some Cities and San Francisco.* Resurgam, NY: Bancroft, 1907.

Banks, Charles E. *The History of the San Francisco Disaster and Mount Vesuvius Horror.* San Francisco: C. E. Thomas, 1906.

Barker, Malcolm E. *San Francisco Memoirs, 1835–1851: Eyewitness Accounts of the Birth of a City.* San Francisco: Londonborn Publications, 1994.

———. *More San Francisco Memoirs: 1852–1899.* San Francisco: Londonborn Publications, 1996.

————. *Three Fearful Days: San Francisco Memoirs of the 1906 Earthquake and Fire*. San Francisco: Londonborn Publications, 1998.

Barth, Gunter. *Instant Cities*. New York: Oxford University Press, 1975.

Boorstin, Daniel J. *The Americans: The National Experience*. New York: Random House, 1965.

Brechin, Gray. *Imperial San Francisco*. Berkeley: University of California Press, 2006.

Bronson, William. *The Earth Shook, the Sky Burned*. Garden City, NY: Doubleday, 1959.

Brooks, James, Chris Carlsson, and Nancy J. Peters. *Reclaiming San Francisco, CA: History, Politics, Culture*. San Francisco: City Lights Books, 1998.

Browning, Peter, ed. *Yerba Buena San Francisco, CA: From the Beginning to the Gold Rush, 1769–1849*. Lafayette, CA: Great Western Books, 1988.

Bruno, Lee. *Misfits, Merchants, and Mayhem: 1849–1934*. Petaluma, CA: Cameron + Company, 2018.

Burns, John F., and Richard J. Orsi, eds. *Taming the Elephant: Politics, Government, and Law in Pioneer California*. Berkeley: University of California Press, 2003.

Caen, Herb. *Baghdad by the Bay*. Garden City, NY: Doubleday, 1953.

Carpenter, Patricia, and Paul Totah, eds. *The San Francisco Fair: Treasure Island: 1939–1940*. San Francisco: Shotwell Associates, 1989.

Chandler, Arthur. *Old Tales of San Francisco*. Dubuque, IA: Kendall/Hunt, 1977.

Chang, Iris. *The Chinese in America*. New York: Penguin Books, 2004.

Chase, Marilyn. *The Barbary Plague: The Black Death in Victorian San Francisco*. New York: Random House, 2003.

Chen, Yong. *Chinese San Francisco, CA: 1850–1943*. Redwood City, CA: Stanford University Press, 2000.

Clary, Raymond, H. *The Making of Golden Gate Park*. San Francisco: California Books, 1980.

Conrad, Barnaby, ed. *The World of Herb Caen: San Francisco, 1938–1997*. San Francisco: Chronicle Books, 1997.

Covert, Adrian. *Taverns of the American Revolution*. San Rafael, CA: Insight Editions, 2016.

Cummings, Judy Dodge. *Tomb Raiders*. White River Junction, VT: Nomad Press, 2018.

De Tocqueville, Alexis. *Democracy in America*. London: Saunders & Otley, 1838.

Dicksen, Samuel. *Tales of San Francisco*. Redwood City, CA: Stanford University Press, 1947.

Dillon, Richard, *North Beach*. Novato, CA: Presidio Press, 1985.

Egan, Ferol. *Last Bonanza Kings: The Bourns of San Francisco*. Reno: University of Nevada Press, 1998.

Ehrlich, Cindy. *Cypress Lawn: Guardians of California's Heritage*. Colma, CA: Cypress Lawn Memorial Park, 1996.

Evanosky, Dennis, and Eric J. Kos. *Lost San Francisco*. London: Pavilion Books, 2011.

Evans, Lorraine. *Burying the Dead: An Archaeological History of Burial Grounds, Graveyards, and Cemeteries*. Yorkshire: Pen & Sword History, 2020.

Ferri, Jessica. *Silent Cities San Francisco: Hidden Histories of the Region's Cemeteries*. Lanham, MD: Globe Pequot, 2022.

Flamm, Jerry. *Hometown San Francisco, CA: Sunny Jim, Phat Willie, and Dave*. San Francisco: Scottwall Associates, 1994.

Fracchia, Charles A. *When the Water Came Up to Montgomery Street: San Francisco during the Gold Rush*. Virginia Beach, VA: Donning Company Publishers, 2009.

Gentry, Curt. *The Madams of San Francisco*. Garden City, NY: Doubleday, 1964.

Gould, Milton S. *A Cast of Hawks: A Rowdy Tale of Scandal and Power Politics in Early San Francisco*. La Jolla, CA: Copley Press, 1985.

Gutkind, Lee, ed. *True Crime*. Pittsburgh, PA: In Fact Books, 2013.

Hamburg, Terry, and Hansen, Richard, *Quotable San Francisco*. Charleston, SC: The History Press, 2021.

Hansen, Gladys, and Emmet Condon. *Denial of Disaster: The Untold Story and Photographs of the San Francisco Earthquake and Fire of 1906*. San Francisco: Condon and Company, 1989.

Hansen, Gladys, Richard Hansen, and Dr. William Blaisdell. *Earthquake, Fire, and Epidemic: Personal Accounts of the 1906 Disaster*. San Francisco: Untreed Reads Publishing, 2013.

Helper, Hinton. *Dreadful California*. Edited by Lucius Beebe and Charles M. Clegg. New York: Bobbs-Merrill Company, 1948.

Hittell, John. *A History of the City of San Francisco*. San Francisco: Bancroft, 1878.

Holdredge, Helen. *Firebelle Lillie: The Life and Times of Lillie Coit of San Francisco*. New York: Meredith Press, 1967.

Holliday, J. S. *The World Rushed In: The California Gold Rush Experience*. Norman: University of Oklahoma Press, 1981.

———. *Rush to Riches*. Berkeley: University of California Press, 1999.

Hucke, Matt, and Ursula Bielski. *Graveyards of Chicago*. Chicago: Lake Claremont Press, 2013.

Jenner, Gail L. *What Lies beneath: California Pioneer Cemeteries and Graveyards*. Lanham, MD: Globe Pequot, 2021.

Johnson, Robin C. *Enchantress, Sorceress, Madwoman: The True Story of Sarah Althea Hill, Adventuress of Old San Francisco*. California Venture Books, 2014.

Kamiya, Gary. *Cool Gray City of Love*. New York: Bloomsbury, 2013.

Kammen, Michael. *Digging Up the Dead: A History of Notable American Reburials*. Chicago: University of Chicago Press, 2010.

Lavender, David. *Nothing Seemed Impossible: William C. Ralston and Early San Francisco.* Palo Alto, CA: American West Publishing Company, 1975.

Lewis, Oscar. *Sea Routes to the Gold Fields.* New York: Alfred A. Knopf, 1949.

———. *The Autobiography of the West.* New York: Henry Holt and Company, 1958.

Lloyd, B. E. *Lights and Shades in San Francisco.* San Francisco: A. L. Bancroft, 1876.

Lockwood, Charles. *Suddenly San Francisco, CA: The Early Years of an Instant City.* San Francisco: San Francisco Examiner, 1978.

Lotchin, Roger W. *San Francisco, 1846–1856: From Hamlet to City.* New York: Oxford University Press, 1974.

Manna, John Salvatore. *To the Land of Promise.* Burson, CA: Calaveras History Publishing, 2023.

Martini, John A. *Fortress Alcatraz: Guardian of the Golden Gate.* Emeryville, CA: Ten Speed Press, 2004.

McGloin, John Bernard. *San Francisco, CA: The Story of a City.* San Rafael, CA: Presidio Press, 1978.

McWilliams, Carey. *California: The Great Exception.* Berkeley: University of California Press, 1949.

Melville, Greg. *Over My Dead Body: Unearthing the Hidden History of America's Cemeteries.* New York: Abrams Press, 2022.

Mitford, Jessica. *The American Way of Death.* New York: Random House, 1963.

Moffat, Francis. *Dancing on the Brink of the World: The Rise and Fall of San Francisco Society.* New York: G. P. Putnam's Sons, 1977.

Morris, Charles. *The San Francisco Calamity by Earthquake and Fire.* Facsimile edition of 1906 book. Secaucus, NJ: Citadel Press, 1986.

Mullin, Kevin J. *The Toughest Gang in Town: Police Stories from Old San Francisco.* Novato, CA: Noir Publications, 2005.

Muscatine, Doris. *Old San Francisco, CA: The Biography of a City from Early Days to Earthquake.* New York: G.P. Putnam's Sons, 1975.

Nasaw, David. *The Chief: The Life of William Hearst.* London: Gibson Square Books, 2003.

Neider, Charles, ed. *Life as I Find It: A Treasury of Mark Twain Rarities.* Garden City, NY: Cooper Square Press, 1961.

Older, Cora Miranda. *San Francisco, CA: Magic City.* New York: Longmans, Green & Company, 1961.

Purdy, Helen Throop. *San Francisco as It Was, as It Is, and How to See It.* San Francisco: Paul Elder, 1912.

Rawls, James J., and Richard A. Orsi, eds. *A Golden State: Mining and Development in Gold Rush California.* Berkeley: University of California Press, 1998.

Reeves, Richard. *Infamy: The Shocking Story of the Japanese American Internment in World War II.* New York: Henry Holt and Company, 2015.

Rhoads, Loren. *199 Cemeteries to See before You Die.* New York: Black Dog & Leventhal, 2017.

———. *Wish You Were Here: Adventures in Cemetery Travel.* San Francisco: Automatism, 2013.

Richards, Rand. *Mud, Blood, and Gold: San Francisco in 1849.* San Francisco: Heritage House Publishers, 2009.

San Francisco and Its Municipal Administration. San Francisco: City of San Francisco, 1902–1904.

Sappol, Michael. *A Traffic of Dead Bodies: Anatomy and Embodied Social Identity in Nineteenth-Century America.* Princeton, NJ: Princeton University Press, 2022.

Saxton, Alexander P. *The Indispensable Enemy: Labor and the Anti-Chinese Movement in California.* Berkeley: University of California Press, 1971.

Scharlach, Bernice. *Big Alma: San Francisco's Alma Spreckels.* San Francisco: Shotwell Associates, 1990.

Shelton, Tamara Venit. "Unmaking Historic Spaces: Urban Progress and the San Francisco Cemetery Debate, 1895–1937." *California History* 85, no. 3 (2008): 26–47, 69–70.

Sloan, David Charles. *The Last Great Necessity*. Baltimore: Johns Hopkins University Press, 1991.

Smith, Dennis. *San Francisco Is Burning: The Untold Story of the 1906 Earthquake and Fires*. New York: Viking Press, 2005.

Smith, James. *San Francisco's Playland at the Beach: The Golden Years*. Fresno, CA: Craven Street Books, 2010.

Soule, Frank, John H. Gihon, and James Nisbet. *Annals of San Francisco*. New York: Appleton & Company, 1854.

Sparks, Edith. *Capital Intentions: Female Proprietors in San Francisco, 1850–1920*. Chapel Hill: University of North Carolina Press, 2006.

Stanford, Sally. *The Lady of the House*. New York: G. P. Putnam's Sons, 1966.

Stannard David E, ed. *Death in America*. Philadelphia: University of Pennsylvania Press, 1975.

Starr, Kevin. *California: A History*. New York: Random House, 2005.

Starr, Kevin, and Richard J. Orsi, eds. *Rooted in Barbarous Soil: People, Culture, and Community in Gold Rush California*. Berkeley: University of California Press, 2000.

Steffens, Lincoln. *Upbuilders*. New York: Doubleday & Page, 1905.

Stewart, Robert, Jr., and M. F. Stewart. *Adolph Sutro: A Biography*. Berkeley, CA: Howell-North, 1962.

Stoddard, Tom. *Jazz on the Barbary Coast*. Berkeley, CA: Heyday Books, 1982.

Svanevik, Michael. *City of Souls*. San Francisco: Custom & Limited Editions, 1995.

———. *Pillars of the Past*. Colma, CA: Cypress Lawn Memorial Park, 2023.

Tarnoff, Ben. *The Bohemians*. New York: Penguin Books, 2014.

Taylor, Bernard. *Eldorado; or, Adventures in the Path of Empire.* New York: C. W. Benedict, 1850.

Thomas, Gordon, and Morgan Max Witts. *The San Francisco Earthquake.* New York: Stein and Day, 1971.

Trobits, Monika. *Antebellum and Civil War San Francisco, CA: A Western Theatre for Northern and Southern Politics.* Charleston, SC: The History Press, 2014.

———. *Bay Area Coffee: A Stimulating History.* Charleston, SC: The History Press, 2019.

Ungaretti, Lorri. *San Francisco's Sunset District.* Charleston, SC: The History Press, 2011.

———. *Stories in the Sand: San Francisco's Sunset District, 1847–1964.* San Francisco: Balangero Books, 2012.

Valente, Francesca. *A. P. Giannini: The People's Banker.* Temple City, CA: Barbera Foundation, 2017.

Valentine, Alan. *Vigilante Justice.* New York: Reynal, 1986.

Walsh, James P. *The San Francisco Irish: 1850–1976.* San Francisco: Smith McKay, 1978.

Winegarner, Beth, *San Francisco's Forgotten Cemeteries.* Charleston, SC: The History Press, 2023.

Yalom, Marilyn. *The American Resting Place.* New York: Houghton Mifflin Company, 2008.